Dear Rick,

It was wonderful to see you
at the launch. I have so many happy
memories of you & Simon taking especial
care of my car.

Jim

# Forsyte
## *and*
# Hindsight

*or*
**Screen Directing
for Pleasure and Profit**

## *The Memoirs of*
## *James Cellan Jones*

# James Cellan Jones

James Cellan Jones was born in Swansea and educated at St John's College, Cambridge where he read the Natural Science Tripos. He served in the Royal Engineers in Korea (after the war) and joined the BBC as a call boy; he slowly worked his way up to become a director, then resigned to become a freelance producer/director.

His many productions include *The Forsyte Saga*, *Roads To Freedom*, *Jennie*, *The Ambassadors*, *Fortunes Of War* and *Harnessing Peacocks*. He spent three years from 1976 to 1979 as Head of Plays at the BBC, where he was responsible for up to 85 productions a year. Among his awards are the Nymphe d'Or at the Monte Carlo Festival, several BPG awards and an ACE award, and the one of which he is most proud: the Directors Guild of America award. He is a former Chairman of BAFTA and of the Directors Guild.

He is married to Margot Eavis, an editor and production manager and has three sons (two of whom work in television) and a daughter.

# Acknowledgements

To the many actors and technicians I have worked with over the years whose courage and creativity I shall always admire.

To my Editor, Chris Perry, for his wise advice, and the invaluable help of Simon Coward and Rob Moss, who is a wonderful designer.

But most of all to my family: Maggie, Rory, Simon, Din and Vinny whose patience and support over the years has been wonderful.

***

Edited by Chris Perry and Simon Coward.

Layout and design by Rob Moss (www.robmossdesign.co.uk).

Photographs are © James Cellan Jones and their respective owners.

Text © 2005 James Cellan Jones.

First published by Kaleidoscope Publishing, 2006.

Kaleidoscope Publishing
93 Old Park Road
Dudley
West Midlands
DY1 3NE
www.kaleidoscopepublishing.co.uk

ISBN 1-900203-21-9

Printed by The Basingstoke Press, Basingstoke, Hampshire.
http://www.basingstokepress.com

# Foreword

'It's absolutely fascinating, but it's nothing but a collection of anecdotes,' said a friend after reading this book.
'Don't knock it,' I said, 'there's a lot of mileage in anecdotes.'

When my friend Jim Leheny asked me to teach at the UMass Summer school in Oxford, like all non-academics I became a little self-conscious and tried to make my course more difficult and more scholarly than others. Jim sat in on a few of my lectures: I found myself drifting into anecdote and felt it necessary to excuse this tendency. Jim was insistent that anecdotes had a real place in the learning process and should be tempered only a little by didacticism.

I think my students learned quite a lot anyway. They certainly showed considerable enthusiasm. This book may be of use to aspirant and practising directors, but this is not its main purpose. It is, for me, a simple and selfish way of celebrating many years of greatly satisfying work. Much of this has been destroyed; some of it is preserved, due to the efforts of people like Steve Rogers and Gavin Collinson to whom I and my contemporaries owe a great debt.

I hope you enjoy it as much as I liked writing it.

# Contents

# Chapter One

# Entrée

It was my second day at Lime Grove. The first had been idyllic, a West Indian Steel band playing *Yellow Bird* and some clever jugglers. Now I was in at the deep end doing final calls for a play: it was ten minutes before transmission.

I was knocking on dressing room doors and saying 'Five minutes, please.'
At the end of the corridor, I knocked on the Distinguished Actor's door. It opened in a flash and I was confronted with a stark naked figure in a condition of excitement.
'Five minutes please,' I stammered.
'Come in, dear boy,' he said. 'There is a lot one can do in five minutes.'

Fifty seconds later, when I had run up two flights of stairs to studio B, the floor manager asked:
'Well, is he coming?'
'Probably,' I said.
'What do you mean, probably?'
Then in came the actor, fully dressed, touched me lightly on the shoulder and said, 'Saucebox!'

I was a call boy: I earned five pounds twelve and six pence a week. I had a room off the Portobello Road at 35 shillings and was happier than I had ever been in my life.[1] At last I was doing what I wanted and the spectre of exams no longer kept me awake at night, sweating. I had got a bad third at Cambridge in medical subjects which I hated and finally got the courage to refuse to go on. My poor father, a surgeon and an emotional Welshman, cried for five days without stopping. My mother, who was Irish, said, 'This will kill your father.' It didn't.

While I waited to be called up for National Service, I worked on a sheep farm in Scotland. My employer, George Gilroy was a retired air ace and he was as mad as a hatter.

George had a great nostalgia for the old ways and we were the only farm for miles around making rucks of hay and stooks of corn. He hated combine harvesters and most machinery. He used to say, 'Early start, tomorrow, old boy.'
When I got up at about five o'clock, I would hear him waiting by the Land Rover; as soon as he heard me, he would drive off in a hurry, leaving me to walk five miles to work. When I staggered into the field, he would say, 'Thought I said early, old boy.'
He was a wicked old bastard and I liked him very much, though he put me off agriculture for life. We got on very well, really, though there was a certain froideur when I was caught snogging his daughter in the haybarn.

---

[1] Five pounds twelve and six pence is £5.62½p; 35 shillings is £1.75p.

# Forsyte and Hindsight

After six months of wallowing in sheep shit, a call came. I was to join the Royal Engineers at Worcester. Hosing the sheep shit off my boots, I took the train south. Much of my army life wasn't interesting, but there were a few incidents that probably influenced my later career as a director. We'll come to those later.

I passed out of the School of Military Engineering by the skin of my teeth; I got away with a good deal by producing and acting in a revue which wasn't that great, though it made the inspecting general laugh immoderately so everybody followed suit.

I should say that the Lime Grove studios, where I started my story, were the subject of a visit some years before. I was in the Footlights at Cambridge. The one revue in which I acted was in the old style, with a big cast and sumptuous décor by Malcolm Burgess, a Russian scholar, who later died tragically young. It was later, in the time of Miller and Bennett, that the cast consisted of five or six razor sharp semi-professionals.

The year may be guessed from the opening chorus:

*The Festival of Britain*
*Really has begun*
*Don't you come to see*
*Our austerity, but come for the sun.*
*And if you find it's raining,*
*It's no use your complaining,*
*Our visitors will find that the posters remind them the sun shines most of the year.*
*Springtime in Britain really has begun*
*Don't you come to see our austerity,*
*But come for the sun!*

It is easy to forget that there was still rationing and that austerity was the watchword in 1951. Half the cast did an extract from the show at Lime Grove.

Gilchrist Calder was the director. The cameras were big and heavy with optical view finders which gave upside down images. The camera tubes were CPS (Cathode Potential Stabilised) which gave a rather sort of soft grey picture. I much preferred when comparing them later on, the EMI tubes which were described contemptuously by old stagers as 'Soot and Whitewash'.

The *Daily Sketch* did a piece on me headlined 'Singing Student Takes the Television Trail'. It said that I rushed each night from the dissecting room to the rehearsal room and was destined for stardom. It didn't impress my father much.

I had a horrible object lesson during the run of *A Flash In The Cam*, for so it was naively entitled. I had been to a party at my Tutor's and was slightly drunk, on sherry for God's sake. It showed slightly on stage that night; not much, but enough. The directors, Ian Kellie and Peter Jeffrey, gave me the father and mother of a bollocking. Two nights later, someone else was seriously pissed and rolling about on the stage. Peter said, 'Right, you and Chris Pym get on and ad-lib for three minutes to cover the scene change.' We did, and somehow managed to make them laugh. A more sophisticated audience would have howled us down.

*A Flash In The Cam* was unbearably exciting, but we were all studiedly cool about it. At Cambridge I had not been a great success as an actor, I was too awkward and shy. I still have nightmares where I find myself standing on the stage, tongue-tied and with hands as big as hams.

In one act plays, giving the new members of the Amateur Dramatic Club the chance to shine before an audience, I played Master Salathiel Pavey in *Spring 1600* with Sasha Moorsom, with whom I instantly and hopelessly fell in love. John Barton played a walk-through part as Mr Shakespeare and Peter Hall was in a gloomy Strindberg piece called *After The Fire*.

I was trying to swim as well. I got a half blue in my first year and neglected my work shamefully. In 1951, I was selected for the British Universities team for the International Student Games in Luxemburg. It was a very post-war austerity sort of affair. We were sent two Union Jack badges and told to sew them on to blazers and track suits. We also had to contribute £10 towards the cost of travel.

We did rather well in the first few days and won a Silver medal in the relay; after that we had little to do but watch the track and field sports. Chris Brasher, who was at my college, concerned us a lot. He was hot favourite for the 10,000 metres, but was a great worrier and was always popping pills - not, I hasten to add, anything druggy, but various healthy vitamins. We decided we had to take him in hand. The night before his race, we took him to the fair. After several beers we took him on the roller-coaster, then to a shooting gallery where if you hit a little statue of the Manneken-Pis in the navel you won a bottle of Riesling. We won a lot of these and he drank many of them and we put him to bed smiling beautifully. The next day he romped home and won the Gold Medal.

I fell in love with a beautiful zoologist called Joyce Finlay. I took a swimming team to Guernsey and beat the island record. I did no work. I was elected Captain of Swimming and eventually into the Hawks club. Everything seemed to be coming up roses.

In my last year, the chickens came home to roost. It looked as though I would fail my finals. I had to give up acting and work a bit.

I had a wonderful Director of Studies called Roland Winfield. He'd been an RAF doctor in the war. He had flown eighty bombing missions to study air crew stress and then became a parachutist. He was given a Fellowship, but did no research and not much teaching: this might be acceptable at Trinity, but not at St John's. At supervisions we used to talk about old silver and English Literature instead of physiology.

As Finals came closer, Roland gave me some blue pills and some pink pills.
'The pink ones are to give you three hours of sleep a night, which is all you can afford,' he said. 'And the blue ones are to keep you awake while you do in a few months all the work you should have done in three years.'

# Forsyte and Hindsight

I had a miserable last year. I graduated with a Third, luckily, and went to Scotland to look after the Blackface sheep. Eventually and inevitably, Roland's Fellowship was taken away and he killed himself. I still mourn his passing.
Back to the army - I hope you don't mind me dodging about like this; it seems a little eccentric and I persuaded my Editor that it works!

When I passed out of the School of Military Engineering, I was sent to Korea. The war was over, but they wouldn't let me to go Malaya, where it still smouldered on. I had what must have been one of the last wonderful voyages of the century. I went in a small troopship, called the Captain Hobson, through the Mediterranean and the Suez Canal to Colombo, Hong Kong, Singapore and Japan. There was a short stop at Gibraltar and Malta (where my father had served in the war). And the passage through the Red Sea was stupefyingly hot. We wore white bum-freezers, in the evening. I'd bought mine in Port Said for 17/6 and I had to starch it every night. After a few days some sailors set themselves up as Dhobi-Wallahs and we got our clothes washed very cheaply.

We were crammed four to a tiny cabin. We showered in salt water and all got prickly heat. It was a red-letter day when the temperature was less than 105°F. It was much worse for the soldiers. The hold of the ship was converted into a troop deck packed with hundreds of bunks full of suffering men. I was amazed that they were so forbearing. The officers' mess stewards were all smiling Goanese who had become used to gentle cruising. They didn't know what had hit them when confronted with crowds of noisy officers bawling for gin. When I asked for a gin and tonic someone said, 'You'll drink gin and onions the same as the rest of us'.
Gin cost tuppence a nip and a bottle of tonic was sixpence.

Just as the heat became unbearable, (we were doing four knots, but had a following wind of four knots which made us effectively stand still in the sultry air), we came round the Gulf of Socotra. It was as if a giant hand had grabbed hold of the ship and thrown it upon the Indian Ocean. Dolphins played in the bow wave, flying fish flew right over the deck sometimes crashing down and gasping until we threw them back, the temperature changed to temperate and the poor sods with heat stroke, whom we thought we would have to bury at sea, came to life again.

As we drew slowly into Kure in Japan, I started chatting with an old captain leaning against the taffrail. 'I'm a bit worried about going to Japan' I said. 'Those nasty little slant eyed people'.
'Ah,' he said. 'It's a very ancient civilization, one that might repay your study.'
'Oh you've been there have you?'
'I was a prisoner of theirs for three years.'
I felt deeply ashamed and about six inches high.

My first job on landing was to be Prisoner's Friend to a very old bombardier who'd been arrested by the Japanese police. 'What do I do?' I asked the adjutant.
'You look after him and every now and then you say 'I don't think you need answer that question'. It's a piece of cake.'

So I was locked in with two detectives and the poor old bombardier who seemed at least 60. He was accused of stealing some money and a clock from a tart. The interview went on all day. Every now and then we stopped and drank green tea, pouring a little libation onto the floor.

Eventually one of the detectives said that if he pleaded guilty he would be dealt with at the Magistrates Court and fined, provided - and this was the key - he made full restitution. Otherwise he would go to the High Court where he may well be imprisoned.

I took the bombardier aside and said, 'What do you want to do?'

'I don't know sir.' he said.

'You did do it, didn't you?'

'Yes, of course I did.'

'Well you'd better say so and get it over with.'

He gave a sigh of relief and seemed to calm down. The detective dictated a statement which started 'A devil entered into me' and ended 'I make full restitution of what I have stolen and humbly apologise.' I don't know what happened to him, as I flew to Korea the next day, but I hope he was all right.

In Korea, one of my most pleasant jobs was blowing up things, for which I developed a real taste. On one occasion, we had made a large pile of landmines and dud mortar shells packed them with gun cotton and detonators, laid out the cable, retreated to a safe distance and pressed the button. Nothing happened. I said to my sergeant, 'What do we do now?' He said, 'What YOU do now is go and find out what's happened. What I do is sit and wait, (pause) Sir.' I sweated quite a lot as I followed the wire up to the detonator, put things right and returned to press the button. The explosion was very satisfying.

Every now and then, we would dig up a minefield. It required a certain concentration and I thought' I wonder what it's like doing this under fire?' The American anti tank mines had a booby trap underneath, so when you lifted them, they would go off in your face. Once, a lance corporal who obviously hadn't listened to the briefing, said 'Look, Sir, there's a bit of string under this one'.

'LEAVE IT!' I said. We blew it up in situ. It made a hell of a noise.

The months passed, a captain with ten years' service came to take over the troop. I felt very lost; I did little jobs like Intelligence Officer and Dog Troop commander. The dog troop was rather splendid. We had guard dogs, mine dogs, who stood transfixed when near a mine and a red cross dog called Search who was supposed to seek out wounded men; he had a field dressing strapped to his back. The only trouble was, when he found one, he bit him.

I was soon to be demobbed. I said goodbye to what had become my second family and Prince, the little dog which I had rescued from the pot. I was very queasy about the idea of eating dog. When we went to lunch with a Korean battalion we had some particularly vile stew. I said to the Korean Colonel, flapping my arms and making hen noises: 'Chicken?'

He shook his head and barked liked a dog. I smiled weakly and forced the stew down.

We felt we were doing something useful in helping to bring the land back to normal by cleaning up the mess and re-irrigating the paddy fields. The infantry, on the other hand, felt bored and were doing nothing, but parade drills and platoon attacks.

It was soon time to go. We boarded a verminous little steamer for Pusan to Kure and then embarked on a larger, but less friendly troopship called the Dunera.

# Forsyte and Hindsight

As we were coming into Port Said, and the Gully Gully men were coming on board 'Nothing up my sleeve, gully gully, you like my sister?'

There came an announcement over the Tannoy: 'We are asking for volunteers to fly home. We need the berths for a general. Who wants to be in England before any of us?' I led the rush; it seemed that within moments we were on our way to the transit camp. This had a peculiar sort of out of time atmosphere. I soon found out why. For some old stagers it was the land of lost content: they lived on in a dream: they made the desert bloom with little flower gardens and had rather maternal Egyptian mistresses.

'When am I going to get out of here?' I asked.
'Probably never, dear boy' I was told.' First you have to find the camp commandant, who's almost never here, and then you have to sober him up enough to sign a movement order, then you have to bribe or blackmail your way on to some transport'
'But I'm due for demob in three days.'
'Dream on, dear boy,' they said.

Two weeks later, I was still there. I had met a kindred spirit, Julian Pettifer, and we whiled the time away, though Port Said had few fleshpots. Finally, we ran the Camp Commandant to earth, got him blotto and guided his hand into a shaky signature.

Fortunately I still had a .45 automatic which I had been given by an American Marine and, by dint of cleaning it in a rather ostentatious manner, managed to persuade a somnolently drunk driver to take us to the Air Base. We boarded a slightly creaky Avro York, flew over the desert for miles, landing at El Adem, a tiny oasis five hundred miles from anywhere, to refuel, and then, at last, homeward. When the York flew over the south coast of England, I burst into tears. I had forgotten that it was so green.

After a few days with my parents I began to get restless. I now knew what I wanted to do. I decided on television: the theatre, for which I had almost an absurd reverence, seemed so far away and I was 22 years of age, far too old I thought, so I wrote to the BBC for a job, any job.

While waiting, I joined the TA and did a parachute course. When I arrived at the parachute school the chief instructor said, 'Has this officer had a medical?' Of course I hadn't. Fortunately there was a doctor on the course. 'Feel all right?' The doctor said.
'Fine,' I said.
'Not got weak ankles or anything?'
'No.'
'Well, give me that paper.' And he signed it.

The five seconds before a parachute jump are one of the most terrifying moments in the world. It gets much easier the more jumps you do. For the first few descents you lie awake the night before worrying about it. Later on you can go to sleep in the aircraft and it's only when someone shouts 'Action Stations!' that terror takes over again.

Curiously, often repeated choruses of the school song:

*'They scraped him off the tarmac like a piece of strawberry jam (repeat twice)*
*And he ain't going to jump no more'*

had a soothing rather than a terrifying effect.

The course was beautifully structured: our sergeant instructor became like a mother to us; he would tap us on the shoulder when it was time to jump and shout 'GO'.
When we landed we took no notice of the chief instructor's sneering criticism of our landings but said, 'Was I all right, Sarge?'
'Not bad, not bad.'

Next day, full of confidence we turned up at the balloon. A new unforgiving face greeted us.
'Let's get on then,' he said,
'Where's our sergeant?'
'Gone, you won't see him again. I've been hanging about all day, waiting for you lot, get in.'
It was a silent ascent. At 600 feet, the new instructor dropped the gate with a clang;
'Right; in your own time, sir.'
'Excuse me sergeant, could you hit me on the shoulder and say go?'
'No.'
I trickled over the edge like a cup of cold sick.
One evening the whole school went to see *The Red Beret* (emphasis on the last syllable) with Alan Ladd. When they came to the line 'Nobody laughs at the red beret twice, soldier,' the cinema erupted in derisive cheers.

Later, in the TA I used to subsidise my meagre BBC pay with TA weekends at £1.00 a jump. The only time I wasn't terrified, was when I did four jumps in an afternoon. At the end I was so punchy I would have jumped without a 'chute

On one occasion, I was last out of the door of the aeroplane when I found myself falling rather fast, faster in fact than the man who was first out. I looked up: my parachute was inside out and, quite quickly, tearing in half. I should have pulled the reserve. As it was I hit the ground hard and broke my coccyx, which was not funny as I had to go on a recce next day

Another time the pilot dropped us onto Frensham great pond which was frozen over as we cracked through the ice I thanked God he had chosen the shallow end.

Being a call boy was a wonderful starting job. If you were seriously keen you could earn overtime. Like the civil service, the BBC was divided into a triple hierarchy. First the production people, Producers and PAs[2] who were mainly recruited from university and were destined for Great Things. Then the middle men, floor managers and the like and, finally, the manual grades, scene hands, sparks, prop men, tea ladies and call boys. Manual grades got overtime and, if we

---

[2] Production Assistants

were obscenely keen, we could earn more than £20 a week with no time to spend it. The head call boy was Michael Hurll, afterwards a distinguished light entertainment producer.

I was a source of worry to the management. I was the only one with a degree, albeit a lousy one, and they were at great pains to tell me that promotion was out of the question. It would mean crossing a barrier. I didn't care, I was loving it and learning more every day. I learnt from the scene hands how to cleat a flat and brail a hanging border. I learnt about lighting from the sparks and composition from the cameramen and every one was anxious to help me because I was so obviously and naively interested in their jobs. I worked with wonderful directors, Michael Elliott, Alvin Rakoff, Ned Sherrin, Rudolph Cartier, Kevin Sheldon (they were all called Producers, then). Ned Sherrin likes to portray himself as a sort of dilettante. Nothing could be further from the truth. He is a highly skilled director technically as well as artistically. At the time I was a callboy, he directed *Tonight*, the popular current affairs programme.

One day, while staying with his parents who were farmers, he was driving the cattle home when he was approached by a man with a beard and a clipboard. The man asked, 'Do you have a television?' 'Yes,' said Ned. 'I'd like to ask you some questions,' said the man. 'For example, what is your favourite programme?' '*Tonight*,' said Ned. 'That's interesting' said the man, 'what is it about *Tonight* that you like?' 'The quality of the direction.' 'Ah,' said the man, gratified that a mere cowman was so well informed. When I asked Ned if this was true he said: 'Mostly. But they were sheep, not cows'.

Kevin, who was an inspired maker of children's programmes took a show on location and I went with him, I don't know how he managed it; I did my first piece of directing for him. He and the crew were on a steamer which took some of the actors on board at Southend pier. I was left with the rest of them, a dozen character ladies, (Judith Furse, Hilda Fenemore, Gretchen Franklin et al.) all of some dangerous distinction. Kevin had a camera on board and while he shot some sequences at sea, I would rehearse the ladies. As the boat came back he would run the camera and the ladies would rush to get on board, all with sticks of rock, bottles of Guinness and Kiss-me-Quick hats. The boat left, I turned round and said, 'Now, ladies.'

There was no one to be seen, they had all disappeared in search of gin and cockles leaving me with a skipful of props and a cynical pier manager who said, 'I knew this would happen.'

Time went by - not a sign of them. There was a distant hoot and a plume of smoke on the horizon. Gradually the actresses began to filter back, many of them the worse for wear. I thrust the props into their hands and the hats onto their heads and as the boat came up to land I hid behind the stanchion and cued them. They surged towards the gang-plank, one of their number effecting a spectacular rescue as the oldest lady was nearly thrown into the sea. Kevin said, 'Cut' and my career was saved.

'Nice bit of business you introduced with the rescue' Kevin said.

Stephen Harrison was a kind, agreeable, old homosexual who had had a startling career. As a very young man he had gone to Russia at his own expense and worked for Eisenstein as a location manager and then as assistant director. He then went to America where he worked on silent films in Upper New York State. This was before Hollywood was really established. He became a first assistant and then an editor, and finally came back to England and edited *The Private Life Of Henry VIII* for Alexander Korda. He was being groomed as a director. In 1936 they sent him to Alexandra Palace where TV was just starting up, reasoning that he could make mistakes there and no one could notice. He was one of the world's first TV drama directors. Two of the others were Desmond Davis and George More O'Ferrall. Only *The Mausoleum Club* (q.v.) would be able to tell you the other one. When World War II started he went to BBC Radio News as an Editor and stayed on the staff of the BBC for the rest of his working life.

Sadly, he was an extremely boring director. He worked everything out in great detail and remained absolutely obdurate when the actors wanted to change a move. The productions worked technically but were devoid of any excitement. I was later to be Stephen's assistant. I liked him very much: he was charming and treated me like a colleague, rather than a servant, which some of the other directors did. He had a wonderful collection of Roman glass and some exquisite Hokusai prints. When he was young, his stepfather, Lord Duveen the art dealer, gave him £100 and sent him to Paris to buy a picture. He returned with a Modigliani.

'I don't think much of that,' said his stepfather, and it spent the next twenty years hanging in the lavatory. I was present when Stephen extracted it and sent it to Christie's where it sold for £26,500 pounds, quite a large sum in those days. When he died he left small sums of money to my children which moved me greatly.

One of the most exciting jobs as a call boy was on *This Is Your Life* which was always live and took terrible risks. On one show I was sent out to Shepherds Bush Green and told to stop a taxi and bring a guest into the theatre.
'What happens if it's the wrong taxi?' I asked.
'Shut up and don't argue,' said the producer.
I found the cab somehow and right on time brought Hugh Oloff de Wett, the sculptor, into the studio. The programme had many more interesting subjects then, not just cheesy minor showbiz personalities.

I cannot describe to you the excitement of a live broadcast in those far off days. The final run-through might be technically perfect and smooth and organised, the transmission was quite different. Every person in the studio felt the tension: the silence was eerily complete. When things went wrong, as they sometimes did, they had to be forgotten at once and we got on with the rest of the show. I don't suppose live broadcasting made any difference to the audience, but we found it wildly exciting. I don't think it's a coincidence that the real labour troubles in television started with the onset of tape recording.

# Chapter Two
# Up The Ladder

My next step was to be made an AFM[3]: I was rather a snob and would only go to the drama department. I should be so lucky to be going anywhere, I was told. It was now 1955 and I found it much harder to live on my new wage of £12 per week as there was no overtime. We did classical plays, Francis Durbridge serials, Thrillers, not, in spite of the certainty of nostalgic commentators of today, a great many new plays; those came later. One such rarity was called *Without Vision*; it was Elaine Morgan's first. Most plays of an hour or more camera-rehearsed for two days. Not this one: the director, Peter Lambert was only allowed one day. It had a splendid Welsh cast, and told about how a housewife had been seduced by the wonderful things she saw on the screen and neglected her housewifely duties. Nowadays, this sounds far-fetched, but in those days, TV was still a magical experience for most people.

*Without Vision* had to be rehearsed at great speed. The floor manager was Marguerite Young, a wonderful old bat who became a close friend: she just managed to keep sober from hour to hour and got us through before she hit the gin hard. One scene ended on a group in the dining room, faded out and immediately faded up on a family of eight having high tea with ham and chips 'How do we do it?' I asked.'
'False table top, dear,' she said shortly.
So we laid a piece of five-ply covered with a lace cloth and a vast meal with ham, eggs, chips, steaming teapots and pickles on top of the table, shoving the actors aside, and got out, all in two and a half seconds. As if by magic, the scene changed to a family at tea; the actors looked a little shell-shocked.

I was sent up to Glasgow to work on a play called *Green Cars Go East* by Paul Vincent Carrol about a poor Glasgow family in the depression. To start with, I found the dialogue incomprehensible: 'Come a step nearer and ye'll get a moufu' o' beasties.' This translates as: 'If you approach me further, I shall smash my head into your mouth and you will ingest my head-lice.' Quite simple, really.

I got to know a brilliant architect called Jack Notman, who designed the show for peanuts, compared with his usual fees, and with whom I afterwards worked as a director. I scoured the junk shops for set-dressings, furniture, etc. The money was laughable. If I'd held onto those props I'd be very, very rich. As it was, I bought a very elegant elm bible chair for £4 which I afterwards lent to the BBC for a show with Alec Guinness and which I still have.

---

[3] Assistant Floor Manager

We moved into a gym in Edinburgh for the transmission; it had a curiously long and vibrant echo, which made the living room scenes sound a bit odd. The young lead was played by Bill Simpson, later to become *Dr Finlay*, but then unknown. The drunken father was played by that fine actor Andrew Keir.

Before his first entrance in a rage, he would grab me by the throat and shake me like a rat, murmuring imprecations in my ear. 'For fuck's sake, Andrew,' I would whisper, 'I'm trying to prompt!'

Prompting was a highly-developed skill which had to be learnt; an AFM who couldn't do it wouldn't get far. It was probably most important during the rehearsal period when one would learn the actor's inflexions and establish a relationship of trust with him or her. In the transmission one lived in fear of prompting during a dramatic pause, though if you'd established a good relationship, this wouldn't happen. During Michael Elliott's production of Anouilh's *Antigone*, I became rather wary of Basil Sydney who was playing Creon. During rehearsal if I tried to prompt him, he would snarl at me. On transmission he dried, definitely and spectacularly. Very quickly I belted out a prompt, and he carried on. Afterwards, he came up and said, 'Thank you, Jim; I was as dead as a doornail.'

In the very old days, one just belted the word out, and hoped they would pick it up. Later, we used a cut-key which cut the studio sound during the prompt. But this caused a complete silence which was unnerving. Finally, after a lot of experimental work by the sound department, a system was devised where just before transmission, we would record an endless loop of studio silence, which took over when you pressed the button, and that did the trick.

I was still parachuting at week-ends, and even trying to learn to fly. This cost £4 an hour and I couldn't afford it. To my great chagrin, I never went solo, though I did a spectacular spin in a Miles Magister, which unnerved the instructor somewhat.

Part of my commitment to the TA was a fortnight's annual camp. The BBC, like other employers, was supposed to give me paid leave to do this. I was summoned to the office of Elwyn Jones, the drama administrator, and told that I had to make a choice; leave the TA or my career would be in the doldrums. I did, though as you will see, I landed in the doldrums anyway.

I began to be spoken of as a coming man. Alvin Rakoff did a production of Thornton Wilder's *Our Town* cleverly adapted for TV using no scenery or props, except what you might find in a studio - lamps, ladders, chairs, brailing ropes etc and, occasionally, a false door as was used in rehearsals. I was asked to direct the experimental session. Heather Sears played little Emily, the heroine. At the audition I fell violently in love with her and wanted to cast her. Alvin's fastidious Puritanism wouldn't let him make the decision, as he was in love with her too. We discussed it backwards and forwards for days, until Kay Fraser, Al's secretary, who afterwards worked for me, said 'Oh, for heaven's sake you both want her, why don't you cast her?' We did.

I played the ASM on screen, with quite a lot of lines, in what I hoped was a New England accent. John Welsh played a superb SM and the show was a great success. Bessie Love who was in DW Griffith's *Broken Blossoms* and who must have been of a great age played the mother.

We used to build and strike sets during a live broadcast, although it was rather noisy at times. During a drama documentary about the U.N. we had over 30 sets, 11 of them being struck and four set up during the 90 minutes. We used moving back projection a lot. The noise during the quiet scenes was severe.

On *Z Cars* they would use two moving BP screens for the front and side views of a car, which the actors had to pretend was in motion, timing the turns, stops and starts with the BP. Because the throw of a BP machine was up to 70 feet the image had to be bounced off a mirror, sometimes twice. It was our continual nightmare that someone would cross the beam during transmission and destroy the illusion.

ATV had started a twice weekly serial called *Emergency Ward 10*, one of the first soap operas, certainly the first medical one, and it was very successful. Gerry Glaister, who died recently, was a very lively Producer-Director who was anxious to do an up-market soap: he got hold of two distinguished writers, Bill Naughton, who had written *Alfie*, and Allan Prior, and commissioned them to write about two families, one the managing Director's and the other that of a skilled craftsman working in the factory. Bill was to write the working class family and Allan the middle class ones. Michael Barry, the head of drama, said, 'Yes, Gerard, what a good idea, *Emergency Ward 9* is so good.'

We started casting. The show was to be called *Starr And Company*, and was to be broadcast twice a week live.

I put my flat mate Michael Murray up for the part of the Managing Director's son. He got the part and was suddenly earning £80 a week. Because I was now a floor manager I was earning £18 with little time to spend it. Michael and I both looked for a new flat. It was quite difficult, as I could afford only a small amount of rent. Finally Michael found a very nice place in St James. It was only big enough for one and he said so, so I moved out into a bed sit in Notting Hill, an area not as chic in those days as it is now.

Bill and Allan started writing scripts. Later on, when the conventions of producing a twice-weekly serial had been established, the producer took care that not more than six sets were used per episode, but at the beginning the writers were under no restraint. They would write 12 and 14 sets into a show and there was frantic building and striking. We were all very hard worked - four days rehearsal and two days in the studio. The seventh day was meant to be free but was always taken up with preparation or administration.

I did 52 episodes on the trot, with no days off and became seriously fatigued. At the end I started drinking before a show; at first it was just a Guinness and an Irish Whiskey and after that it was two Irish Whiskies. There was a pleasant little pub opposite Riverside Studios which did very well out of the cast and crew. Thank God I stopped drinking in time; otherwise I could have been in serious trouble.

One of the older actors in *Starr* was Arnold Ridley, the author of *The Ghost Train*. The rights of which he had reputedly sold for £25 and watched others get rich on the proceeds for the rest of his life. Apart from this crucial error he was a wise old bird. When the actors and the director were endlessly arguing about the script, he handed me a note:

*'O what a tangled web we weave*
*When the poor author's words we cleave.'*

I later worked with Gerry Glaister on a live show where quiet scenes in a house alternated with noisy scenes in a pub. The leading actor, Percy Herbert had to drink a pint of beer in one go, and then cause massive trouble in the pub, shouting at everybody. In those days the Method, a watered down version of Stanislavsky's way of working, which had found its way to England via New York, even more watered down, was very strong and Percy felt he had to do the drinking for real at every rehearsal. The beer was flat and warm and disgusting and Percy became rather ill.

On the transmission, when two ladies were talking quietly in a scene on the other side of the studio, Percy suddenly started noisily vomiting and spraying it all over among the extras. Gretchen Franklin grabbed hold of me, 'What are we going to do? What are we going to do?' I said, 'We are all going to shut up; get back to your seat.'

Percy continued to vomit noisily. The ladies at the other end of the studio continued the scene very professionally but a close observer might have seen the look of panic in their eyes. I managed to get a message up to Gerry Glaister in the gallery, saying that if Percy was fit to go on I would put a thumbs up in front of one of the cameras otherwise we would have to fade to black and reassess the situation, which probably meant cutting to the *Potter's Wheel* [4]. This was a dreamlike piece of film where a potter built up a pot, destroyed it and started again and continued ad infinitum. It was used to calm the audience whenever something disastrous happened on air.

Gerry, like the former fighter pilot that he was, remained entirely calm and composed throughout. Percy was still vomiting copiously and I shook him a little and said, 'Are you OK to go on?' He nodded. We had five seconds left. I put up my thumb in front of a camera and Gerry calmly said, 'Cue and cut.' The following scenes worked quite well except for the rather strange sight of the actors fastidiously picking their way between the pools of sick.

I went back to being an AFM. Every now and then, I was advanced to production assistant/floor manager at £18 per week: It seemed I could do no wrong, but the Gods were waiting to punish my hubris. Young and immature, I had an affair with a much liked and older secretary. She became pregnant and I was cited as co-respondent by her husband, who had not even seen her for ten years. It became public knowledge and my career took a dive. The lawyers behaved badly, as they will, and made unpleasant threats. I was advised to break contact with her except for the weekly payments. To my eternal shame, I cravenly did so and didn't see our son, Rory, until he had grown up and wrote to me and made contact. I had tried to forget his existence for many years, wondering what he looked like. Eventually we met several times and began to get to know each other; I wanted to introduce him to our family. I told Simon, our eldest son, who said, 'Hey, leave it out, dad.' Next time I came home he said, 'Well, I rang Rory and we went out for a drink.'

---

[4] An interlude film used by the BBC as a time-filler in schedules.

Trust a young and sensible man to cut through all the nonsense. We all became firm friends and Maggie my wife talks of him as our stepson. He is now the BBC's Business Correspondent, and immensely distinguished. When he married Diane he made us all so welcome at the reception that I had difficulty controlling my tears. They now have two splendid boys, Adam and Rufus.

Alexandre Dumas Fils wrote to his father about a success he had had: 'So great that I thought I was at the premiere of one of your works.' He replied, 'My dear son, the greatest of my works is yourself.' I feel that about all of them.

Michael Elliott did a powerful production of *The Lower Depths* by Gorky with Wilfrid Lawson and an outstanding cast including Eric Thompson, the father of Emma. I was PA/FM on a temporary basis. When Wilfrid made his first entrance with pots and pans tied all over him, singing a song which went 'In the dark of the night, with no light to find you' in his own very nasal peculiar voice, I could see that it was interrupting a love scene between Eric and Diane Aubrey. Eric was seething and about to explode.
I said, 'Wilfred, I'll give you a cue for that little song of yours'.
'What little song?' he said.
I was always a good mimic and I did an exact imitation of him, which made the whole studio laugh.
'Oh,' he said, 'Understudying me, are you? Well, you're not going on tonight, I can tell you, you sod.'

The next day I was due to start work on a dramatised documentary in Cornwall, centred round the ill-starred Penlee life-boat, later to be lost with all hands. Curiously, that was the day after television had come to the region, *The Lower Depths* was talked about in all the pubs 'Did you see that old man, weren't he wunnerful?' This is what I mean about the excitement TV generated in those distant days. It is difficult to imagine a modern audience paying as much attention to an obscure Russian play.

I went doing PA work and being demoted between jobs; I was getting very little money for a lot of hard work. This went on for three and a half years. Maggie, my wife and an outstanding AFM, went to see the Drama Administrator. Fiercely she asked, 'Is it because of the scandal that Jim isn't getting promotion?'
'Yes I'm afraid it is.' he said shame-facedly, 'and it doesn't look as if he ever will.'

During this time, I became attached to BBC Wales at Cardiff. It was run almost entirely by former schoolmasters, the sons of Free Church ministers, who whispered in corners in Welsh. Being a South Walian, I had very little Welsh, and most of that unrepeatable.

We did a series called *Signal Box*, with many fine London-resident Welsh actors and a healthy leavening of talented local amateurs, led by Jack Walters, a local builder. One day, we were in the studio and there seemed to be a lot of rushing about by the staff of a current affairs programme called *Beunydd*.
'What's the matter?' I asked.
'We're doing a programme about Cyprus,' they said, 'and nobody knows the Welsh for compromise'

My wife Maggie, formerly Margot Eavis, and I had worked together on *Starr And Company*. She was obviously very talented and would have leapt ahead in the BBC, probably overtaking me, if we hadn't got married and had children. We now hardly ever worked on the same show, it was thought unsuitable. Thus, when we got married in Pilton church, my address was 7 Senghenydd Road, Cardiff, theatrical digs formerly occupied by Emlyn Williams, as the landlady never tired of telling me: 'Mr Williams had his supper at ten o'clock. I presume you will?' I did.

This address gave rise to some complications when we got married. John Walker, the Vicar of Pilton, Maggie's childhood home, whom I disliked intensely, said he couldn't marry us, as neither of us was resident in the parish, and besides, it was a mixed marriage. Maggie's family were Methodist so we had to go to London to get an Archbishop's Special Licence which involved going to The Sanctuary in Westminster, swearing an oath and paying £25, quite a lot of money at the time. We got to chatting pleasantly with the administers of the oath; in those days, everybody was interested in television, and then went and had a slap up lunch.

John Walker was the man who, when he visited an old lady and she said, 'Vicar, you're such a snob' replied: 'Now, Mrs so-and-so, if I were a snob, would I be sitting here talking to you?'

In 1962 I was having an Annual Interview (how very BBC!) with Norman Rutherford, temporary Head of Drama. He said, 'I don't think you have much creative talent, we would like to groom you as an Administrator?'
I let him know forcefully what I thought of that idea. Many years later when I was directing a rather grand Classic serial, I found Norman was one of the extras. I was very nice to him.

I started looking for another job, anywhere, in or out of the BBC. I wasn't normally very good at selection boards; Al Rakoff gave some advice. He said, 'When you go in, before they get a chance to say anything, point at one of them and say 'What do you do?'
He'll say, some Goddam admin job, then you point at the next one and say 'And You?'
He'll whine on about what he does and by that time you've got it so you're asking the questions, not them.

Eventually a post came up in Bristol. I went to the Board not caring whether I got the job or not; I was pushy and arrogant. Apparently this was the secret. I got the job and took a room in a Regency house on the edge of Clifton, but its postal address was Bristol 7 instead of 8.
'You can't live there' said my mother in law, 'It's Hotwells, and nobody lives in Hotwells.' I did, and very nice it was too.

I suppose I selfishly assumed that Maggie would follow me wherever I went. I certainly wouldn't get away with that nowadays.

We racketed about between Bristol and London for months. It grew ever harder for Maggie, holding down a job in London, while I travelled back and forth, and she soon became pregnant with our first child, Simon.

We bought a house in Axbridge at the ridiculously low price, even then, of £2,350. It had five bedrooms, a big garden, lots of outbuildings and walls which were plastered with lime and horsehair. We found a wonderful builder called Mr Chubb; we never knew his first name. Much later, when our son Simon was three and very articulate, he told us, with great amusement, that Simon had asked him, 'Mr Chubb, can I borrow your hammer?' When he refused, Simon said, 'Mr Chubb, if you don't lend me your hammer I'll say "Bloody Shit".'

When we painted the outside, we dug some ochre from the mine on the hill and put it in a dustbin with quicklime and water. It boiled up most satisfactorily and came out a lovely tawny colour.

We wanted to buy some strawberries, but there were none in the village; everybody grew them and sent them to market. We thought we'd better grow some ourselves and asked our neighbour, Mr Whatton, what he thought of a variety called Redgauntlet?
'How can I put it,' he said, 'It's a very good strawberry for market, but not so good for eating.'

BBC Bristol was a charming little enclave of talented and underpaid people. There were two producer/directors in the drama department; Brandon Acton Bond who played the page in *St Joan* at Birmingham Rep in 1926, I afterwards found, and Patrick Dromgoole. There were first class film cameramen and editors who mainly served the enormous Natural History unit. It was a charming little set-up run very professionally by Desmond Hawkins and Pat Beech which was later to be destroyed in one of the BBC's pathetic re-organizations. I found it pleasant to be regarded as something of an expert in my field and to be invited to programme review board, and settled down happily for the first time for some while.

It was January 1963 and the country was covered with the deepest snow for 300 years. Maggie was also very pregnant. Someone at the BBC remembered that they had planned to do *Lorna Doone* in the summer, although no scripts had yet been written. He also cleverly remembered that there were a lot of scenes of sheep being rescued in the snow. I was told to go to Exmoor on Friday and shoot about 20 minutes of snow scenes. 'The script?' I began.
'Write it yourself, design some clothes, find the locations, go out on Thursday and don't stop shooting till you've got it.'
This was Tuesday.

I got some clothes together from the wardrobe, mainly sheepskin, took two cameramen to Oare in Somerset; the blizzards came down thick and locked us into the moor. Everything happened as if by magic. Oare Ford farm, the first we looked at, was totally unmodernised since the seventeenth century and it was beautiful. They had Red Devon cattle, Exmoor horned sheep and a wonderful dog that was a real star.

I played Gurt Jan Ridd with my back to the camera; Bill Travers was later to repeat the actions in close-up and the two would be cut together. We dug the sheep out of the snow (some of them we'd dug in first), and everywhere we directed the camera the land was sparkling white and glorious.

I say elsewhere in this book that a director should be able to do anything his crew can, if not as well. I saw a half-frozen waterfall above a pond which looked ravishing. I said to the cameraman, 'What we really need is for someone to get into the water and shoot upward.'
'You do it,' he said and handed me the camera. I did it, and bloody cold it was too. It was a beautiful shot, but it ended on the cutting room floor.

The final shot was of Gurt Jan Ridd walking along a pristine landscape with a ewe under each arm. This had to be done first time, as the footsteps from earlier takes would spoil the shot; I just managed it.

We packed up, fought our way out of the valley and I got home just in time to take Maggie to Weston Super Mare hospital to have our son Simon. Sliding on the ice all the way, I was frightened witless. In those days I wasn't allowed anywhere near the delivery room and I mooned about in the time-honoured way worrying myself sick. It was a long and difficult birth but she has great strength and got through it well.

Maggie and Simon came home. The weather continued very cold; there was no bread to be had and Maggie's cousin Michael lost several hundred gallons of milk trying to drag the churns through the snow with a tractor. I went to work on a second hand scooter which bore a shameful L sign. I had failed my scooter test the day after passing my Advanced Driving test. When the tester leapt out from behind a van for the emergency stop I braked too hard, did a full 180 degree turn, coming to rest two inches from him.
'Try again later,' he said, 'Much later'.

I tried making rock cakes; there was no yeast for bread. They seemed a little hard but I gave one to Betsi the dog (no one else would eat them) and later found her surreptitiously trying to bury it in the snow.

The months went by, my first real experience of directing receded into the background. But now we had a son to look after or, rather Maggie did, men could get away with much more in those days. I went back to Exmoor as a First Assistant and found the locations even more beautiful in the summer. I got the local stag hunt to ride for us at £5 per day per man plus horse. They treated it as a lark and got fiercely drunk more often than not. Andrew Faulds who played Carver Doone was terrified of his horse and the farmers used to go behind him and whack it on the quarters until it bolted. I got myself a horse as Assistant Director and fell off spectacularly going down hill.

We eventually got into the studio and did a live episode every week playing in the location film. In this my dear friend John Bennett played Tom Faggus, the romantic highwayman. When John was young, he had an uncle who owned a string of race horses and let him ride them in the holidays; He became really expert. This stood him in good stead for Tom Faggus. The director, Brandon Acton Bond, made him gallop into close up and keep focus, something a stunt rider would hesitate to do. He did it.

When the winter sequences were being shown Sydney Newman, the head of drama, came down. I had been pressed to give him a jar of my home made wine which he swigged copiously during the day. 'I didn't think much of that last episode.' he said, 'except the snow sequences, they were brilliant.' Cue dagger looks from the director.

As I had a few days off, I was asked to direct (produce) two episodes of *The Luscombes*, the West Country radio drama series, written by Denis Constanduros, which was twice as good as *The Archers*. The management tended to play this down, but I was very excited. I was working in a new medium, and I thought the scripts were very good and very funny. A new director is always under a certain disadvantage, the actors know so much more about the show, and if they wish to they can make your life a misery. The cast of *The Luscombes* were very nice to me until we had one hiccup: I suggested that at a poignant moment the clock should strike.

'Oh, no, dear,' said Phyllis Smayle who played Mrs Luscombe, 'The clock broke down about three years ago, November, I think it was, and it's never been mended since.'

I gracefully withdrew the idea, and substituted a passing aeroplane, which they gratefully accepted. I would amaze them occasionally by falling about with laughter at something they found very ordinary. When Dad (Hedley Goodall) said to his daughter, 'Dot, make a long arm for the tomato sauce,' I fell off my chair. They looked on in amazement, but treated me with great kindness.

After *Lorna Doone* I began to be talked about. People would consider me in connection with classic serials. I wasn't thought trendy enough for *Play For Today*. Eventually I had a message from Donald Wilson, Head of Serials: 'I want you to start on *Compact* next month,' he said.

*Compact* was the worst sort of twice weekly romantically rubbishy serial about a woman's magazine. The writers were reputed to get £250 per half hour script which very often they would farm out to be ghosted by an impecunious hack for £100. I hated the idea. I rang Donald and I said, 'It's not that I am too good for it. I think everybody is too good for it and it's meretricious rubbish.'

There was a pause. He said, 'You will either do this, or you will do nothing and I will personally see that you direct nothing for the rest of your life.'

'Well,' I said, 'If you put it that way...'

Bridging the Imjin River in Korea.

*Above:*
*A Flash In The Cam*, Footlights Revue 1957.
JCJ centre.

*Right*: Joyce Finlay,
the beautiful zoologist.

*Below*: Making up for the
Cambridge Amateur Dramatic Club
Nurseries, with Roger Jenkins
on the left.

*Right:* As a callboy with Floor Manager Geoffrey Manton.

*Below:* As Assistant Director filming aboard the ill-fated Penlee lifeboat.

*An Enemy Of The State*

*Esther Waters*

*Opposite page*: Meg Wynn Owen and
Gordon Gostelow.

*Above*: John Bennett.

*The Hunchback Of
Notre Dame*

*Top:*
Peter Woodthorpe.

*Left:* Emrys Jones
and James Maxwell.

*The Portrait Of A Lady*

*Above:*
Richard Chamberlain as Ralph Touchett.

*Right:* Suzanne Neve as Isabel.

*The Scarlet And The Black*

*Above:*
John Stride and
George Roderick.

*Left:*
Preparing to duel.

*Opposite page:*
Karin Fernald and
Gerald Cross.

A selection of Tele-Snaps taken by John Cura.

*Compact*

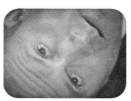

1: Meg Wynn Owen. 2: Richard Chamberlain. 3: Dallia Penn.

*The Forsyte Saga*

*Right:* Kenneth More
*Below:* Susan Hampshire and Martin Jarvis.

*Opposite page (clockwise from top left:*

Eric Porter and Susan Hampshire;
Martin Jarvis and Susan Hampshire;
Betsi, the director's dog.

The author and Glenda Jackson discuss the next scene in *A Bequest To The Nation*.

# Chapter Three
# Back To The Smoke

*Compact* was broadcast live on Tuesdays and recorded as live on Wednesdays for transmission on Thursdays. There was no time or money for editing, so unless one of the cast said 'fuck' (and it did happen) the show went out as recorded.

I was due to start rehearsing my first two episodes on Boxing Day. This meant that we had to travel up from Axbridge on Christmas Day with Simon in his cradle and Betsi the boxer dog (named after the Queen's name in Welsh).

John and Pat Bennett had offered to put us up. They lived in a very smart flat in Swiss Cottage and were wonderfully tolerant of four ragamuffins moving into their beautifully decorated apartment. We lived in agony because the dog was in season and bleeding on the carpet and we cleaned up frantically after her.

On Boxing Day morning I went to the rehearsal room in Putney. As was the custom then, I had worked out every move, every camera position and every lens. When I walked in they said, 'Change of plan, Bill Kerr's been run over and we have to re-write everything.'

The hacks were called in; I threw the camera script away and started from scratch. It was the best thing that could have happened. Robert Flemyng played the Editor. He was a superbly composed actor of the old school, who took his position as leading man lightly, but very seriously. He supported me gently without making it obvious. The rest of the cast were very supportive; when I decided to stage a scene in a gents' lavatory, (very daring in those days) Bobby Desmond said, 'You want to be known as the Alain Resnais of Putney Bridge South.'

Somehow we got through the rehearsals and after three and a half days we moved into the studio. It was all going to be all right. Somehow, I had got a couple of shows together and I knew they would work. Then incipient disaster struck.

Gretchen Franklin, who was a very successful character woman and who would continue to look just the same for the next thirty years button-holed me. The last time we had worked together was the vomiting episode.
'What time do we go out tonight dear?' She said.
'7.30 on the dot.'
'You do know I am in the theatre in *Gentle Jack*, and we go up at 7.30?'
I was dumb struck. Booking a tape machine to play in a scene was a very long wearisome business. Because of the seriousness of the occasion, we got the machine in the next half hour and pre-recorded Gretchen's scene, let her go and continued with the rehearsal.

When 7.15 came around we were sitting in the gallery and the network was on the monitor. I wished they would turn it off, I wanted to concentrate. Suddenly I remembered that at 7.29 someone would say 'One minute' and at 7.29 and 45 seconds someone would say 'Stand by' and at 7.29 and 52 seconds I would say 'Run Telecine' and at 7.30 precisely we would be on the air.

It all happened, we seemed to be going well; and then I remembered Gretchen's scene. I croaked 'Stand by VT.' It needed 10 seconds to run up and giving a wild guess I cued it, 'Run VT.' It turned out more or less right and we played the scene and we finished the show. When Sydney Newman saw the episode, he said, 'This is brilliant,' which pleased me, though I thought it a bit over the top for a soap opera.

The next night went smoothly, I seemed to get on with the cast and I started a run of 18 episodes over several months. On the night BBC2 started, we had rehearsed and were ready to go. Suddenly all the lights went out, there had been a power failure. I was called up to Planning and agreed to record the first episode in the morning and spend the rest of the day rehearsing the second and record it at night. Nothing on *Compact* was ever quite the same again.

John and Pat Bennett generously let us stay in Swiss Cottage until we found somewhere to live. Amazingly, we found a big house in Kew and bought it with a massive mortgage. I was still getting paid on a temporary basis, so we had to take lodgers. Many were students; we lived on the ground floor and let the rest of the house. Over the years it got worse, and then better, we thought we were now on an even keel. When we went away for a few weeks in the summer, we returned to find the place full of drug addicts, none of whom we had ever seen before. They used to aim their disposable syringes at next door's dog and the lawn looked as though it had sprouted a harvest of hypodermics. The police weren't helpful. They said, 'We like having them here, we can keep an eye on them and eventually arrest a dealer.'

Eventually we got them out, long after they had ceased to pay any rent at all.

Meanwhile, my unaccustomed humility on *Compact* paid off. I did a six part serial of George More's *Esther Waters* with John Bennett and Meg Wynn-Owen. It was taken quite seriously and praised. Then I did a spy thriller called *An Enemy Of The State* starring Dallia Penn, an Israeli actress who later went back for the Six Day War. She sent me a postcard of Masada and a message saying 'Hopes are high.' She stayed for a while in the army and returned to work on *The Forsyte Saga* (qv) then made her home in Israel where many years later, I met her on my British Council tour (qv).

We made Kingston Power station look like a vast steel factory. We had a splendid cameraman called Peter Bartlett, who handled a 35mm camera with such steadiness that it looked like a crane shot. By sheer guess work we managed to make Wandsworth Town Hall look like the KGB headquarters complete with red flag, and impress the management and a few other potential employers.

Then, for the first time I did Henry James's *The Ambassadors* with Bethel Lesley whom we sneakily got over from America, for no money to speak of: my first encounter with Henry James was to prove very fruitful later on. That fine actor Bruce Boa came to be interviewed for Strether, the lead. After I had spent some time asking what he had done he said, 'And what have you done?'

'Nothing much' I was forced to say.
A very good lesson in humility. *The Ambassadors*, in three parts worked well, but I resolved, some time in the future to do it again

John Stride next played Julien in Stendhal's *The Scarlet And The Black*, his first television after doing *Romeo And Juliet* for Zeffirelli. When we did the scene where his lover buried his heart in a great cave in the mountain we pointed the camera out of the studio doors (no filming allowed) and had the extras cross a bridge carrying flaming torches and singing the Dies Irae. Very exciting. Henry Oscar played the priest and Carl Bernard was unforgettable as a veteran of Napoleon's campaigns. What am I talking about? Television is ephemeral; the whole production is forgotten now. Karin Fernald was a delectable heroine.

John had great pride in being able to cry at will. We were shooting a scene of him in a box at the opera. I said, 'I want to see a tear rolling down your cheek as the soprano reaches her high C.' He did it twice during the rehearsal, but couldn't on the take. A very bad, selfish piece of direction.

The drama department had been trying for years to get the rights to *The Forsyte Saga* and its follow-up trilogy, *A Modern Comedy*. MGM were quite willing to sell them, except for *The White Monkey* which they had sold to someone else years ago. Donald Wilson, who produced the 26 hour epic, was desperately trying to find a way around it when they rang up. They did own the rights. They had bought a firm to which they had sold *The White Monkey* and only when they checked did they find that they had owned it all the time.

It is difficult to remember that all those years ago, we treated *Forsyte* as just another show. We had no idea that forty years on it would still be watched by thousands, or that it would be regarded as the BBC's first Classic serial and indeed would be part of the title of this book. We had done plenty of Classics before that we thought were rather good and we reckoned that this was just another job, though a bit longer. We were wrong, weren't we?

In early 1967 we started work.

David Giles was to direct the beginning and I would do a big chunk in the middle starting with young Jon and Fleur. I cast Martin Jarvis and Susan Hampshire. She was very nervous and frightened and was concealing profound dyslexia. When I got the scripts I was in despair. The series was already underway, I was to direct eight weeks of location filming and the scripts were drab, boring and conventional. I said to Donald, with my heart in my mouth, that I couldn't direct them. Donald said, 'I'll write you the location film sequences and by the time you have finished I will have the studio scripts ready.'

We proceeded. I made up a lot of introductory shots, one for each episode. Many of them we threw away later. The filming went spectacularly well. When we were filming Jon and Fleur on Chanctonbury Ring, where Susan sang, enchantingly, 'O who will o'er the Downs with me?'

Donald arrived in a rage: 'What's this I hear about you overspending and commissioning music?'
'Two oboes only,' I said crisply. 'I'm not bloody made of money,' he said.
There was a roaring and a rattling sound from above.
'And what the hell's that?'
'That's the helicopter I've ordered for the next shot. May we get on?' I said.

When we got into the studio things began to turn a bit funny. Eric Porter was a superb Soames. He was a militant, but self hating homosexual, whose ruthlessness soon became apparent. In the middle of a scene with Sue Hampshire, he stormed off and said, 'I can't work with this girl, she has no technique.'

The trouble was she had tons of technique. She lacked confidence, was sneered at by some because she was thought to be middle class but she was, and is, a superb actress.

After a while Eric turned his attention to me: He would refuse all direction both in moves and in mood. It made chaos of ensemble scenes. The other actors, many of them very distinguished, wanted to be told where to go and Eric would try and direct them which made them very uncomfortable. We would eventually sort something out, but I would come home night after night quite distraught and sleep only for an hour or two.

By this time we had another son Deiniol (the Welsh for charming) known as Din. He was born very prematurely when I was in Glasgow shooting *The Scarlet And The Black*. Thankfully Maggie was able to stay in hospital for a few days. Din looked exactly like the Giles child in the *Daily Express* with a great shock of black hair. Poor Maggie put up with all this. She was working herself, much of the time, and also had the responsibility of finding someone to look after the children. I was being paid £3,000 a year and had resigned from the staff of the BBC. I was told I had £700 in the pension fund less £30 for which I had had tax relief. They told me I could leave it with them and at the age of 65 I would have a pension of 30 shillings[5] a week. I drew the lot out and bought a Bristol car.

Maggie made me sign a piece of paper saying I wouldn't work with Eric Porter again for however much money. I was glad to.

Kenny More was a delight to work with and acted as leading man in the absence of any input from Eric. I remember him telling a young actor to go away and shave 'That's no way to come to rehearsal.' He did so at once, he loved Kenny as we all did. We nearly fell out over his death scene. The cameramen came and whispered, 'He keeps beckoning us to come in closer, what shall we do?'
I said, 'Do it, and flip the lens to a wider one.'

The last rehearsal was very slow. I said to Kenny 'You've got to take it faster.'
He exploded 'You know bugger all about acting or anything else. I'll take it at the pace I like.'

---

[5] £1.50

On the take, he took two minutes off a seven minute scene, was twice as moving as before, died, then came over and embraced me.

None of us was prepared for the explosive success of *The Forsyte Saga*. Kenny gave an interview to the press and said, 'David Giles and Jimmy Cellan Jones are the two directors most in demand in this country.'

I had been out of work five weeks at the time.

*Forsyte* was nominated for a Guild award (the precursor of BAFTA). No one asked us to the party. When the *Saga* was announced as the winner, the award going to *The Production Team*, Donald stepped up and took it. David and I read about it the next day in the newspaper.

Every time someone thinks of doing a new production of *Forsyte* I get interviewed by *The Sunday Times*. When Granada did it recently, I was asked what I thought of the idea. The article said: 'Why can't they think of something new, fumed James Cellan Jones.'
I thought of ringing up and saying, 'Sneered not fumed.'

In the event, the Granada production was very good except for one ghastly performance. The only thing that disappointed me was the nice things in the story that they left out, because we had done them before, like the scene on Chanctonbury Ring, the meeting in June's gallery and Fleur running across Marsh Lock. When we shot it, she couldn't run fast, as she was wearing high heels. So she said, 'Let me run in my bare feet; they'll never notice.' They didn't.

# Chapter Four
# Notre Dame De Paris

Victor Hugo's book talks of a door high up in the Cathedral, with the Greek word ΑΝΑΓΚΗ carved on it, meaning Fate. I have seen it. We were given a comprehensive tour around Notre Dame by Philippe, Le Petit Gardien as he described himself. We leant over the gallery next to a gargoyle where a woman had thrown herself off the previous week landing on an American tourist and killing her. Philippe took us into the roof space where massive timbers, some original, some replaced by Violette Le Duc held up the heavy slates. Philippe called it La Foret.

All this was to get to know the building for a production of *The Hunchback Of Notre Dame* which was to be shot mainly in the studio and of which Vincent Tilsley's scripts were very unsatisfactory and had to be re-written.

Peter Woodthorpe, a fine character actor played Quasimodo. James Maxwell played Frollo the mad monk, Wilfrid Lawson was Clopin, King of the Beggars and Gary Raymond the young troubadour. Wilfrid, an incorrigible drunk, was one of the finest actors of his generation. He had been blacked by Binkie Beaumont of HM Tennant, then the most powerful person on the English theatre, for drinking too much. Beatrix Lehmann who was also in the cast had also been blacked for being a communist. HM Tennant had, I thought, a lot to answer for.

I had been a call boy on many shows with Wilfrid. I had had to chase around all the pubs in Shepherds Bush and he would leave little notes saying 'Ha Ha!'. I had also, you may recall, worked with him on *The Lower Depths*. He had a long speech which started 'I, Clopin, King of the Beggars ask you Hugo de Beaumont, Bishop of Paris...' On all the rehearsals and at least one take, he addressed him as Binkie de Beaumont.

He kept pretty sober except for one day when Gary Raymond and Emrys Jones were playing a scene where they argued across his face. Wilfred had hardly any dialogue and sulked, then got drunk. I told him that most of the scene would be shot on him in close up but he didn't believe me. The climax came when he rose to his feet and shouted: 'To arms!' And someone threw him a sword from across the room which he was meant to catch.

Because he was so drunk he missed the sword and it skeetered across the floor. Everything stopped. There was huge embarrassment. Wilfrid sobered up as if by magic. We re-shot the scene. He was sparklingly different and caught the sword with great panache.

Poor Peter had a fake back made to protect him during the flogging scene. His winces and squeals during it were at times too real.

This was the first screen appearance of my son, Din. He played the baby Hunchback with a tiny fibre glass hump. Frollo baptised him. He was playing a mad sadistic monk but for one moment he became very quiet and gentle as he said, 'Quasimodo.'
He was named after the first word of the daily office of the day he was found, which was the Sunday after Easter.

We were not allowed to do any filming in France. The sets, though enormously ambitious, were not really like the actual thing apart from an enormous pair of fibre glass bells which Peter balanced on. They, and he, looked wonderful.

I managed, I think, to break new ground by shooting Frollo in close up screaming his head off against a moving BP[6] shot of a zoom-in to the ground, thus giving the illusion that we were following him down on his suicide dive. We had the BP on a loop, and he had to repeat the screams so much that we ended up corpsing. It looked pretty good except when we overcranked and he drifted down very slowly

*Hunchback* was six months out of my life. It is one of the few shows I feel should be allowed to rest in peace.

Colour was just becoming to television and experiments were made. I was aksed to direct something in colour and I chose to do an adaptation of Saul Ansky's *The Dybbuk*. I transferred all the action to a Welsh chapel and it was a very Grand Guignol sort of production. I fell out with the Costume Designer because I wanted everything in plain black and white so the fleshtones would stand out. And when a young girl made her entrance with a bunch of red flowers it would have an instant impact. I wonder if it still exists?[7] Bits of it were rather good.

---

[6] Back Projection
[7] It doesn't exist, sadly.

# Chapter Five
# **Station Street**

Peter Dews, who had done a beautiful production of *An Age Of Kings* with an extraordinary cast including Sean Connery as Hotspur and Maggie, my wife, as first assistant director, had taken over Birmingham Repertory Theatre which had nurtured almost every great talent on the English stage. In early 1967 he had had a great success with *Hadrian The Seventh* and was going to the Mermaid to put it on. I was to look after the Rep - still in the old and beautiful Station Street theatre - and do a production of Shaw's *St Joan*.

There was a mischievous and talented company. Anna Calder-Marshall as Joan, Michael Gambon as the Bishop of Beauvais and Timothy Dalton as Dunois. I asked the stage management whether the play had ever been done here before. 'I think so,' they said and found the original prompt script. It had been done in 1926. James Stewart, later to become to Stewart Granger, played Dunois and Elspeth March, whom he later married, played Joan.

I threw myself into the production with immense enthusiasm. I'd had to extricate myself from a TV play by Maurice Edelman which would have paid three times as much. I fell in love with the Theatre, both the building and the concept. When I had got rehearsals underway, the stage manager said 'I want you to meet Mrs Shakespeare.'
'Who's she?' I asked.
She was a veteran programme seller.
'How long dooz this plye last, luv?' She asked.
'The original production with Sybil Thorndike was nearly four hours long,' I said.
'They won't stand for that here,' she said. 'They'll miss the last booz. Yer'll ave to coot it.'

I thought about it and cut half an hour out of the English Tent scene and speeded up the rest. It improved the show immensely. It ran in repertoire over six weeks.

Simon was now five. I took him to Brum to see the play. We had a puncture on the motorway and he helped me change the wheel: then we went to a matinee and he watched entranced throughout. We went backstage and he met the cast and the Stage Manager let him press the buttons. We had a Chinese meal (which he'd never had before) and went home. He came back from school next day and said, 'We were asked about something we'd done in the holidays. I didn't think I'd done anything much so I pretended I'd been skiing.'

After the first night party, we all went to a night club. My friend Vernon Dobtcheff, who had paid me the great honour of coming to the first night, was wearing his usual garb, a faultless black suit with a black silk soutane. The bouncer wouldn't let him in.
'He's not wearing a toy,' he said.

Unusually, I was wearing a tie, a rather farouche blue number.
'Cinderella shall go to the ball,' I said
I borrowed a penknife and cut the tie in half, giving the smaller half to Vernon. Honour and the bouncer were satisfied and we were admitted.

Part of my job during these few weeks was to keep a leery eye on the other two productions in the repertoire: *Romeo And Juliet* and *Othello*. Mike Gambon played Othello with Brian Cox as Iago. I first saw a schools' matinee of *Othello*. The kids were absolutely merciless. It was a fine production with two very strong performances, but the kids sniggered all the way through, the boys setting the girls off and vice versa. It was very shocking for the actors, who had been well received by the grown up playgoers, and they finished in a lather of sweat. Fortunately, their confidence was restored by a very positive reaction from an adult audience in the evening.

*Romeo And Juliet* went well most evenings. Peter Dews had a partially deserved reputation as The Prince of Darkness, due to the low lighting of many of the productions. The tomb scene was especially gloomy. Gambon, who was playing the Duke, would mischievously enter each evening carrying a different object and defy the audience to see it. Once he came on with a bicycle and another time, when one of the Assistant Stage Managers brought her baby backstage, grabbed the child and made his entrance with it in his arms. Nobody appeared to notice.

Gambon gave a stirring performance in *St Joan* as the Bishop of Beauvais. In rehearsal he asked me why his character was subject to apparently insane bouts of rage, I thought for a moment and replied, 'It's because he has a very painful syphilitic leg'. He looked at me a bit suspiciously, but from then on he preceded each outbreak by clutching his tibia.

When a play is in repertoire over a long period the cast can get lazy. I mostly left them alone but occasionally would go up and see the show unannounced. One Wednesday matinee I could see that they were just coasting through the play and to my horror I saw Sybil Thorndike and Lewis Casson, who had created the parts of Joan and de Stogumber, sitting in the front row. They were at the King's Theatre in Birmingham and their matinee was on a different day. In the first interval I went backstage. The cast looked very nervous and shifty. 'You don't know the half of it,' I said. 'Sybil and Lewis are in front, I was ashamed of you.' The performance got much, much better. Gambon became a friend and we'll hear more of him later.

# Chapter Six

# Quadrille In A Sentry Box

Henry James once said that 'Most English conversation is like a quadrille in a sentry box.'

This can be very true of some of his novels, to which I was inexplicably attached. You may remember that in 1965 I had directed *The Ambassadors* in black and white. It was now early 1968. Colour had just come to BBC2. There was a snarling dislike between those who put on downbeat serious *Plays for Today* and those who did classic serials. The plays stayed on for some time being shot in black and white. Colour was reckoned to be camp and a bit silly and not real. I wanted to do both, but got firmly stuck in the classics.

The second colour serial to be produced was to be *The Portrait Of A Lady* by Henry James, beautifully adapted by Jack Pulman. I liked the scripts even better than the book and conceived the outrageous idea of casting Richard Chamberlain who had just finished a massive series of episodes of *Dr Kildare*. There was a certain amount of opposition to this, though Shaun Sutton now Head of Serials backed me up. Obviously we had to get a labour permit and he had to accept a very small fee.

When he arrived at Heathrow, Jane Annakin and I, then his agent and soon to become mine, went to meet him. She had brought a copy of the labour permit with her. I scoffed a little at this. We waited at the barrier for quite a long time and an official came out and said, 'Does anyone here know a Mr Chamberlain? He's got no labour permit and he's going straight back on the next plane.' Jane produced it and all was well.

There followed an exciting period of rehearsal. Alan Gifford played Mr Touchett, Beatrix Lehmann was his wife. Bea's sister Rosamund, the novelist and John Lehmann the editor used to come and sit in the gallery during the recording. A beautiful English girl called Suzanne Neve who'd been in *The Forsyte Saga* played Isabel. Edward Fox played Lord Warburton.

On the first day's filming Edward was rather nervous. We were filming at Hatfield House which is rather intimidating and we were all a bit shaky. I told him a filthily scabrous Welsh joke. He laughed so much I thought he'd never stop. Then he pulled himself together and gave a performance of such truth and delicacy that it left us breathless. One day he spoke a speech so perfectly that he dried the rest of the cast up, they were so moved. We used to eat at Carlo's Place in the Fulham Road which was cheap and very good. One day Beatrix said, 'I think Carlo is so attractive, I wish I was a man.'

Just before we went into the studio, on Christmas Day in fact, Maggie gave birth to our daughter Lavinia. The cast generously sent telegrams to the new lady.

We were very nervous; the critics were licking their lips and waiting to butcher Richard. Remember, television was still big news and you could rely on notices, good or bad, in all the national dailies.

The show worked like a charm. Richard got stunning notices and it was repeated twice. When the Guild Awards came around we were nominated. I was irrationally excited and wondered who had won. Llewellyn Rees, an old friend said, '*The Parachute*, I thought everyone knew that.'
I was upset, not only because, I didn't think it one of David Mercer's best plays, but because I naively thought that the name of the winner was a secret until someone opened the envelope. I vowed that if ever it depended on me in the future it would be a secret and readers will see in later chapters if I kept my promise.

I had now become a distinguished director of classic serials. When I was offered a single play *Albinos In Black* by Alun Richards, I jumped at it. I offered the part of the materfamilias to Gwen Ffrangcon-Davies for no other reason that she was bright, very old indeed and I remembered vividly the old records of *The Immortal Hour* when she sang *Etain* with a wild untrained pure voice. For the play I got her to sing *I've Got A Lovely Bunch Of Coconuts* in Welsh. I had a chorus of Welsh fox hunting miners who sang *Abide With Me*, so beautifully that there wasn't a dry eye in the house.

Michael Bakewell, who was Head of Plays, a job I was to do many years later, wrote a very sarcastic report on me, that I needed to learn how to pace a full-length play. I hated him not only for that, but for marrying the beautiful Joan Rowlands. She eventually ditched him. A woman of great taste.

The next year I did *The Way We Live Now* with Colin Blakely and a young brash enthusiastic cast. The scripts by Simon Raven, who'd been to the same school and university as me, were certainly better than the recent version.

Also I did two Somerset Maugham stories. One was *The Creative Impulse* with John Le Mesurier, Brenda De Banzie and Megs Jenkins.

Verity Lambert, the producer, had warned me about Brenda, she proved capricious, difficult and malicious. When I laughed at some particularly inventive business by John Le Mesurier she drew me aside and said:
'I noticed you laughing at John's gag. Please ask yourself, will the audience laugh? I leave you with that thought.'
John said, 'I'll cut it, I'll cut it.'
'No you won't,' I said, 'Over my dead body.'

Brenda became as difficult as Eric Porter, but now I had the confidence to deal with her which I did with a kind of breezy insouciance. Just before a run through she started crying. I took no notice but let the cast (who hated her) carry on. She blubbered her way through the whole hour. I affected not to notice the tears and said, 'Splendid, Brenda.'

The other Somerset Maugham story I did was *Olive*, originally called *The Book Bag*. It was almost impossible to adapt, though. David Turner did his best. We filmed quite a lot of it in Swansea which was meant to represent Malaya. I filled the shots with waiters from Chinese restaurants in lampshade hats.

We photographed Eileen Atkins and Eddie Fox galloping along the beach and going to sea in a very dangerous little yacht and a good time was had by all, including me who stood in for Eddie galloping along the beach. We found ourselves having to drag a big clinker built boat up a cliff to the next bay to catch the tide. We could never have done it if the electricians hadn't decided to break the habit of a lifetime and help. It would never have happened at all in ITV.

Verity had sensibly counselled me against casting a young man who had played a pretty boy in an Italian film. Foolishly I cast him. He proved to be awkward, to say the least. In one important scene, he was in the foreground being wooden with Eileen being brilliant and playing the piano in the background. I could have restaged it; instead, I turned up the backlight and Eileen's key and killed the boy's keylight[8] so one couldn't see his face, and all the attention was focussed on Eileen.
'Right,' I said, 'We'll go for a take.'
'Wait a minute,' he said, 'There's a light missing that should be on me.'
'No there isn't,' I said, 'Let's get on, shall we?'
We did. If you look closely you can just see the suppressed laughter in Eileen's eyes. Or perhaps it's only I that can see it.

By now it was 1970 and although the explosion of French youth had started in 1968, there was still a white-hot revolutionary feel among English students.

Many producers and agents were ruthless Marxists, many less directors. Like many I somehow wanted to be part of the revolution, but hated Marxism. When the students of the RCA film school locked up all their lecturers in their offices and refused to be taught by them, they decided to choose their own teachers and I was one of them. Feeling foolishly and dangerously flattered, I started a series of six lectures (unpaid of course, money was so bourgeois) and after two or three I began to feel rumblings of discontent. Somerset Maugham apparently was an old reactionary not fit to be produced.

One of the students, Mireille Danserau asked me to take part in a discussion programme which they would record. I naively agreed. I got into the studio and found we were to sit on the floor (chairs were so decadent). Mireille was in tears: 'All the cameramen are giving me the same shot; when I try to direct them they say I am a fascist.'

It was eventually sorted out and the discussion started. It droned on for twenty minutes. Then the door opened. A terrifyingly bearded person carrying a small child burst in and took over the discussion. He was Steven Ben Israel of the Living Theatre (not his real name). It was a notorious group which courted publicity by shouting at their audiences and physically assaulting them.

---

[8] The main light on an actor's face

He sat down and talked non-stop for 15 minutes, the word 'shit' appearing monotonously often. 'All television is shit, you people are all shit.' It was a set up, of course. The two year old child was pleasant and affable, so I was chatting quietly to him. The chairman said,
'What do you think about that, Jim?'
I replied 'I have never heard such a lot of old shit in my life, I've been far more interested in talking to this little boy.'

Steven erupted like a volcano, abuse poured from him, he slapped me across the face again and again and spat in my eyes and wiped it round with I noticed rather dirty hands. I was quite frightened, but kept smiling which enraged him further. Finally, after twenty minutes or so, he picked up the little boy, spat very accurately into the centre of the camera lens said,
'The message is fuck,' and walked out.
I was shaking quite a lot but trying to appear cool. The students bombarded me with questions.
'Why are you so calm?'
'You should have engaged in dialogue with him.'
'Why didn't you hit him? It would have shown you loved him.'
I said, 'But I didn't love him I thought he was dreadful.'

So ended my association with the RCA film school. Ironically, many of the students were French sons and daughters of the rich bourgeoisie playing at Le Film before going to work in Daddy's silk factory.

I needed a few days of convalescence after that. Quite soon I forgot all about it. I was rudely awakened a year later by an invitation to the Forbidden Film Festival. On the cover of the programme was billing for a film called *Forum* starring James Cellan Jones. They had transferred the whole thing to 35mm and here it was. Maggie and I attended. We watched the film through. There was considerable applause; I got some curious glances from the audience on the way out. Maggie was very supportive but I needed another couple of days of convalescence.

Now back to Henry J. Being now established as a director who understood him (I am not sure that that was ever so. I followed my instincts and felt his ghost smiling paternally and forgiving my lack of intellect), I was offered *The Golden Bowl*. As usual, it was to be shot almost entirely in the studio and written again by Jack Pulman who captured the astringent quality of the dialogue without the long sentences.

We discussed how to tell the story; Jack was keen on a narrator. I had great misgivings until I thought of Cyril Cusack, who could be almost hypnotic at times. He insisted on using an autocue (just as well). Kathleen Byron played his wife. Charlotte was played by Gayle Hunnicutt quite stunningly well. Dan Massey played the Prince and Barry Morse the father, Jill Townsend his daughter. Dan and Gayle had a tendency in common - to start with a brilliantly instinctive approach to the part and then by an intellectual process to tear it to pieces. Fortunately Gayle, a consummate professional, was able to put her intellectuality in the cupboard and bring it out occasionally for an airing, Dan followed.

On one of the few days of location filming on Brighton Pier, Gayle was late on the set. It was beginning to rain and I was shaking with fury. When she arrived, I shouted intemperately at her

and criticised her professionalism and much else besides. She began to cry and said,
'If we're late and we are losing time, why are we standing here with you shouting at me?
Shouldn't we be getting on with shooting?'
Abject collapse of foolish director. We shot in driving rain and it was magnificent.

*The Golden Bowl* was accepted without much fuss by the critics and the public. They were perhaps over-used to the sumptuousness of costume and scenery. In contrast it was very well thought of in America and is still talked about and written up by Academics. Cyril Cusack was electrifying and squeezed all the humour out of it. Years later when I went to a Henry James Symposium in Dallas, Texas, I met Leon Edel, the great Henry James scholar. We had tremendous laughs together. There was a band playing slightly out of date numbers and picked out in flowers above them, the words HENRY JAMES.

There were black tablecloths and white lilies on the table. It looked like a mortician's convention. We all gave lectures. Mine was rather adlibbed and made too much use of flamboyant hand gestures. The ones by the academics were a bit constipated.

# Chapter Seven

# Sous Les Ponts De Paris

David Turner, the distinguished writer and I had fallen out. He had written a life of Jesus whom he saw as a bloody revolutionary playing at guerrillas with all the disciples. I couldn't go along with this, though I had agreed to do it and as more scripts came in I felt more and more worried. I told Shaun Sutton, now Head of Serials, that I would have to walk out. I said this with a sinking heart. I had two children and no money. He refused and said, 'Leave it over the weekend.' I said I wouldn't change my mind. He said, 'Bugger off home, there's a good chap.'

I went home and Maggie and I gloomed through the weekend. On Monday morning I went into work: Shaun had pulled the show. The BBC was now obliged to pay me for the length of the contract and find me something else. This was an act of generosity on his part. I still think of it.

Some years later, in 1970, David Turner was commissioned to adapt all three volumes of JP Sartre's *Roads To Freedom* in thirteen episodes. He was a little wary at first. 'I hope you're not going to run out on this one.' But we got on very well. It is probably the closest collaboration I have ever had with a writer. The role of Mathieu was a towering leading part. It was also in danger of being dull and boring. I cast Michael Bryant who never was. Daniel the ruthless and tortured homosexual was brilliantly played by Daniel Massey and Lola the cabaret singer by Georgia Brown.

This was the beginning of an enormously fruitful collaboration with Dick Holmes, a composer of outstanding range. I did an immense amount of research into French Café Concert songs. Georgia didn't speak much French but sang faultlessly. During one session Stanley Myers, the arranger, made her wear headphones to balance the seven piece orchestra. She hated this and after rehearsal took the cans off and went through each of their performances very critically indeed. Then she sang it beautifully.

I couldn't find the right opening music, I tried Les Six (Poulenc, Milhaud, Georges Auric, Germaine Tailleferre and I can never remember the other two) but none of them was right. I even cut the titles to a piece of Messaien, it sounded horrible.

Suddenly I thought why not compose a tune myself? I could write a lyric in French, no problem, so I tapped out the tune with two fingers on the piano and played it to Georgia.
'Can you sing this?' I said.
'When?'
'In a couple of days.'
'For fuck's sake, OK.'

So Dick arranged the tune for oboe and cello and Georgia recorded it two days later. The lyrics were:

*La route est dure, la vie est morne*
*Mon ame n'est sure d'aucune borne*
*Je ne sais que faire avec ma vie*
*Quand toute la terre m'est endurcie*

Not a very cheerful piece, but it captured the admiration of a lot of people. The BBC paid me £25 for 26 transmissions including the repeats. Fortunately my agent got me to join the Performing Rights Society and I had a stake in it for the future. One day I got a letter from them saying 'Total receipts from all sources 2p. We will add this amount to your next receipts, if any.' Next time I got £2,950.

The cast managed to dig their way into their characters and became supremely confident. We did quite a lot of location shooting in France. Villenauxe-la-grande which stood in for the town devastated in the final battle took us to their hearts. On the recce Ken Riddington my PA accompanied me around over forty villages. I said to him, 'You remember the second one we saw? I want you to go back and book it. I'm going back to London to carry on with the casting.' Ken went to Villenauxe, called a meeting of the mayor, the town council and had them at his feet. We got permission to take over the whole town for three days to blow off the doors of the Mairie and to set fire to the church tower. The whole population joined in, often providing their own period clothes and props, though some were scared out of their wits when they saw our German actors in Wehmacht uniforms.

In Paris you have to get detailed permission from all police forces and there are five including the Beaux Arts police. When we were challenged by a policeman, the French electricians took him around the corner and filled him in until we'd finished shooting.

There was a very important shot of Michael Bryant as Mathieu in a deserted Paris deciding whether or not to throw himself off a bridge. We had forgotten that it was Easter and Paris was full of tourists, mostly German. It was almost impossible to keep them out of the shot until Michael said 'Raus, schweinhunde!' and they disappeared.

This was the first speaking performance of my son Simon; he played Pablo the son of the character played by Andrew Faulds. He was shown looking out of a window and describing all he saw below, soldiers, horses, tanks, artillery: he was very convincing. When the actress who played his mother had to smack him, she was frightened of hitting him across the face. She hit his arm instead, which hurt much more. He was very stoical indeed. It was also the first appearance of our mad boxer dog Chips. Our cleaner, Mrs Saby, took him to the studio. He ran around a flat and knocked over a microphone. The Sound Mixer was livid. Mrs Saby said, 'Silly place to put it, I told him.'

*Roads To Freedom* was well thought of, despite the seriously downbeat subject matter although we put as much humour into it as possible. Perhaps its surprisingly naïve socialism and simplistic philosophy appealed to the young. I still meet middle aged men who can sing the theme song.

Georgia was wonderful, she died tragically young. Michael and Dan, both of whom I worked with often later are both now dead, I miss them very much.

## Chapter Eight

# O Dark, Dark, Dark, Amid The Blaze Of Noon

*Eyeless In Gaza*, which I had made in 1971, was Ian Richardson's first television after leaving the RSC[9]. Michael Gambon was another lead actor. The action took place mostly in the South of France and Mexico. As I was building a house in Portugal at the time I insisted that this was the only possible location. The BBC reluctantly agreed. We took a cheap charter flight to Faro. Maggie, who came to supervise the building, was mortally afraid of flying and was preparing to drink herself into oblivion. Michael Gambon, who had a private pilot's licence kept her falling over with laughter with lines like, 'I don't like the sound of that port engine' and 'God, did you hear the undercart? I hope it's not fallen off.' She laughed so much she was never frightened again.

Much of the filming consisted of John Laurie and Ian travelling through mountainous countryside on muleback. John, a master at upstaging ad libbed, got off his mule and moved closer to the camera. He called his mule 'hen' a Scottish word for dear. The mules, contrary to rumour, were wonderfully placid. Gambon dug his spurs into his once only to get it above a trot. 'I couldn't bear it,' he said, 'his little heart was beating so fast,' so we confined ourselves to walking shots. The rain started coming down and we had to leave without the mule riding close ups. We shot these later with John and Ian sitting on stools in my back garden.

We had one technical difficulty. We had to shoot a sequence where Ian and Lynn Farleigh were making love on a roof top when a passing plane dropped a dog out which landed on the roof beside them and burst covering them all in blood. It was piece of bizarre imagining by Aldous Huxley or perhaps it originated from a real news item.

We obviously had to do this without harming a dog and this is how we did it. We found the only suitable biplane in Portugal, pointed the camera at a revolving mirror, telling the pilot by radio where to fly for the best shot. We had a quarter inch model of a fox terrier which we put on to the mirror and revolved it so it looked as though it was falling through the sky. We had two prop men standing by with fake blood and John Baker the cameraman swung a woolly toy past the lens so that it looked like a blur, then the prop men threw the blood onto the actors and we cut to a made up corpse with celluloid ribs sticking out and dubbed on the noise of flies. It was very effective.

We shot a sequence of Philippa Markham being raped by Ian; she was very nervous as she had been in a similar scene in a film directed by Ken Russell. The scene went well. Philippa is now a very important agent. Gambon and Richardson were both wonderful. I will never forget Gambon speaking Chesterfield's lines:

---

[9] Royal Shakespeare Company

*Then old age and experience hand in hand*
*Lead him to Death and make him under stand*
*That all his life he had been in the wrong*
*Huddled in death the Reasoning Engine lies*
*That was so proud, so witty and so wise.*

When he spoke the lines, Ian, a wise fellow and a distinguished Shakespearian said, 'This boy is going to be very, very good.'

# Chapter Nine
# To Sea In A Sieve

Hal Wallis was a fierce, famous old American producer. He offered me a feature film of Terence Rattigan's *A Bequest To The Nation*. It wasn't one of Terry's best works, but had had some success as a theatre play.

I was to be paid £10,000, riches beyond the dreams of avarice. Terry was to get £70,000 for the rights and another large sum for the adaptation. He was ill at the time with the beginnings of cancer which was later to kill him. I went to see him in Albany and he was unfailingly courteous but not really well enough to do much.

I soon found that if any adaptation was to be done it had to come from me. There were no battle scenes written. We had to shoot everything on the big stage at Shepperton and build a quarterdeck and one gun deck which were to be hurriedly redressed to become numbers One, Two and Three gun decks.

We did have a couple of days on location in Bath and one day at Dartmouth. For the next few weeks it was the designer Carmen Dillon who kept my nose to the grindstone. I had done quite a lot of research on the Battle of Trafalgar but I now had to produce a coherent shooting script. I dictated a lot of it to Carmen and she was such a good listener and so demanding of detail that I ended up with quite a good battle which was to be seen almost entirely from the lower decks. We were to use a small amount of library film which was later to cause massive trouble.

Peter Finch was to play Nelson. I desperately wanted Elizabeth Taylor for Emma Hamilton. She was quite plump at the time and prepared to get plumper (the real Emma was 14½ stone). The reason Nelson was in bad odour with the establishment was a general disgust that he should be infatuated with such a grotesque creature, not that he was an adulterer.

Elizabeth was probably too beautiful but would have been wonderful in the part. Hal was set on Glenda Jackson, then at the height of her popularity. She was to be paid £70,000 (a seemingly magic figure) for three weeks' work and the schedule was constructed around her. Tony Quayle was to play Minto and Margaret Leighton whom I admired enormously Lady Nelson, Dominic Guard played the boy and Michael Jayston, Captain Hardy. I was highly involved in the casting for all of these.

Maggie Leighton had the obsession that the left hand side of her face was the only acceptable one and she wanted the shooting to accommodate this. I had pleased Carmen by settling for a two walled set for Lady Nelson's house - I knew how I was going to shoot it so I could save some money. When I rehearsed with Maggie, the right side of her face was the more prominent.

'It won't do,' she said. I was in a quandary. I decided the only thing to do was to turn the set around making the right hand wall left, and vice versa using only the same flats. This satisfied Maggie whom I enjoyed directing very much and also the producers as the extra cost was nil.

There were ominous signs of trouble early on. Glenda and I seemed to get on all right, but she was giving Finchy a hard time. We were in Dartmouth shooting our only day at sea. When Finchy was upset, his lip swelled up on one side and I had had to shoot his left side only, but he seemed fairly calm.

We continued to shoot. One day I said to George Frost, the superb make up artist, 'George, I'm very worried about Glenda, she's got a whole network of little red veins all over her face.'
'I know,' he said 'I just spent two hours putting them on.'
Collapse of director, not for the first time.

The next day I heard a sharp voice saying, 'Hey you director! I want to talk to you in my caravan.' Thus started a bitter row and we never afterwards exchanged a friendly word. To this day I don't know what the trouble was: perhaps it was because I said, 'Could we have the voice a little more Wirral, and a bit less Royal Shakespeare Company.'[10]

The shooting continued. Terry saw a rough cut of the first fifty minutes, professed himself delighted and kissed me on both cheeks.

It wasn't a bad film when it was put together, the battle scenes were enormously impressive, and the fibre glass guns were manned by a lot of very suspect stunt men. Finchy didn't want to do the scene where he prayed before the battle which was historically correct. He said, 'I'm a Buddhist.' I explained that Nelson's father was a vicar and he really had to do it. Eventually it was one of the most moving scenes in the film.

I made a very short Hitchcockian appearance in the film as one of the gun crew. The special effects people wrapped a kerchief around my head and put a tube with a lot of fake blood underneath the kerchief. When we turned over they had prepared a special clapper board with Take 27 on it and when the gun exploded next to me about a gallon of blood appeared to spurt out of my head. It was so over the top that I only used twelve frames of it in the film.

Finchy died most movingly in a shot which reproduced the famous painting. I allowed myself to be persuaded to use some Library film from other feature films. In the end we only used 65 seconds, but this enraged the critics. I didn't know how cruel they could be. TV critics tended to be patronising but not vicious. It was as though I had committed High Treason.

*The Western Daily Press* said, 'This is Mr Cellan Jones's first film; let us hope it is his last.'

I did a whistle stop tour of America doing up to six interviews a day. All the journalists wanted to know what it was like directing a fleet of battleships. Unwisely I hadn't the heart to disillusion them. Glenda went public and said it was a lousy film and she didn't like her own

---

[10] Glenda and Emma Hamilton shared a birthplace near Liverpool.

performance. Terry Rattigan also went public: 'I notice she didn't offer to give back any of the money,' he said.

At the Premiere attended by Princess Alexandra and Lord Mountbatten, Terry and I and Maggie couldn't get to our seats without clambering over the Princess so we sat in the Manager's office drinking gin and eating popcorn.

One of the pleasures of the film was working with Michel Legrand. He wrote a fugue which is marvellous and we had a 70 piece orchestra. The associate producer was terrified that Michel would not turn up and he was frantically telephoning France. The session was to start at 9.30. At 9.25 Michel walked into the studio lifted his baton and said, 'Messieurs, numero un.' Ten minutes later we had recorded the first cue.

When we were dubbing the sound I discovered something for the first time. Actors and directors can do anything under pressure. I wanted to avoid music over the opening of the film and use a bosun's call, (that's the real name for the pipe) My grandfather, who had been in the Navy had given me a silver call which I taught myself to play and it sounded really spooky and strange.

We needed a lot of odd voices for on board ship. I asked Michael Gambon to do a day's dubbing and he made a very convincing whole battleship crew.

We flew first class to Los Angeles. It was my first visit to a vanishing world. Hal took me to a party at the Beverley Hills Hotel. We sat with Robert Mitchum and his wife and Susan Heywood. At the next table were Cary Grant and John Wayne. Half way through the meal I found a hand groping my upper thigh. I won't say which of the ladies it belonged to but Martha Wallis said, 'I shouldn't let her do that, Bob'll punch you in the face.'

I was flushed with enthusiasm after the American premiere at the Directors Guild which went quite well. The company was going to fly me first class from Los Angeles to London. I had arranged to do a little television play by Evan Jones with Ted Ray. The plane was delayed for fourteen hours because of a bomb scare and I was shamefully late for rehearsal after no sleep for 36 hours. Michael Bryant was playing the lead and led the recrimination: 'Oh your Lordship we are honoured by your presence, are you sure it's not too much trouble now you're so famous?' I smiled grimly and did a full day's rehearsal before collapsing in a heap.

There is a little post script to this chapter. Many years later I had a script about Edith Cavell which I thought was rather good. Glenda and I had not spoken for many years. I wrote to her and asked her to lunch. I thought it was time we could speak politely to one another. We got on quite well, I offered her the script, she liked it and we made some alterations. I said, 'I need a letter from you showing interest. Not the usual one from your agent but in your own handwriting, saying you'll do the script for almost no money because you think it's wonderful.' She laughed and sent me the letter. Sadly I couldn't raise a cent either on her name or mine. She later went into politics.

# Chapter Ten
# Moor Street And After

Maggie Smith is one of the actresses I admire most. We met in the 50s when I was briefly sharing a flat with Michael Murray in Moor Street, Soho. Maggie had lived there before and came back to stay. She would always describe the windows of 16 Moor Street as looking out through the O of the advertisement for Damaroids a supposed aphrodisiac. Not strictly true, but quite a good story. The building was owned by a retired whore's maid. In order to avoid being given notice I would sycophantically take her giant poodle, Beau, for walks and be greeted by all the street girls.

'Hello Beau,' they would say, and to me, 'I know where you live, darling.'

The landlady had some amazing stories. She and her mistress were catering to a very strange man who only achieved fulfilment if he were tied into a frog man outfit and his air was cut off at the crucial moment. On one occasion he seemed to have passed out and they discovered he was dead. They were at a loss what to do, but bundled him off still in his diving kit and put him in the Round Pond in Kensington Gardens.

Upstairs lived Bobby Burns and his girlfriend, Ros. Bobby was a talented musician who conducted and played the accordion in a night club. He would come home at four in the morning and persuade me to go and drink beer in Covent Garden where the pubs were open for the porters.

One New Year's Eve I was watching Bobby playing the piano in the Cottage, a musicians' club (not a gay one) and two hard faced men came in. 'Bobby' said one, 'The governor's waiting for the band.' They were members of the Falco gang who were known to be a bit active with the razor. Bobby had forgotten that he had promised a band for the Falcos' New Year Party. In panic he stopped playing, grabbed hold of me and we left followed by the imprecations of the manager.

The music market was free and easy at the time; you could pick up musicians at the Red Lion in Windmill Street any night of the week. We went into the bar and in seconds had found a bass player, a saxophonist and a guitarist without any trouble and got them to wait by my Morris Minor. But there were no drums. Bobby made a swift decision. We burst into the Skiffle Cellar in Greek Street, climbed onto the stage and removed Fat John the drummer and all his kit. The band and the customers were furious. We hustled all the kit upstairs and crammed everyone into the car with the bass sticking out of the window and made for the East End.

When we arrived the two heavies were looking at their watches. One of them said, 'Just in time, Bobby, just in time.'

Maggie Smith soon left Moor Street. She was at the beginning of an enormously successful career. We met from time to time and I got to know her then husband Robert Stephens better.

I was asked by Cedric Messina to do a production of *A Midsummer Night's Dream* on location at Scotney Castle. Betty Hussey, who owned it and was just giving it over to the National Trust, became very enthusiastic. It was madness to try and shoot it in four days, but I foolishly agreed. We managed to get a remarkable cast including Robert Stephens as Oberon, Eileen Atkins as Titania, Ronnie Barker as Bottom, John Laurie as Quince, Lynn Redgrave as Helena, Jeremy Clyde as Lysander, Edward Fox as Demetrius, Michael Gambon as Theseus and Eleanor Bron as Hippolyta. Ronnie Barker proved himself a wonderful actor, not just a comic.

The location was impossibly beautiful and we nearly got away with it.

It was not until 1983 that I worked with Maggie again. William Trevor had written an enchanting story called *Mrs Silly*, adapted by Bob Larbey, about a divorced woman whose idolised son was sent away to a smart prep school by his upper class father. James Villiers played the head master in a wonderfully abstracted manner. Maggie as Mrs Silly had to disgrace herself in front of everyone including the Bishop by falling over. The most affected was her son, a difficult part for any young actor. She insisted on doing the fall which was brutally hard off screen, over and again, for the boy's benefit and it helped his performance enormously. It was a real example of unselfish professionalism.

Later I asked this very classically trained actress to ad lib a scene with the boy in a long tracking shot. 'I'll try anything once,' she said. She was superb, it was a very fresh and exciting performance. The sound mixer wanted another take, but got a flea in his ear from both of us.

Bob and I became friends. Some years later we were to go to the National Theatre and see Michael Bryant in *Love For Love* and have dinner afterwards. Michael rang and said Bob was coming as well.
'I am not having dinner with Bob Stephens,' Maggie said.
'Yes you are,' I said.
She was very much into the crystal pendulum at the time and asked, 'Am I going to have dinner with Bob Stephens?' The pendulum said no.
'There you are,' she said.
I said, 'Rubbish.'
We went to the theatre. Bob came on for the first act and his performance was decidedly dodgy. At the end of the act, the stage manager came on and said, 'Mr Stephens has been taken ill; the rest of the play will be played by the understudy.'
'There you are' said Maggie.
'You're a bloody witch,' said I.

I'll write more about Bob later on. Our last meeting was extraordinarily dramatic.

# Chapter Eleven

# A Lee Shore

Lee Remick was idyllically beautiful and enormously professional. Martin Gilbert wrote a biography of Jennie, Lady Randolph Churchill which was dramatised by Julian Mitchell. Stella Richman, one of the earlier independents, produced it and I was asked to direct it. My agent at the time, Larry Dalzell, fought savagely to get me £200 a week and Stella said, 'You should change your agent, he's not asking for enough money.' I don't know what else he could have done other than belt her one.

Lee, who was to play Jennie, and I met for lunch. The public often think there has to be a romantic liaison between directors and actresses for the magic to work. It isn't quite like that. As we walked down the road together we both felt a strong mutual attraction, not a word was spoken and almost at once our feelings changed to a deep sincere and entirely innocent friendship.

The first scene we shot was of her and her father riding through the woods. I didn't know that Dan O'Herlihy who played Dad had been in a western soap opera for many years but was terrified of horses and had it in his contract that he wasn't to come within ten feet of one. With great courage he mounted up and followed Lee, a superb horse woman at the trot.

Randolph Churchill was played by Ronald Pickup, in a beautifully understated performance. Lee showed her professionalism when I did a scene of her running down the hill to meet Randolph. She fell very hard and cut her knees badly. Everyone ran forward to help her. She got up and said, 'I expect you'd like to shoot that again,' and went back to the stand-by mark.

I didn't like Blenheim or the Marlboroughs right from the first Sarah Churchill onwards. I found them a decadent, spoilt family and Blenheim was a monstrous vulgar piece of fantasy created by an otherwise good architect Vanbrugh, fatally influenced by a sulky and spoilt woman.

Even one of the senior servants, who was brought in to talk to the crew, insulted our senior lighting director, Luigi Bottone, by mocking his Italian name and calling him an ice cream seller.

We had done some good work however, and shot an amazingly long ball scene as if on the Royal Yacht with Thorley Walters being an excellent Prince of Wales.

We had a good company and mostly a good crew. Thames was going through a particularly bad patch of labour relations, mainly through their own cowardice and wish to avoid rocking the boat. We were hopelessly overstaffed, we had overlong meal breaks and there were dozen of extra payments for dressing time, soft soled shoes allowance and who knows what else.

At Blenheim we had three scene men, three prop men and three facility men. There was no scenery to move, the props were mostly handled by the palace staff and what, I asked, did the facility men do? I was told that the prop men weren't allowed to wash the cups up after a tea scene and the facility men did it. In fact most of them sat around playing cards and plotting mischief and we ran the show with one prop man who was very keen. Rumours started to fly around; there was going to be a prop mens' strike. It made everyone very edgy. I asked our man, 'Fred, what's the matter, is there anything I can do to help?' Of course, he hadn't heard anything about it and wouldn't until the little Hitler in charge told him to stop work.

I learnt a lot from Chris Cazenove who played George Cornwallis West, Jennie's second husband. The scene where he left her was supposed to be played in a drawing room. I decided to play it outside, with Chris trying to start his car, a beautiful old De Dion Bouton. It would not turn over as Jennie was getting more and more contemptuous of them. I said, 'Kick it!'
'Oh no' he said, 'he wouldn't do that.'
He leant over it and stroked it and said quietly, 'Come on, old girl' and we started the engine by remote control at once. The scene said quite a lot about the failure of the relationship.

I had a chance to fulfil a life's ambition towards the end of the shooting. Jennie was supposed to go up in a 1917 Vickers Vimy bomber. She said pleasantly: 'There is no way I'm going up in that thing.' I grabbed her coat and helmet and leapt into the cockpit, hesitating only momentarily when I was told the maximum compensation Thames would pay in the event of my death was £10,000.

We took off. It was a wonderful experience with the hot oil spraying back in our faces from the engine. I understood why those old pilots wore silk scarves, it was to wipe their goggles. We looped the loop and returned to earth overjoyed.

I asked Lee to drive a governess cart through the gates and up to the front of the house.
'Can you do it?' I asked.
'I can drive and have driven a coach,' she said very positively, and drove it at a very scary rate.

The labour troubles which had been brewing for sometime came to a head later. Thames Television had taken on some make up men who were well qualified. There was a convention that in film, make up was done by men who were represented by the ACT (Association of Cinema Technicians). In TV the make up was done by women who were members of NATKE. There was a great deal of silly demarcation between the two. NATKE decided that they should go on strike. The day they chose to do so was when we were shooting the House of Commons, a full size replica set which went the rounds between the companies. Of course, 150 or so extras all had wigs, beards and moustaches. Lee finding no one to help her, put on her own wig, they begged her to take it off or she would be blacked.

A day's filming, costing tens of thousands of pounds, was wasted. We could re-shoot after the strike was over (which it almost immediately was) on a Sunday. I tracked the set down and it was being used until 10.00 p.m. on the Saturday at the BBC. We arranged for a fleet of lorries to collect it and bring it to Thames when it would be re-erected over night with enormous overtime and shot the next day.

I wrote a rather pompous letter to Jeremy Isaacs then Head of Programmes saying that I thought the labour relations were a disgrace and it was largely the fault of Thames for being so weak. He replied rather aggrievedly. It turned out that he didn't think *Jennie* was in the first class of programmes anyway.

*Jennie* won quite a lot of awards including three Emmies. I, amazingly, won the Directors Guild of America award, of which more later. Jane Robinson, won the Emmy for costume design.

The moment I remember best was the scene where Ronald Pickup as Randolph tells Jennie that he has syphilis. She puts her arms around him and says, 'You poor, poor dear, why didn't you tell me?' He falls into her arms and his body is racked with dry heart-breaking sobs.

In England this led to a commercial break and the next voice heard was that of Stratford Johns saying, 'I've been looking for a really moist dog food.'

# Chapter Twelve

# Big Al

Let's rewind my career a little: I had just started work on the massive thirteen hour adaptation of Jean Paul Sartre's *Roads To Freedom*, when I was offered two little solo performances with Sir Alec Guinness. He was to choose them, and he chose *Little Gidding* by TS Eliot from the *Four Quartets*, and some poems by EE Cummings. We met over lunch at the Gay Hussar and got on well. The BBC said I was already under contract for Sartre so they would not pay me any more. I wanted to work with Alec so I swallowed my pride and agreed.

We started rehearsing, but we couldn't break what I like to call a 'barrier of boredom' in *Little Gidding*. Alec's reading came over as a little cold and withdrawn. There was no money for film, but I drove Alec up to the village and we looked around the church and graveyard. It suddenly seemed that he had seen the words of the poem for the first time and after that in every rehearsal he brought it vividly to life. I took a still photographer up with a tin of shaving cream and we recreated the snow covered trees with this (no designer or prop men allowed). We got a splendid set of stills which enriched the recital and helped to remind Alec of what he had seen.

The producer, Cedric Messina had arranged a lunch for Alec the next day with some BBC bigwigs. I wasn't invited. After rehearsal Alec said, 'See you at luncheon tomorrow.'
I said, 'No I'm afraid not, but I'll see you the next day.'
His face was quite impassive. That evening I got a call from Cedric: 'Your friend - Sir Alec Guinness refuses to come to lunch unless you're invited too, so I suppose you'd better come.'
I said, 'After so charming an invitation, how can I refuse?'

Maggie and I used to go and stay at Kettlebrook Meadow: Alec's home near Petworth. He was hugely amusing, he had a pony which he was sure had rheumatism and had given it a copper bracelet. I saw nothing of the viciousness which Piers Paul Read said he showed Merula. He proudly used to show off her paintings. I thought Alec was probably gay but it didn't affect our relationship. I was able to give Matthew, his son, a part in *Roads To Freedom*. One afternoon we went for a long walk through the woods and he told me about his commitment to the Catholic Church. When Matthew was five he had polio, Alec said he made a pact with God that if Matthew recovered he would commit himself to the church. Matthew did and Alec did.

Six years later I was offered Shaw's *Caesar And Cleopatra* by Hallmark. The producer David Susskind left me alone to get on with it. We were to shoot at Southern Television in Southampton. Eileen Diss designed wonderful sets. The first scene required a ton of sand and an enormous polystyrene sphinx. How, I wondered, after all that expense could she build a throne room? Easy! She sliced the back off the Sphinx, sprayed it gold and stuck a throne between its paws, brilliant.

I offered Jane Robinson the contract to design the costumes, she was on the staff of Thames Television at the time and I said, 'It's time you went freelance. I can only offer you one job but it will be quite well paid.' She did the job brilliantly and never looked back.

I did a terrible thing to Michael Bryant who played Britannus. We gave him a Welsh accent which he did very well. Five minutes before the first long take I had terrible doubts. I said, 'Michael, please cut the accent.' He went very pale but he did it and played the part beautifully.

Genevieve Bujold, the Canadian actress, played Cleo superbly and on the third day she was ill with ghastly stomach trouble. She would run off and vomit in the corner and come straight back to the set. We would turn over and she would give a wonderful feisty performance. When it came to the last day we were a little behind and they were building a boat in the next studio for the giant set for Caesar's departure. I made a speech to the crew and said we would now be moving next door and carrying on. I went to the next studio and saw a group of men scratching their heads and the boat in a hundred pieces on the floor. We had a long pause while they built the boat and by this time it was eleven o'clock at night. Alec had a £20,000 penalty clause in his contract if we overran. He wanted to stop at midnight. David insisted on going on and working all night. He won, but Alec cussed Susskind loudly in front of the whole studio. In fact, on close examination of the contract, the overrun started at midnight and Sir Alec got paid anyway.

Although it was well received Alec, always a harsh judge, didn't like his own performance much. We never worked together again, but met every now and again and exchanged Christmas cards.

# Chapter Thirteen
# The Mausoleum Club

Quite recently I was approached by Gavin Collinson, late of the BBC, who was interested both professionally and emotionally in old television programmes. There are small and devoted groups of people who try to track down lost shows. Many, of course have been destroyed but these groups still love to research them. One of the destroyed was *Beach Head*, from the *Out Of The Unknown*[11] series, for which I won a diploma (the lowest award) at the International Science Fiction film festival in 1968. It was quite a bold production. Tony Abbott, a brilliant set designer, designed a space-ship in gold instead of the more conventional metallic grey. The female lead, described as blonde, was played by a black actress who was superb. Ed Bishop played the male lead.

I had the spaceship crew dressed for dinner in gold lame served by robots. My friend Vernon Dobtcheff played a dyspeptic officer who asked the robot waiter for bread and when presented with it said, 'No, brown bread, you fool.'

The spaceship was wonderful with a great sixty foot plastic tube running down the middle of it which Ed which ran up and down when he was going potty.

Another contemporary show made by me was *The Murders In The Rue Morgue* with Edward Woodward and Charles Kay. It was the first performance of my son Simon who was feeding an orang-utan at the zoo. I had to stand in for the Orang for Simon's close-ups. As I capered around, the crew, for some reason found it funny.

When Ted Woodward asked me why his character was so preoccupied and depressed I thought for a moment and said, 'accidie' (as you will know, the French for a profound and dispiriting boredom). That seemed to do the trick.

Another series I contributed towards was called *The Edwardians*, produced by Mark Shivas. It was a series of biographical plays which, after the convention of the time, concentrated on bringing the subjects into disrepute. My two were rather different. One by the brilliant Ken Taylor was about E Nesbit, the children's writer, played by Judy Parfitt, who turned out to have an amazing private life, living in a ménage a trois with Hubert Bland, secretary of the Fabian society (James Villiers) and her housekeeper (Jane Lapotaire). Both of them had children by Bland. One of the most terrifying scenes was when one of Nesbit's children had died and they were burying it in the garden (bizarre, but accurate) Nesbit screamed and tried to grab the little coffin from Bland and said to Jane's character, 'Why couldn't it be one of yours that died?'
I don't think I've ever seen a more terrifying scene.

---

[11] *Out Of The Unknown*, written by Mark Ward, published by Kaleidoscope Publishing

Some time after, the other play, Daisy, about the Countess of Warwick, mistress of Edward VII was broadcast. Virginia McKenna who played Daisy, wanted a copy to show to an American film producer. She, rightly, thought she had been rather good. David Turner and I had turned it into a musical, with a group of singing miners and a septet; Dick Holmes arranged the music. It ended with Daisy leading the cast in a chorus of *The Red Flag*, (Daisy was a fervent communist as well as an outrageous snob). The BBC, had, for some reason, allowed them both to be wiped. All the others in the series were preserved.

# Chapter Fourteen

# Wonderful Town

In 1976 WNET Channel 13, the New York PBS[12] station, which normally imported the posher BBC output, decided they wanted to do something of their own. They commissioned *The Adams Chronicles*. Not a horror story, but the history of America in the first years after the revolution. The producer, Virginia Kassel decided she wanted to employ me and fought long and hard against considerable opposition. The US Immigration department were less enthusiastic.

'Is the guy educated?' they said. I telephoned the registrary at the university and asked them to send a copy of my degree certificate which I had lost. They did.

'Is this guy known outside England?' they asked. I sent them some foreign press cuttings including some Russian ones which neither they nor I understood.

Virginia wore them down with ruthless persistence and eventually they gave way and granted me a permit. I shall always be grateful to her. I couldn't direct the first two but arrived at the studio to prepare numbers three and four and watch the shooting. They were filming an early meeting in Philadelphia: there was a carved coat of arms on the wall. I ventured to say it wasn't right. In fact it was Belgian with the motto Je Maintiendrai. The director, Paul Bogart was visibly annoyed and shooting stopped. After a while they came up with another coat of arms with English lions quartering the fleur de lys, the lion and the unicorn as supporters. It, too, was wrong: It should have been impaled with the White Horse of Hanover but Paul said:

'Well, your Lordship, does that satisfy you?'

I hurriedly said yes it was fine.

I had to join the American Directors Guild; it's a wonderful organisation and I am proud still to belong to it. Anyone could join as a director if he or she paid $500. It was a different matter if you wanted to join as an AD or production manager. The entry fee is now $5,000. Fortunately I managed to make WNET13 pay my subscription. I was now in a position to nominate something of my own for the awards. I nominated *Jennie* and forgot about it, and got on with the rehearsals.

American actors are no different in the main from English ones. They were amused and amusing, committed and hard working. When we went on location to Newport Rhode Island we had a little problem. The town is full of palaces and chateaux built by fabulously rich families in the last century. We were to film in one which was to represent Versailles and looked very good. One of the leading actors said he wanted a trailer.

'Look,' I said, 'you have a big room of your own in a fake French Chateau chock full of real 18th century French furniture.'

'It's a matter of principle,' he said.

---

[12] Public Broadcasting Station

He refused to work, so I had to shoot around him which was difficult especially as he came on the set and watched. 'I like the way you are shooting that,' he said. After three days he cracked and we got on fine.

In the rehearsal room the lift opened right out into the hall. The elevator boy was keen to be in the business and every time I was working near him he would make suggestions, some of which I used. This was America, the land of opportunity. By the end of the shoot he was an associate producer.

Meanwhile, out of sentiment, I had decided to live in the Chelsea Hotel, a famous old place where Dylan Thomas stayed before he died and where William Burroughs had lived for years. It was much cheaper than anywhere else. I had a suite and although the hotel was miles downtown opposite the Empire State Building this seemed to matter more to my employers than to me. There were cockroaches; that's usual in New York, but I was more disturbed by the mice and I asked if they could do anything about them. 'No problem,' they said. That night a lot of little foil trays full of blue crystals appeared. Early in the morning I put my foot out of the bed and trod on the small still pulsating corpse of a rodent. I didn't have to stay much longer in New York so I moved out to a Baptist Hotel on 58th Street. Maggie came to stay. She had a long trip and was a little bit jet lagged and she said what she would really like is a cup of tea and some toast. No problem I said and telephoned the local Deli who appeared with tea and toast in five minutes which amused her greatly.

I went back to England for a short time and in the early autumn prepared to go back for another episode. It was the last to be shot though not the last in sequence. I had noticed that many of the other directors had a credit as producer as well as director. I asked if I could have one. No problem they said. It didn't cost them anything more. It made a lot of difference in fact. Directors didn't get Emmys for a show. Producers did, which is why you often see seven producer credits or more on American TV series. I went back to New York and this time the whole family came too. We had a suite at a hotel on Central Park West. It was old fashioned and really nice. Maggie made a marvellous collage of bus tickets, throw-aways and odd bits of paper which we still treasure.

*The Adams Chronicles* had got as far as the American Civil War. We were to do a little in the studio in New York and then we were to move 1,500 miles to Charleston, South Carolina. The company very generously proposed to bring the family and I said that I would use them all playing parts in the show. It was agreed.

I discovered that the song planned for a little musical interlude for the show was written long after the 1860s. It had to be junked and I needed to write something fast, I tossed this out one morning:

> *Heartsease and silverthorn my love gave to me.*
> *Hedge roses newly born, harebells one two three.*
> *She met another boy and made a new bouquet.*
> *With speedwell and traveller's joy to send me on my way.*

This song is still on the ASCAP Register.

Charleston had to represent Ealing, where Charles Francis Adams, Minister to Great Britain, had a country house, Little Boston Manor. It also had to represent Boston Mass and itself. I think we got away with it. To open the episode, I set up one of those foolish scenes that directors use to cover up the lack of money and extras with frenzied activity. A newspaper boy, played by Simon, in what I hoped was a New England accent, ran towards camera throwing newspapers at front doors and eventually exchanging dialogue with Mr Adams. A dog dashed across the frame and a coach and pair came into the foreground and receded. There were various single extras cued in to make the place look busy. The assistant director couldn't get the cueing right, it was a mess. After three unsuccessful takes Simon came and said quietly to me, 'Look dad, if he cued the coach, counted three and then cued the dog I could take my own cue after a count of two and...'

'Yes, yes,' I said, 'You're a dear clever boy, but you must let him do his job.'

Eventually the Assistant Director got it right. It was the first inkling I had that Simon might become a director.

Din wasn't so keen on filming. I said to him, 'Take this small horse across the shot.'

'I can't,' he said. 'He'll bite me.'

I became impatient. Not so the local news stations; they crowded round taking close-ups of him. 'Well,' said one of the actors, 'I suppose to get a close-up around here you have to be the director's child.'

Charleston is a ravishing town. The pavements are all beautiful stone brought from England as ballast. The lady who looked after us and her friends found the British more congenial than the New Yorkers, who couldn't get used to the heat and what they perceived as the essential foreignness of the place. I said to our hostess,

'During what I should probably call the War between the States...' she interrupted. 'Y'all can call it the War of Northern Aggression if y'all like.'

We had a few war scenes. I needed a military drum and fife band and got them together and asked them to do something awful.

'Will you please dress in blue uniforms and play *Marching Through Georgia*?'

Their faces fell, but they agreed. The shots went well and they turned up in the afternoon wearing grey uniforms and playing Dixie.

Our last day of shooting was the last of the whole series. We were a very well suited and pleasant crew and very happy together. We spent the night before playing poker all night until 7.50 a.m. when we started shooting. One of the electricians got a bit drunk and truculent and the Director of Photography put him in a bath full of ice and he nearly froze to death. After the last shot the Assistant Director approached at the head of the fife and drum band and after a short speech presented me with a Grand Union flag, like the Stars and Stripes, but with a union flag in the corner. It was first used in 1775 and never again. I left Charleston with a lump in my throat.

I was then offered a commercial pilot written by Reginald Rose and produced by Buzz Berger and Herb Brodkin. It concerned a young woman recently widowed with three children and no insurance who came to live in New York. It was a good script but we had endless interference from the ABC network. Instead of a cold water flat they wanted her to live in a brownstone, even then a wildly smart and expensive house. They didn't want to show any garbage on the streets. New York was snowed under with garbage at the time.

I had to do screen tests on six actresses one of whom was Carroll Baker a woman of some distinction but not recognised by the network. Sadly she was wrong for the part but I would have liked to have worked with her. A battery of network people stood behind me criticizing the shooting.
'Why doesn't he take a close up for Christ's sake?'
Eventually I turned around and told them all to shut up; this was apparently how I was expected to behave from the start. We made quite a good film, sadly not good enough to be made into a series.

The police in New York are extraordinarily co-operative with film makers. We had a cop with us the whole time. I asked him if we could close the 59th Street bridge for a minute or two? 'You'll get me shot,' he said, but he did it.

When we had finished shooting, Maggie was going to spend the weekend on Fire Island. I couldn't, I was editing. Buzz suggested I edit all night and at eight o'clock in the morning I could go down to the East River and catch a sea plane. They had an account with a sea plane company and it would only cost $60. I worked until 7.50 a.m, finished the show and went to the East River. I met the pilot who had a two-seater sea plane. I got in; he pointed it at the 59th Street bridge and took off. It seemed to me that we just cleared it. The flight which was beautiful only took half an hour. When we landed the pilot said, 'do you mind taking your shoes and socks off and getting into the water? Then you can grab the tail and turn me into the wind.'
I did so and he took off. I got my pay cheque next week minus sixty bucks for the sea plane.

At this time I asked my children whether we should come and live in America as I was likely to be offered enough work. Simon said, 'Come on Dad, it's lovely to come to New York but you can't live here.'
'Right, son,' I said, 'We'll go home.'

A while later I came over to promote *Jennie*. It was the end of the year and it and *The Adams Chronicles* would be highly eligible for awards. We had breakfast at the Pierre Hotel with a lot of reporters. Just before we started Jac Venza, the executive producer said, 'I want you to introduce the thirty minute trailer we've made.'
I said, 'Hold on, what's in it?'
He said, 'Well, there's the scene where we … and a scene where … oh you know.'
I said, 'Give me a very large Bloody Mary.'
I drank it fast and managed to bludgeon my way through the speech. *Jennie* was enormously well liked and *Adams* was also well received.

The awards were held simultaneously in New York and Hollywood. I went to the New York party and *Jennie* won best director of a mini-series. It was the most pleasing award I'd had or ever would have, the approbation of my peers. Bob Fosse presented it and I made a rather too emotional speech.

At the Emmys a week later we collected a whole heap of nominations, including me as producer and director. Girish Bhargava, my editor, won an Emmy for *Adams* and the camera crew did too. Jane Robinson won an Emmy for the costumes for *Jennie*. It was quite a jolly evening with a big British contingent including Chris Hodson who had directed *Upstairs Downstairs*. Nominees are feted ridiculously until the award is decided. Then the winner is God and the nominees cease to exist. It is a very sobering experience.

# Chapter Fifteen
# Head Of Ashtrays

Mockingly, this is what I called the job which Shaun Sutton offered me in early 1976. The official title was Head of Plays, the senior of the three drama departments. I refused. Well, he said there was no hurry; I could just think it over. I was very flattered but didn't want to give up directing.

I thought about it for several weeks and asked Maggie. She said I should do it. It was such an important job, even though we would lose a lot of money because it was not well paid. She had an uncomfortable properly serious attitude to life and is nearly always right.

Shaun took me to see Alasdair Milne the managing director. He was abrupt, sharp and unshakeably honest and a superb administrator who was afterwards treated with contempt by people unworthy to lick his boots. I said I would do the job for two years.
'No, three,' Alasdair interrupted brusquely. I also said I'd want to direct two plays a year. This proved optimistic.

I was to get £12,000 a year, a lot less than I earned as a freelance. I wasn't going to start for a while so I went to America to do *The Adams Chronicles* (q.v.)

When I started the senior men said, 'It's all fixed except for the formalities.' I didn't understand. It was carefully explained that one had to be vetted by MI5 who had an office in Broadcasting House and my appointment couldn't be confirmed until this was done. I was to hear more of this later. Then I had to meet the governors. Alasdair said, 'You will wear shoes won't you?'
'Of course,' I said, though I hadn't thought about it.

I took over from Chris Morahan, a brilliant director whose conscience had been pricked into doing the job. His way of working, though very successful, was a little different from mine. During the fourteen day takeover I had a small desk in the corner of his office; people would be wheeled in and stand in front of his desk and queries would be settled in double quick time. It worked very efficiently, but it wasn't my way. After three days we agreed that he should go and that I should take over prepared or not. He gave me a file containing all the memos he had sent in the last six months. It was very heavy.

There were twelve producers in the department and almost as many script editors. I thought that a good producer was his own script editor. I got rid of many of them except, curiously, I found it important to have a script editor for classical plays; someone with an encyclopaedic knowledge of the drama. I appointed Stuart Griffiths, a former leader writer for *The Evening Standard*, whose enthusiasm was immense.

Many of the producers were bone idle, never appeared until 10.30 in the morning and tried to take all the credit. One exception, whom I had appointed, was Margaret Matheson (formerly Margaret Hare, David's ex-wife) she was young, beautiful and had a real zest for hard work and, although fashionably left wing, had surprisingly personal opinions about many subjects. She was a fervent proponent of fox-hunting and had been a successful amateur rider before breaking her back.

A few weeks after I took over, Ian Trethowan the Director General, came to see me.
'I want you to sack Ken Trodd' he said. 'He is a communist and his contract is coming up for renewal.' I hated Ken Trodd, who had changed his name from Kenneth to Kenith. He was a particularly ruthless Marxist I thought, and I had worked with him at Granada very unhappily.

At a meeting of ACTT, the technicians' union, attended by all of thirty members, he moved that we should go on strike to stop Britain joining the Common Market. I said a few pathetic words against it. He made a rousing speech saying we should lose no opportunity to strike against our management who were unspeakably vile. It was put to the vote. Over half voted for it including one distinguished producer, for who knows what reason. The strike never happened.

Of course I couldn't possibly fire Ken and a couple of days later I rang Ian and told him so. He accepted it with no argument. A few weeks earlier Ken had produced a play called *Your Man From Six Counties*. In spite of having a distinguished author and director, Colin Welland and Barry Davies, the show was a mess. Ken wanted an extra £3,000 to go back to Ireland and re-shoot. I refused on the ground that it would be throwing good money after bad.

Later, when I was on holiday, Ken prevailed on Graeme McDonald, who was standing in for me, to give him the money. It made no difference, the show was a mess.

In the *Play For Today* series I managed to rescue a Charles Wood play about rape that Chris had turned down. Margaret was coming up with a striking series of plays. We had to decide which one to start the season - remember that in these days *Play For Today* got a respectable audience of around eight million and on one occasion seventeen million. It was thought of as the flagship of BBC drama and the first play was vitally important.

I thought the Plays Department was the aristocracy of the drama group. I thought it right that they should produce anything I felt like including plays, series, serials and readings.

Ken Trodd came to see me. Dennis Potter, possibly the most distinguished television dramatist ever, had said he would never work for the BBC again after a play of his was banned. Ken brought Dennis in. I said the banning was nothing to do with me - could we start afresh? I gave Dennis an enormous glass of whisky. I couldn't help noticing his poor hands, clutching the glass awkwardly.

He had an idea for a series, it was to be called *Ghost Writer* and to be about a man who was pulled in to write 'autobiographies' for famous but illiterate people. He discovered that, uncannily, the fictitious stories he wrote for the famous seemed to come true. Was he in some mysterious way writing their lives instead of their books? The confusion of fantasy and reality was an old theme of Dennis's. It was a fascinating idea and I said so. I commissioned him to do six hour long programmes, told Ben Travers Junior, the Authors' Contracts man, to write him a contract which would give him six half fees, the other half payable on delivery. Ben jibbed at this. He suggested one half fee for the first episode and so on. I insisted. I knew Dennis's Methodist conscience would keep him to delivery dates.

When the scripts came in they were a big surprise; they consisted of a murder story in serial form: every now and then the action stopped and the actors mimed to gramophone records of the 1930s. It was a breathtakingly original idea and I found it brilliant.

When we had several scripts, I took the project to Michael Checkland. I begged him for enough cash to put it on.
'We can't,' he said, 'We just haven't got the money.'
I grabbed him by the lapels and lectured him for about ten minutes telling him what an exciting project it was. Then he showed his great strength, or weakness, depending on where you're standing. His eyes gleamed and he became as enthusiastic as I was.
'It sounds wonderful I'll get it for you somehow,' he said and he did.
The show was of course *Pennies From Heaven* which was superbly directed by Piers Haggard.

The department was beginning to be reckoned as a place where things happen. The Chairman of the BBC, Sir Michael Swann, paid us a visit. After all, we were a dangerous lot and we needed an eye kept on us. Michael Swann was a pleasantly humorous man who ran the Board of Governors urbanely and with great skill.

I circulated the producers; I said just for once could they be in a little bit earlier than 10.30 as it would look rather bad if no one was there. When the Chairman arrived at ten o'clock, the offices were all empty. I had to give him coffee and bluster on about everybody being on location.

I had always intended to take him to the rehearsal rooms, where, I explained, the real foundation work went on. Before we left, I gave him a gin and tonic and sat him in a chair which promptly collapsed under him.
'I'm afraid the Chairman has been too much for the chair,' he said.

I drove him to the rehearsal rooms and we went to see various productions including *Tussy* written by Andrew Davies, one of his first jobs for the BBC and directed by Jane Howell. She was properly pugnacious and let us know she expected us to leave after fifteen minutes or so. We left showering her with apologetic compliments. After we visited a couple of more rooms, it was lunch time. It had been suggested that I take him to the executive dining room. I decided to walk him upstairs to the canteen and we would queue for our lunch. We could also have a glass of wine.

The red haired lady behind the counter said, 'Why don't we see you any more, you haven't been here for ages?'
She said to Sir Michael, 'E's taken some sort of admin job. I don't know why he bothered. It can't be much fun.'

# Forsyte and Hindsight

Every month I had a routine meeting with Alasdair Milne and with the Controllers of BBC1 and BBC2, separately of course. I, and I imagine, the other heads of department were regarded as experts in our own fields and expected to produce the goods unsupervised. The autonomy I enjoyed I tried to pass down to the producers and directors, with varying results.

Alasdair was a joy. His irreverence and contempt for the chairbound functionaries was like a breath of fresh air. He would take off his shoes, and put his feet on the desk and wiggle his toes. You could feel the disapproval of the suits. He would say,
'I think it's time for a toot,' and reach for the whisky. I once said,
'I'd rather not have that cheap grain whisky I know you've got a bottle of Glenmorangie in there.
'Right,' he said, 'Break out the Water of Tain.'

Brian Cowgill, the Controller of BBC 1 was a blunt northern Outside Broadcast Director who wouldn't stand any nonsense. We fell out, not seriously, over *Play Of The Month*. He wanted to call it something else. I stood my ground. There were already seven per year instead of twelve and if the title were changed they would have the perfect excuse to cut down even further.

He behaved beautifully over my first season of *Play For Today*.
'What are you going to give me for the first one?' he said.
'I don't know yet,' I replied, 'I'm waiting to see how they turn out.'
He muttered but agreed. Eventually, just in time for the *Radio Times* Press Date, I told him the first play was to be *Barmitzvah Boy* by Jack Rosenthal. It was an enormous success and he was gracious enough to acknowledge it, not only in a memo but in front of the Programme Review Board, a weekly gathering of Heads of Department.

Programme Review was an odd meeting: people were very keen to make their mark. Shaun Sutton and I tended to be very outspoken especially about drama produced by other departments like Music and Arts.

At the end of my first year I had to make two very important appointments. Margaret Matheson decided she wanted to leave. She was by far the most talented and hardworking producer and would be greatly missed. We discussed who her successor would be and decided to offer the job to Richard Eyre, who was finishing some very good seasons at Leicester. The trouble was, that he was a director by inclination and he would want to direct too many of the productions.

However he was a very worthy successor and he put in a challenging and exciting season of plays. One of them was *Licking Hitler* by Ian McEwan with Harriet Walter and Bill Paterson. She was superb and I later worked with her, but there was an anomaly which Richard did not want to face. A girl who had joined the ATS and had a Higher School Certificate would automatically be considered as an officer. The character she played didn't appear to have been, and it only needed a few lines explaining that she had turned it down early in her military career to make sense. I think Richard felt this would have been an improper interference with the writer's intentions. However, the show was a great success and my reservations didn't seem to be shared by anyone else.

Trevor Griffiths had written a stage play called *Comedians*. Richard bought it and mounted the TV version. I disliked Trevor and his work intensely, but felt and still feel, that programming is not about the personal taste of the programmer, though when they do coincide it makes for great success.

The play contained a particularly vile joke using the word 'fuck'. I felt Richard should have asked for it to be removed, though like a wet liberal he unloaded the decision on to me and, like another wet liberal, I agreed to let it stand. After the decision had been taken, I was irritated to hear Trevor slagging me off on the radio.

Richard later became director of the National Theatre, a job he did with great success. He afterwards published a diary, saying he had been miserable all the way through and had to take Valium. I couldn't understand it. Why do the job if it isn't going to be fun? My job was less important, though I was responsible for eighty-five productions in the first year, but I had a ball, even though I seemed to lurch from crisis to crisis.

I also needed a producer of classical plays for the *Play Of The Month* series. David Jones, who had been working a lot at the RSC, came and did the job. He also was at heart a director. Every time he directed I came in as producer, an unfamiliar role though we got on very well together and any suggestions I made were with a humble and hesitant mien. We did three productions together.

*Ice Age* was a strange Norwegian play starring Anthony Quayle and it was wonderful to see him again. I personally thought it rather dull. However, Tony lent the part great authority and got away with it splendidly. There is an apocalyptic story about Tony. He had had a very good war and had worked closely with the Crown Prince of a Scandinavian country and they became great friends. After the war, the Crown Prince had become King and was coming to Britain on a state visit. Tony had a play running in the theatre and invited the king to see the play and meet the cast afterwards. He introduced all the actors and then said, 'His Majesty the King of Denmark.' To which the King replied, 'Norway, Tony, Norway.'

David also directed *The Beaux Stratagem* by George Farquhar. It is extraordinary how many English playwrights and generals are of Irish origin (e.g. Farquhar, Sheridan, Shaw, Wellington, Montgomery, Alexander). This had a sparkling cast, many of whom had been at the RSC. Tom Conti was his usual brilliant self and the big surprise was Ian Ogilvy. It is always easy to underestimate a really good light comedian. He made the performance look effortless and his timing was elegant and perfect.

For some time I had been trying to get the rights to a play by Harold Pinter called *Langrishe Go Down*. Eventually Harold, who had been hoping to make a feature film of it, let us have the rights. We got Jeremy Irons and Judi Dench to play the leads and there was a certain amount of fluttering of the dovecotes among the management, because there was a scene where Jeremy covered her nipples with whipped cream and licked it off. He played this with great aplomb, and the film was a success. This was my first meeting with Judi, whom I admired greatly. We were to work together later. The shooting was done in Ireland. I was too busy to get over there, so I felt it wrong to take the credit as producer and I left the film with only the director's credit.

# Forsyte and Hindsight

Many years later, when Friday Productions (qv) was at its height, we were approached by a producer who wanted to work with us. He showed us an impressive list of credits. The last one he said he had produced was *Langrishe Go Down*. I should have called him a liar to his face but I didn't.

We worked very hard indeed in our office. I would get in well before nine o' clock. This left at least ninety minutes before any of the producers got in, so we were able to get on with letters. I had to dictate above thirty every morning and, if there was time, catch up on reading the pile of scripts which landed on my desk at the rate of about forty per week. I had two secretaries, one of whom was usually a trainee. When poor Margaret Matheson overspent and I had to cancel a film she had commissioned, which was written by Reg Gadney and was in praise of fox-hunting, I dictated a letter of condolence to Reg. I would have loved to make that film, it would have really put the cat among the pigeons.

Unfortunately, I dictated it to a trainee secretary, who was illiterate, and it was full of terrible mistakes of syntax and spelling. I had a letter back from a furious Reg pouring contempt on my literacy and, almost, my legitimacy. I had foolishly let the letter be signed in my absence, as I was going abroad. It wasn't the poor girl's fault, so all I could do was hand-write a grovelling apology to Reg. He was a distinguished author and I felt I had let him down, though I couldn't make money where there was none.

Before I took over it had been decided to mount a series of all of Shakespeare's plays over six years. Trevor Nunn had approached the BBC and suggested a co-production with the Royal Shakespeare Company. This had been turned down and Trevor was not pleased. Cedric Messina was to be the producer; this filled me with foreboding.

When I asked him what his policy was to be, he said, 'I'm an instinctive person and shall follow my instinct.' My heart sank. I managed to get Doctor John Wilders of Worcester College Oxford to be advisor. He was a great Shakespearian Scholar and had been an actor and was supremely tactful. There were to be six plays in the first year. *Much Ado About Nothing* was to open the season directed by the distinguished Donald McWhinnie.

Cedric was finding it difficult to get good directors. There was a lot of work about and he was not over popular. He appointed a very ordinary staff director to do *Henry VIII*. I, for once, trod on this and suggested Kevin Billington an experienced film director who, in the end, shot it at Leeds Castle and made a lovely job of it.

Meanwhile things were looking bad for *Much Ado*: it had good actors, a good director and good designers but it was turning out to be a dreadful mess. As sometimes happens, the mess spread like wildfire and good artists were doing appalling work.

When it was put together I said to Alasdair, 'I want you to watch this; I think it is so bad that we can't put it out.'
'Christ, boy,' he said, 'Do you know how much money that will cost?'
He watched the tape and telephoned me. 'I'm half way through it,' he said. 'You're right, it's absolutely dreadful, we'll have to junk it.'

Cedric was puce with fury. He neglected to tell any of the cast including Michael York and Penelope Keith, who were understandably miffed. Fortunately Al Rakoff's production of *Romeo And Juliet* was well under way. It was ambitious and exciting. Al wanted John Gielgud to do the Prologue but he was being very difficult about money and, understandably, having heard rumours about *Much Ado*, nervous about the whole project. 'I want you to persuade him.' Al said to me. 'I rely on you.'

I didn't want to take Sir John to the Ivy or anywhere else expensive. It would make it look as if we were made of money and we would be surrounded by hangers on. I asked him to have a cold lunch in the office which the catering department did cheaply and very well. He came. After some gentle sparring I said, 'The residuals would be quite good, Sir John.'
'Ah residuals, I always think of those as fairy gold. Besides I am not sure that Shakespeare ever works on television. There was one exception; *Antony And Cleopatra*, directed by someone called Cellan Jones. That was brilliant. In contrast to *Caesar And Cleopatra* with Alec which was dreadful.'
I forced a smile. 'No, Sir John, you have it the wrong way round. I directed *Caesar And Cleopatra*.'
'Oh really,' he said, 'Tee-hee.'

It was, I'm sure, quite deliberate. I eventually persuaded him to do the Prologue which he spoke with wonderful authority. He was worth every penny. As he left the room, he said to me, 'Fairy gold, dear boy, fairy gold.' And he smiled and closed the door gently. Afterwards he played the Prologue beautifully.

Shaun, Alasdair, Mark Bonham-Carter, the Deputy Chairman of the BBC, Cedric, some BBC suits and Maggie and I went to America to promote the Shakespeare series. In New York we went to a smart dinner in the New York public library. WNET were delighted to see us, rather surprisingly after the BBC's rejection of *The Adams Chronicles*.

Marlene, an ebullient and noisy American friend whom we shall meet in half a page, came to see us dressed in seriously grubby jeans and we met in a room full of people in dinner jackets and long dresses. Alasdair didn't turn a hair, gave her a glass of champagne and joked merrily with her. Cedric kept himself a bit apart.

We moved to Washington D.C. and stayed at the Hyatt Hotel opposite the White House. Cedric was summoned to meet the President. We had a splendid dinner in the Folger Library: Richard Pasco and his wife, Barbara Leigh-Hunt, whom I had worked with on *Bequest*, joined us, as did two rich old American ladies who said, 'We're so relieved; we thought we were going to have to sit with Oil People.' Mobil was funding us. The Americans suggested that Richard recite the seven ages of man from *As You Like It*. He said he didn't know it, so we wrote it out on a piece of paper, he climbed up to the high gallery and hiding the paper in one hand and gesticulating with the other gave an inspired rendition to huge applause.

At about this time, Maggie was working very hard and we had three young children. Various Au pairs had come and gone and we were desperate. The labour exchange sent us an American girl, called Marlene Benjamin, who was a hippie bumming her way around the world and who needed a job where she could live in. She came to spend an evening with us and, as one did in those days, we watched television. Jeremy Brett was doing a solo performance as Keats which was brilliant but florid.

'Who is this guy?' said Marlene, 'Did he freak out or sump'n?'

'Famous poet, died young of TB,' I said crisply.

She stayed with us and looked after the kids wonderfully. After a while she decided she wanted to get an education. She applied to St John's College at Santa Fe to do a four year course. She got a full scholarship - everything paid for, though she had to work and eventually graduated Summa Cum Laude (or would have if the college hadn't decided awards were invidious that year).

She went immediately to read for a PhD at Brandeis in moral philosophy, and eventually became a Professor of Philosophy at Stonehill College, a Catholic institution which she described as Stonehenge and did not deserve someone as talented as her. We have kept in touch ever since and marvel at how she has overtaken us in learning and maturity. She is one of our greatest friends and occasionally I go and give a lecture at Stonehill.

When young, she used to swear like a trooper especially in front of the children. It didn't seem to matter; they thought it was a bit uncool. I heard Vinny, at three years old, say to her very kindly, 'Now Marlene, we don't want to hear any more about fucking California'.

The Shakespeare season blundered on with varying results. A few were quite good, partly because of good directors but partly because of John Wilders.

Aubrey Singer, who was now the Controller of BBC2, was a dreamer of dreams and very likeable. He had some strange ideas. For example, he wanted to dramatise a version of *Zen And The Art Of Motorcycle Maintenance*. Regretfully we passed on that one, but he was always supportive and excited by new ideas.

After a year the heads of the channels changed. Bill Cotton, formerly a brilliant light entertainment director took over BBC1 and Brian Wenham at BBC2. There was a different atmosphere. We had been told to give the Controllers information well in advance of transmission so that the trailer unit could prepare a campaign. Seemingly all very laudable. The head of the trailer unit conceived it his duty to warn the Controllers of anything he considered dirty, dangerous or subversive. He became known as the school sneak. Margaret was producing a play by Roy Minton, called *Scum* about a juvenile prison. Alan Clarke, a formidable director, was making it. There were rumblings.

The school sneak kept feeding titbits to Bill Cotton who became very anxious. When the film was finished I viewed it with the production team and said, 'I think it is too violent. I think the frequency of the violence is so over the top that the audience will begin to laugh. I suggest you cut the following moments. I'm not insisting, but this is my advice and whatever you decide to do I will fight on your behalf.'

They cut it very sensitively and I thought they improved it. Bill saw the film and said, 'I'm not having it on my network.' Unwisely I said, 'You're not the only game in town, I'll offer it to BBC2.' Brian Wenham equivocated. I went to Alasdair; he was as always fair and honest.

'I find it deeply troubling,' he said, 'In principle I'd like it to go out but I want to think about it.'
'Well it's not going on BBC1' said Bill.

Alasdair, who had never forced anyone against his will over an artistic decision reluctantly agreed. The film was junked. I unwisely gave interviews to the Press calling it a disgraceful decision. I was cold shouldered by all the others in the executive dining room for at least two days. The irony was that after all the publicity the team were able to raise the money and re-shoot the film in all its entirety with all the violent bits left in. It did very well in the cinema advertised as 'The film the BBC tried to ban.'

The department was now settling down quite well. I inherited a series called *Young Film-Makers*[13] to be produced by Irene Shubik. It seemed to me to be an exciting project and I thought a good learning experience for a young producer. Graham Benson was a very talented production manager. I attached him to Irene. She suddenly said, 'This is not the sort of series I should be doing. I'm a very distinguished senior producer, I refuse to do it.'
'Well, I haven't got anything else for you, you'll just have to leave.' And she did.

Graham was now to be put in charge; he immediately made a plan. Half the young film makers would come from outside the BBC and half from inside. I noted that one of the insiders was to be Roger Bamford, who later directed *Auf Wiedersehen Pet* and was Middle Class and very far from Graham's own politics. For Graham, as I was soon to discover, bore the mark Cain on his file. He had been tried by MI5 and found wanting. When I tried to get him promoted to producer, Personnel said, 'He has a Christmas tree on his file.'
It looked like this:

and indicated that the subject was politically unreliable and probably subversive. I said, 'Nonetheless I want him made a producer.' [14]

There was a great deal of discussion. Personnel agreed that he should be a producer, but that he should resign from the staff and take a six month contract, thus making him sackable. Graham agreed. He was full of self confidence, justified as it turned out. I refused. It was a matter of principle. MI5 and personnel capitulated.

Graham became a producer, made a great success of the series which he called *Premiere* and, not too long after, resigned to pursue a highly successful career as an independent producer.

The one battle I avoided and felt guilty about was the case of Roy Battersby. He was a good director but a fanatical Trotskyite. He, too, had a Christmas tree on his file. I determined that if any producer wanted to cast him as a director I would fight for him. No one did. I regret that I

---

[13] Known as *Premiere* when it was eventually transmitted
[14] This may be true or untrue, but it is included in these memoirs as the personal comment of Jim - and we hope that nobody will raid our offices! - Ed

never tried to get him employed, even though I thought his opinions were dangerously potty. He is now working more than I am in fact, though I think reluctant time that blunts the lion's claws has probably modified his opinions.

Or possibly not.

One of the perks the drama department had was the Italia prize. It was held in a different Italian city every year and was originally given for Radio and later for Television. The prize was substantial, to be paid in Swiss Francs to be divided amongst the creative people. I was instrumental in getting the lion's share paid to the director rather than the producer, but I expect that has changed now.

A whole group of BBC people spent a week in Rome, Venice, Bologna or wherever and saw a lot of television. When we went to Venice the first year the BBC contingent was led by Shaun Sutton, older and wiser than the rest of us. Shaun had been a director and remained one at heart. We stayed, as befitted the BBC, in a moderately priced hotel while the ITV contingent stayed at the Gritti Palace. We went to visit them and I bought a round of drinks for twelve people. Many were kind enough only to ask for a cup of tea, but the bill came to the equivalent of my meagre allowance for two days.

Three journalists always came. Peter Fiddick of *The Guardian*, Sean Day-Lewis of *The Telegraph* and Chris Dunkley of *The Financial Times*. We have remained firm friends with Sean and Peter ever since. Peter became Arts Editor of *The Guardian* and Sean was fired twice by Max Hastings. Sean was later taken on again but fired in favour of Cristina Odone who boasted that she never watched television. Sean was and is a consummate TV critic, he has a great love for the medium, second only to his love for music.

In Venice in 1978 I remember chasing the Director General of the BBC across the floor of a palazzo and when I caught him he said, 'I know, I know, you want to persuade me to allow a repeat of *Days Of Hope*. Yes, yes, you can have it.'
The show had been produced by Tony Garnett, another Marxist, and written by Jim Allen. It was a blindingly fierce portrayal of history as the struggle of the working class against capitalist oppression. Tony and I had agreed that if a piece about Churchill, which I thought to be untrue, were to be removed I would fight for the repeat. The show had been made during Chris Morahan's reign. The fact that a repeat was mooted at all was an indication of the cuts in drama production which were happening and the gaps that needed filling.

The Italia prize coincided with the giant mushroom season, so we watched a lot of outstanding television and ate like kings. Two productions figured largely at the Italia prize. Tom Stoppard had come to see me in London and offered me a script called *Professional Foul* about an English professor who went to a conference in Czechoslovakia where he met one of his brightest former pupils who was now a street cleaner. The professor was shocked. The boy said he had completed his PhD thesis which he had not been able to do before. Would the professor take it back to England? No, he couldn't possibly, said the professor.

Stifling his conscience, he went to find out about how the English team was doing in the international football competition that was taking place. There was a hilarious scene where he was trying to find the result of the match by blundering into journalists' rooms, all of whom were dictating copy to their various papers over the telephone. The result eluded him for some time, but he managed to cobble together the result by synthesising all the reporters' phone calls. Eventually England won, right triumphed and he smuggled the thesis out of the country.

I fell hook line and sinker for the play. I said that we had no money left this year but would do it next year.

'No you won't,' Tom said, 'This is International Refugee year, and if you won't do it, I'll take it elsewhere.'

I begged him for a few days grace. He agreed and I flew to New York. In three days I had raised the money and the play was produced with Peter Barkworth as the Professor and brilliantly directed by Michael Lindsay-Hogg.

It was a great success in England. I wanted to put it in for the Italia prize but was told that it would upset the Russians and the other Iron Curtain countries. I then asked if it could be entered Hors Concours outside of the competition. No, I was told.

I took half a dozen copies of the tape with me to Italy, booked a number of viewing theatres and put up notices everywhere saying due to the unprecedented demand by many delegates wanting to see this production, I had arranged various showings. The delegates began to come in dribs and drabs and by the end of the week most of them had seen it and loved it. It sold well throughout the free world.

I had another dealing with Tom Stoppard. We had arranged a co-production of *Every Good Boy Deserves Favour*, a very inventive musical play in the theatre by Trevor Nunn. It was a co-production with America and Andre Previn was conducting the orchestra. The first sign of trouble was that our co-producers rejected it, saying that it was unsatisfactory. This lost us a great deal of money. It turned out that Andre, with whom I had worked on *Jennie*, was also very unhappy with it.

We held a meeting in my office with Trevor, Tom, Andre and myself. Andre was very definite that it was unsatisfactory. Trevor, whom I never thought much of as a television director compared with his stage work, fought for it and offered to re-cut. I said our co-producer didn't want it at any price. Tom became a peace maker and eventually persuaded us all to re-cut it and show it. I reluctantly agreed; we had already lost all our co-production money and we could ill afford a gap in the schedule. It went out on BBC2 without much fuss.

After being the hero of the radical left over the *Scum* issue, I suddenly found myself on the other side. I had agreed to direct a dramatised documentary for Margaret Matheson about Les Cannon the Electricians' Trade Union leader who was robbed of his job by ballots rigged by the far left. It was a good story. Cannon was a strong left winger though not left enough for some of the brothers, so it wasn't a simple story of left and right, more of a detective story.

# Forsyte and Hindsight

After I had seen several drafts, I didn't consider the script good enough. It introduced a television interview that never happened and it didn't stick closely enough to the facts. I asked for changes. The writer could not give them. I said I could not direct it nor should it be done as it was. Margaret turned pale. There wasn't enough time to fill the space. She got hold of another script. It was the transcript of a trial of a young man in Ireland, held under the Diplock Rules. The play was to be called *The Legion Hall Bombing*. Caryl Churchill was given the task of editing it and, wrongly in my opinion, given a contract as writer. Roland Joffe, later to direct a series of brilliant feature films, was to direct it.

I asked how they had got hold of the transcript of the trial. There was no copyright, of course, in the words, but the actual transcript had not been published. I was told who had obtained it, probably illegally, and agreed not to divulge the name of the person. Then Special Branch got to hear of it. Alasdair summoned me and asked how we had got hold of the transcript. I said, 'I'm sorry, I refuse to tell you.' He said, 'I confirm absolutely your right to protect your source, and I will support you all the way. However it's a very dodgy subject, so be careful.' I said I would.

When I went to rehearsal I found that some foolish mistakes had been made; the worst was that the judge, played by that fine actor David Kelly had a Dublin accent. I protested and he slipped into a Belfast accent with great ease.

The play was intriguing. A boy had been accused of planting a bomb under the local British Legion Hall. It was unlikely that he had actually done it, though he may have been guilty of many other offences. The Special Branch thought he was a member of the Irish National Liberation Army (then in its infancy) and that he had been set up by the Provisional IRA as a loose cannon. True or not, he was found guilty and sentenced to a long term of imprisonment. The play stood on its own and needed no prologue or epilogue but Caryl and Roland were determined it should have one. I went up to Glasgow to see the recording. I was treated with great suspicion by the production team as a potential enemy. They were dismayed to see me greeted by the camera crew as an old friend. I had made many programmes there.

Roland said he had an idea of getting the actors to make speeches to camera along the lines of 'I am just an actor but I think an injustice has been done.' The actors were not keen. I listened to one of them attempting a speech, it was a disaster. Roland agreed. By now the whole BBC was aware of the situation especially the Northern Ireland Office. I went to see the final cut. It had an epilogue which was violently anti-British and used the term 'Freedom Fighters' for the IRA. I insisted it had to be changed. They objected violently. I don't know who wrote the epilogue, but I suspect it was a joint effort by Roland, Carol and the Belfast solicitors for the defence. There was a furious row. I said if they would not change the epilogue I would take the tape and change it myself. They defied me to do so. Stories began to appear in the press. In re-writing the epilogue I consulted BBC Belfast who were most concerned and many others including Shaun. The result was, I thought, quite hard hitting but fair.

The production team took their names off the credits. *Time Out* said it was the worst piece of censorship in television history. Special Branch telephoned to say they had information that the Troops Out Movement was planning a raid on TV Centre to capture the tape. I had a copy made and sent to Birmingham to be used if they succeeded. Nothing happened, of course.

I was now the Voice of Repression, a. mindless fascist and a vicious censor. It was just before the Edinburgh Television Festival, a bean feast for producers who, while staying in smart hotels at their company's expense, slagged them off in public. The companies, including the BBC were sensibly pretty cool about it. This year there were a lot of rumblings. There was to be a great set-piece in front of several hundred people. I was to be brutally attacked mainly by Ken Trodd for my act of fascist censorship and Roland Joffe was to be there as a Christ-like figure to elicit sympathy.

Just before the festival, while we were staying at George Gilroy's farm in Scotland in the gardener's cottage, a seriously tumbledown house on which we had a life rent, I composed the speech I would give. I wanted to rehearse it to Maggie. She sat down and prepared to listen. It was a hot night. The windows were all open and while I was in the middle of the speech a bat flew in and swooped around the room. Maggie shouted and screamed. In vain I said, 'It's all a fallacy that they get tangled in your hair, their radar is too good.'
All to no avail. We eventually got the bat out but the rehearsal was abandoned.

In Edinburgh I prepared for the meeting, I was sick with nerves. My opponents spoke with voices ringing with indignation from the platform. I had to speak from the body of the hall which was packed to capacity. My mouth was dry and I was aware of waves of anger on all sides. I spoke reasonably well. Basically I said, I regretted nothing and would do it again. Fortunately this seemed to take the wind out of their sails. Roland replied with a paean of martyrdom. The audience seemed satisfied and Brian Wenham took us all out for a Chinese meal.

There was an unpleasant post script. Caryl Churchill complained to the Writers Guild that her play had been cruelly ruined by me. I thought she had a nerve, she hadn't written a word of the original play. I was called in to a meeting by some BBC suits and Leon Griffiths spoke passionately on Caryl's behalf. The BBC, who had been on my back throughout, capitulated entirely and I was reprimanded for interfering with an author's script. I was shocked at what I considered a total betrayal.

Next time we went to the Italia prize I entered a film directed by Roland called *The Spongers*. It won. I was able to telephone him and ask him to come out and accept the prize. He was very grudging at first and then agreed. We took him out to dinner. I heaped coals of fire on his head as he thawed. I felt that he had been elbowed into a position where he felt misplaced loyalty to his associates; he remained loyal to them but we ended very friendly.

I was coming to the end of my contract. Shaun and I had a long meeting. Cedric had to go; there was no question. We decided rather nervously on Jonathan Miller, then at the height of his fame, as producer. He wanted an enormous amount of money and to stay for two years and, of course, to direct quite a lot of the plays. We took him to the Etoile for lunch. He ordered ginger beer and we more or less made a deal. When it came to paying the bill however, neither Shaun nor I had any money or credit cards, an embarrassing moment which was a foretaste of things to come.

Jonathan took over and things were not very satisfactory. His production of *Othello* with Tony Hopkins as a light-skinned Moor was an extraordinary contrast with Tony's performance in

*Kean* (qv). The production got lukewarm notices. Jonathan was dreadfully upset. He said, 'I can't stand this, I'm going back to medicine.'
I said, 'They wouldn't have you.'

What we should have done of course was appoint Shaun, too modest to suggest himself, who eventually produced the last two years brilliantly. Loved by all the directors (including me) and giving an object lesson in how to be a producer.

It was now time to decide what I would direct to fulfil my contract. I decided I would like to do *The Ambassadors* again. Lee Remick would be a perfect Miss Gostrey and if I could get the script good enough, I could find a really distinguished actor for Strether. I didn't yet dare to think of Paul Scofield. I asked Dennis Constanduros to write the script. He was a very underestimated playwright, who was based in the West Country. The trouble with adaptations is that the writers get paid by the hour and naturally say, 'This is a very important book. It needs six hours.' Dennis was immune from this temptation. He read the book, which was very long and said, 'I think it would probably work as a single two hour play.' I commissioned him.

When he delivered the script I found it delightful. Where Henry James had left things too vague, Dennis had invented things subtly. Where James had rambled on, Dennis cut considerably and firmly.

Scofield loved the script and agreed to do it. Lee Remick was already on board. The big problem was the casting of Sarah Pocock a formidably well written part but not the lead. I very much wanted Gayle Hunnicutt but hesitated to offer an undeniably leading actress a second lead.

Our mutual agent solved it. She suggested to Gayle that she offer herself for the part. I fell over myself to accept her. For the third of the trio of beautiful women Madame De Vionnet, the older woman with whom young Chad falls in love I cast Delphine Seyrig a wonderful French actress who had so memorably starred in *L'Annee Derniere a Marienbad*.

The *Radio Times* had a great idea. 'We've got the cover,' they said. 'What about taking the three actresses to Paris and getting Clive Arrowsmith to photograph them' and Paul Theroux would like to write the article. My heart sank. I did not like Clive Arrowsmith. I thought he would be trouble and I knew that a well known author like Paul Theroux would regard this piece of journalism as slumming and would write an unpleasantly patronising article.

Fortunately the pictures were good and very few people read the text but Paul fulfilled my fears. Half the trouble was, that in spite of his name, he didn't speak French and we all did. He became sulky. A large chunk of the article was about a fish which in French is Lot and none of us, French or English knew how to translate it. Now, of course, everybody knows it is monkfish. Paul wrote: 'Even the director, James Cellan Jones, all tweeds and fine French idioms was baffled.' Sarky bugger!

However, we put all this behind us when we went into rehearsal. David Huffman, a brilliant young American actor played Chad. He asked me after two weeks: 'Do you think Mr Scofield would mind me calling him Paul?'

'Ask him,' I said. And of course he didn't mind at all. Sadly, David who had a glittering career ahead of him was beaten to death by a drunk when he went back to Los Angeles.

We fixed the date as 1903, the year of the great Impressionist retrospective in Paris. Fanny Taylor and Juanita Waterson did ravishing sets and costumes. How they did it for the money I shall never know. The show was a great success with wonderful notices both here and in America.

A few weeks later Maggie and I went to Madrid for a conference where I was to give a lecture. They were very exciting times. The Falangist era was coming to an end and the streets were alive with excitement. The first election for many years was about to take place. We were swept up in the enthusiasm and made many new friends. During the lecture, I showed some of *Caesar And Cleopatra* and *The Ambassadors*. I got to meet the interpreters whom I came to like very much. They effortlessly jumped from language to language. If one of them wanted to go to the lavatory, he or she would touch the shoulder of a colleague and rush out; the colleague would cover for her, sometimes translating into two languages at a time. You could see the puzzled look on the faces of some of the delegates.

*The Ambassadors* contained a lot of mirror shots. I was asked, 'Why do you do so many shots with reflections?' Jocularly, I replied, 'It saves money on the scenery.' There was a stunned silence. I was supposed to be an Artist. Artists did not talk like that. I hastily explained that in Henry James communication was often indirect and the use of mirrors prevented direct confrontation. They were almost satisfied.

Over twenty years later the British Film Institute decided to show a series of Henry James' adaptations at the National Film Theatre. *Portrait Of A Lady* and *The Golden Bowl* did well. *The Ambassadors* did very well. My friend Vernon Dobtcheff told Paul Scofield about the showing and persuaded him and his wife to come, though normally he hated that sort of thing. He kissed me on both cheeks and was visibly moved. So was I.

*Kean*, which I mentioned earlier, is a comedy by Jean Paul Sartre. It is light, brilliant and sparkling, an amazing contrast to his other work. I had seen Alan Badel play it in the theatre. He was superb, but like the real Kean he upstaged all the other actors to the ultimate detriment of the production.

I cast Anthony Hopkins whom I consider one of the foremost actors of his generation. His agent said he wouldn't be interested, but Tony kept on telephoning from Los Angeles saying, 'Don't take any notice of my agent.'

We had an excellent supporting cast, including Robert Stephens and for a while all went well, until in the canteen Tony heard Diana Rigg make a loud whispering reference to him as the actor who had walked out of *Macbeth* at the Old Vic. From then on everything went funny. After a technical rehearsal Tony walked out. I said to the cast, 'There is very little we can do without him. I'll go and see him tonight and persuade him to come back.'
'You will do no such thing,' said Bob Stephens. 'You will wait for him to ask if he can come back.'
'I'm not proud,' I said, but Bob over-ruled me and went to see him.

Tony was back the next morning. He seemed to suffer agonies all through rehearsals. Cherie Lunghi who played Anna Danby, was wonderfully patient. Somehow we got through it. Robert as the Prince Regent sparked off something in Tony and they played an excellent duologue together.

The finale, shot at the Bury St Edmunds theatre, was an extract from *Othello* with Tony as the Moor blacked up with burnt cork and black tights. He gave an absolutely electrifying performance. Although it was only a short section I never hope to see the part played so well again. I tried to analyse what made it so good. As with all great art it defied analysis.

Overall, I was sad and blamed myself. The show apart from a few outstanding scenes wasn't really very good. Years later Tony wrote to me. It was a letter of apology which brought tears to my eyes especially as I know how bravely he was fighting alcoholism throughout and succeeding magnificently.

One thing that I was able to do as a functionary pleased me greatly. The BBC staff in Northern Ireland were having a seriously rough time and were seriously depressed in spite of the grave-yard humour they exhibited. I went to Belfast to see the Twelfth of July parade. Ron Mason the brave and intelligent man in charge asked me to watch the parade from his office. The Secretary of State for Northern Ireland, Merlyn Rees, was there. Ron nudged me: 'See which window Merlyn's standing at and stand at the other,' he said, 'There may be bullets flying.'
This from a man who had received many death threats himself.

When I got home I determined to set up a series of short plays to be shot in Belfast which would give the local people a bit of a rest from the endless preoccupation with the Troubles. I sent Neil Zeiger, whom I had brought into the BBC as an Assistant Floor Manager and who had been my stage manager at the Royal Lyceum in Edinburgh, as a producer. He was to produce six plays. He managed to commission them all from local writers and directors. Sadly all the plays submitted were grim pieces about the Troubles and the little holiday I wanted to give the staff fell flat. Neil went on to be a successful freelance producer.

All in all I had a reasonably successful three years as HPD (the same initials as the police in *Hawaii Five O*, which amused the children greatly). As we came near the end of the contract Alasdair said, 'Well, boy, what are we going to do next year?'
I said, 'I told you I'm only staying three years.'
'You shit,' he said, 'leaving me in the lurch.'
They started looking for someone else to do the job. Sadly, no one of any talent seemed to want it. Either it was too difficult, or they wanted to go on directing and there was a lot of work around. I tried to get Richard Somerset Ward to apply. He was a brilliant head of Music and Arts, but he was too shy to put himself forward. He was later shifted out of his job and the BBC, but managed to carve out a succesful career in America.

They decided on Keith Williams, who was what my Methodist minister father-in-law would have called a Poor Tool.

Towards the end, Richard Broke had commissioned my old friend Frederic Raphael to do a translation of of the *Oresteia Of Aeschylus*. It was well cast and well directed by Bill Hays. But, in my opinion, not very well written. Alasdair, who was a classical scholar, hated it but they were my people and I felt obliged to defend it. Alasdair grumbled a lot, but said no more.

The time came for my farewell dinner. The BBC behaved handsomely. Maggie and I were allowed to ask twenty-five people of my choice and Alasdair hosted it with Shaun and a lot of BBC officials. I asked Charlie Woolgar, a scene hand who was an old friend and a wide ranging group of people from all over the BBC. I made a reasonably good speech. Alasdair presented me with a beautifully bound copy of the *Agamemnon Of Aeschylus* in Greek with the inscription: 'Get it right next time.'

# Chapter Sixteen

# Back To The Director's Chair

Though the BBC didn't go in for chairs much: one sat on an upturned box or just stood. I was very popular for a short time. I was offered a great many interesting things, some radio, which I would have loved to do, and several plays. Richard Somerset Ward suggested that I should produce, rather than direct, an opera. They already had an experienced director. Foolishly I turned it down. The experience would have been invaluable. I could have learnt enough confidently to direct an opera on television and perhaps later in an opera house.

Instead, I chose to do a three hour Jesus flick for Twentieth Century Fox called *The Day Christ Died*. The producer, Martin Manulis was a very distinguished man, a former head of the American Film Institute. The script was dire. I discovered that Martin had been pushed into employing a cowboy film writer and could only tinker with the script. The money was very good and the whole thing was to be shot in Tunisia. Michael Cacoyannis was at one stage to direct it, but fell out with the studio and was replaced by me.

We moved between Rome and Tunisia at breath taking speed. Martin very sensibly wanted to cast mainly British actors and I cast a good many old friends including Colin Blakely, Oliver Cotton, Tim Pigott-Smith and Harold Goldblatt. Jesus was played by Chris Sarandon in a committedly American accent, and none the worse for that.

We had a casting session in Cinecitta in Rome, even then sadly overgrown and shabby. Many of the actors we saw were old friends like Marne Maitland who had come to Rome to dub, and stayed. I behaved, as usual, politely with the actors. The Assistant Director, Carlo Cotti said, 'Jeem, why you always say how you today, I shake you hand, I offer you role? You should say you, I like you face you stay, you, I don't like you face you go, is quicker.'

When Chris Sarandon had a smart attack of the runs and had to keep leaving for the john, Carlo said, 'Look, Jesus, I build you leetle sheet house on set like I build for Elizabeth Taylor, save time huh?' He did and it did.

The thing I admired most about the Italian crew was their craftsmanship. There were carpenters, painters and plasterers, all artists. When painting was needed everyone pitched in and even the Master Carpenter and Master Painter acted as labourers, and so with each speciality. They built me a whole plaster floor thirty yards long in a Roman temple whose walls were standing but whose floor was made of mud.

The word was that the script had been approved by the Catholic Church and the Jewish Defence League and not a syllable was to be changed. All the rushes went straight to Los Angeles.

Fortunately nobody noticed the total re-writes we did every day. I don't think the suits could read much. The actors worked hard rehearsing every evening without extra payment.

The film starts with Keith Michell as Pilate and Tim Pigott-Smith, as what they called his Aide, riding into Jerusalem. Then cut to a group of tough looking men playing a rough game with a bean bag cheered on by hundreds of children. The players land in a big pile. Suddenly there is a murmur of worry as they detach themselves. At the bottom of the heap is a man in a loin cloth with arms outstretched apparently unconscious. He opens one eye, winks, smiles and gets up. This is the first view the audience has of Jesus.

When the rushes reached California the screaming started.
'Don't let anyone see those rushes, keep them under wraps.'
What was the matter? I asked.
'It's that little pair of undershorts Jesus is wearing, it's disgraceful.'
I said, 'I've got news for you, that's the kit he gets topped in on Good Friday.'
They mumbled and we carried on each day re-writing totally. In the scene where Pilate was examining Jesus we had a statue of Minerva, deeply offensive to any Jew. Chris Sarandon didn't look at Keith Michell but kept his eye on the statue. When Keith asked him, 'What is truth?' he said it quietly and intensely as though he really wanted to know. It was very effective.

Most of the crew had worked a lot with Franco Zeffirelli and were rather frightened of him. Carlo said, 'His name is not Zeffirelli, the gentle little wind, it is Gian Franco Corsi, he would not like people to know it.'

One day Zeffirelli appeared on the set. He said, 'I weesh thees feelm all the bad luck in the world' and left. It rained for four days without stopping. I eventually gathered the crew together and made the sign of the goat with my first and little fingers.
'This drives the curse back to the curser,' I said. It stopped raining.

Maggie came out to Tunisia for a couple of weeks. My driver took her and Colin Blakely out into the desert. Suddenly, a man stepped out into the road demanding that they slow down. Ahmed put his foot on the accelerator and they roared away.
'Why did you do that? 'asked Maggie.
'Bandits,' said Ahmed,' They would have captured you and cut off your arms.'
'What?' said Maggie.
'Or your nose.'
Maggie was a little silent for the rest of the journey.

We had a little contretemps about the board that was nailed above Jesus on the cross and was paraded in front of him on the walk to the crucifixion. I knew the Latin which was Iesus Christos Rex Judaeorum and I had it translated into Hebrew but I didn't know the Greek. When threatened with sanctions by the Catholic Church I had said, 'Who is the Catholic Church I want to meet him.' He turned out to be a perfectly reasonable Jesuit called Terry Sweeney and I asked him about the Greek. He looked very embarrassed. He said, 'When I was at Loyola I had a choice between Greek and ROTC, I chose ROTC'.

We found someone who could translate it and all was well. Terry afterwards left the priesthood and got married.

When we were dubbing some Hebrew at Shepperton under the supervision of Robert Rietty that fine actor and Judaic scholar, we got murmurings from L.A.
'The Hebrew doesn't sound right, it doesn't sound like we hear in the Temple.'
'That's because it's Sephardi, not Ashkenazi,' I said.
They accepted grudgingly.

A year later when Channel 4 were to broadcast the film, I wrote to them. I said I would like to re-cut it, the editing had finally been taken out of my hands and I could improve the cut. What had happened in fact was that the editor Barry Peters had rung me every day from Los Angeles and we had discussed the cut. Channel 4 agreed and generously paid me a fee for doing the re-cut.

It's not such a bad film, we were perhaps a little too careful to avoid too much violence although the moment when the nails were hammered into Chris Sarandon's hands was fairly horrifying.

*A Midsummer Night's Dream:*

*Above:* The audience.

*Right:* John Laurie as Quince.

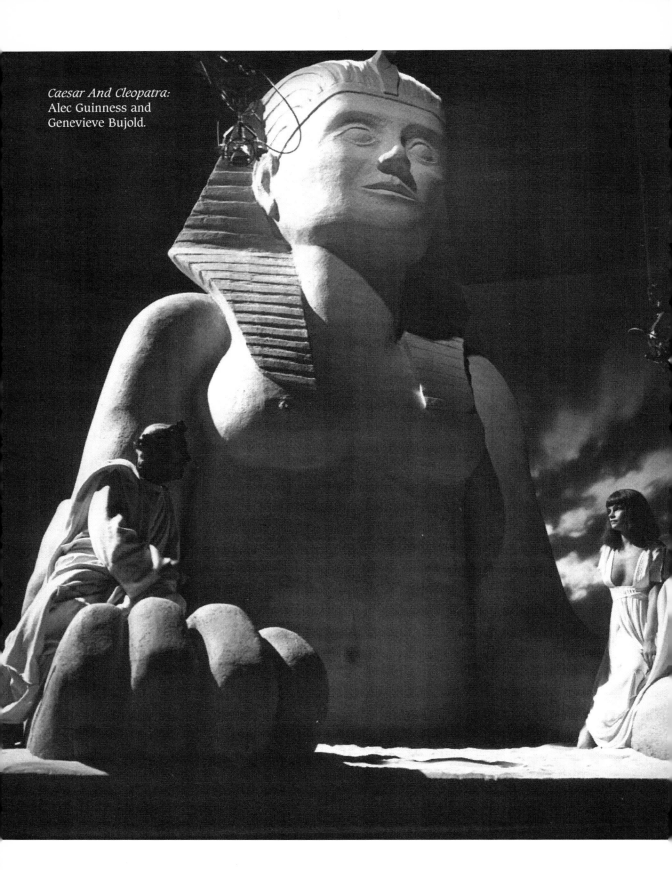

*Caesar And Cleopatra:*
Alec Guinness and
Genevieve Bujold.

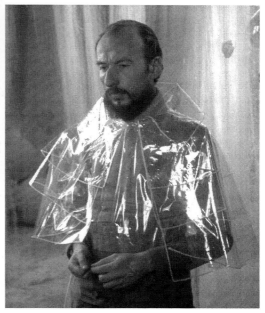

*Out Of The Unknown: Beach Head*

*Above:* Vernon Dobtcheff.
*Left:* Ed Bishop and Robert Lee.
*Bottom*: The inhabitants of planet 0245/B.

*The Ambassadors:*

*Left:*
Alan Gifford as Strether and Bethel Leslie as Maria Gostrey in the 1965 adaptation.

*Below:*
Paul Scofield and Lee Remick take the same roles in the 1977 version.

Paul Scofield as Strether.

*Above:* The crew of *The Forsyte Saga*. JCJ, Donald Wilson and David Giles at the front.

*Left:* Recording *Strife*.

*Kean:*

*Right:* Anthony Hopkins.

*Above:* Hopkins with
Cherie Lunghi and
Frank Middlemass.

*The Way We Live Now:*

*Right:* Colin Blakely as Melmotte.

*Below:* Rachel Gurney, Lila Valmere and Colin Blakely.

# Chapter Seventeen

# $C_2H_5OH$

Which, as all my readers will know, is the chemical formula for Ethyl Alcohol. Earlier in my career, my friend David Turner, with whom I had worked so closely on *Roads To Freedom*, appeared one day at my house in a terrible state of nerves; his hands were shaking dreadfully. He was working quite a lot at the time and he had three contracts to fulfil. He was crying and saying he would never work again because he would not be able to fulfil any of these.

I asked him in and gave him something to eat and telephoned the three producers. I got his deadlines put off for several weeks in all three cases and said,
'Now you can take your time.'
He was obviously exhausted so we put him to bed. Because of the shakes I thought he had advanced Parkinson's disease and I bullied my doctor into coming round and seeing him.
'What's the matter with him?' I asked.
'He's a serious drunk and unless he knocks it off he'll be dead in six months of a hobnail liver,' said the doctor.
I had no idea.

David stayed with us for a few days but went to the cellar and drank a lot of wine every night and was deeply ashamed in the morning. I telephoned his wife and he eventually went home to Leamington Spa.

When I was Head of Plays, David came to me with an immensely long and rambling script about an alcoholic. The man's name was David and during the course of the script he would call him by several surnames including his own. Could I do anything with it? I believed that after some judicious butchery it could be made to work and I offered it to all the producers in the department. Not one of them wanted to take it on. David was now a known drunk and very unfashionable and they did not want to be associated with him.

Eventually I commissioned it, cut it roughly in half and said I would produce and direct it myself. I felt really disgusted at the cowardly behaviour of my producers. There was a scene near the beginning which I thought might be suitable for my son Deiniol. The father, David, was staggering about drunkenly upstairs. His wife said to the child, 'Where's your father?'
The boy said, 'Upstairs in his office.'
'Did he vomit?'
'All over the floor.'
'Get him some water will you?'
'He can't hold a jug because of his shakes. He slops it everywhere.'

I thought Din would be amused to play this and indeed I cast him and he did it very well indeed and rather seriously. Vinny played his sister.

The play's lead character, David, had a wife who was in a wheelchair dying of cancer, whose house was about to repossessed because of debt and who had to keep going to a mental hospital to be dried out. All these things were eerily autobiographical. I had cut the cast to manageable proportions and when we came to have the read through it was a very macabre scene. David and his wife arrived, she in a wheelchair suffering from advanced cancer and he for once sober. Zena Walker and Dinsdale Landon who were to play them on the screen were transfixed at the sight. When we started to read through David started to sob noisily and grabbed my wrist nearly crushing it. His wife seemed to accept it all very coolly. She had been through much worse in real life.

In the event the play was very well received by the critics who still had some respect for David although no producers did. Dinsdale gave a superb performance as David and got very good notices. David's wife died two months later and David not very long after. He was a fine writer and he was my friend and I felt like spitting on the grave of those who despised him.

# Chapter Eighteen
# **Back To Skule**

My first appearance on any stage was at Parc Wern School, Swansea as Prince Charming in *Snow White*. I was confused by the applause and cheers as I rode in on my hobby horse, with my two companions to rescue the Princess who had eaten a poisoned apple. My Godfather swore that I had hit one of the companions with my whip for upstaging me, but I do not remember. Carys Richards, who played the princess, had an enormous apple clenched between her teeth but it seemed to make no difference. The show was a success.

When my father joined the army in 1940 and my mother took a job commanding the local Civil Nursing Reserve I was sent away to the Dragon School in Oxford. It was an extraordinarily liberal establishment. We were allowed to take a boat on the Cherwell unsupervised and roam around Oxford. We worked very hard; at age twelve we had two hours prep a night, but it was made to seem easy. We wrote Latin Elegiacs at ten and learnt Greek and French from eight years old.

J. B. Brown was my English teacher, who also directed the school plays. We did a Shakespeare in the summer, a Gilbert and Sullivan in the winter and a French play at Easter. Bruno was a Communist married to a Conservative city councillor. He was a wonderful director. I was in several plays, but Ross in *Macbeth* was the one I enjoyed most. Antonia Pakenham (later Fraser, later Pinter) played Lady Macbeth and I was wildly in love with her. I used to stand in the wings and sigh a lot. She had a pronounced lisp, so one of her speeches went:
'All the perfumth of Arabia will not thweeten thith little hand.'
The lisp didn't matter at all, I thought she was wonderful.

I was deeply unhappy when I went to Charterhouse. I had failed the scholarship exam and had been put in a form full of duds. My Latin went to hell and I did no Greek. Freddie Raphael was in my house. He wasn't any more unpleasant than any other thirteen year old but there grew up a fashion for mocking his Jewishness. To my eternal shame I joined in and the guilt has not left me for over fifty years. Fred and I made friends and I got to know his mother whom I thought very glamorous. I don't know why it all happened. There were plenty of other Jewish boys who were totally accepted. Freddie never forgot it either. It has coloured all his work throughout his life. I tried to make amends but the scars ran deep.

Fred and I were in *Hamlet* together. I as Laertes and Fred as Osric. I was beginning to get self-conscious about acting and became clumsy and awkward on stage. We both went up to Cambridge. Fred, for reasons I couldn't fathom, was a year behind me. He had stayed at school for a year and became a school monitor. I was in the Footlights Revue in 1951 (qv) and he in 1952. We sort of kept in touch. Years later, he telephoned me and Richard Broke, a producer. He had an idea for a television play about a school. He wanted to call it *School Play*. I read it. It was a barely disguised portrait of our house at Charterhouse. I could recognise almost all the characters who were based on our schoolfellows. Thankfully I couldn't recognise myself. It was very autobiographical and very weird. I felt I had to direct it whether I wanted to or not and I did want to. I decided to use grown up actors to play the boys. They included Denholm Elliott, Tim Pigott-Smith (a slimy monitor) Jeremy Kemp, Michael Kitchen and Jenny Agutter as the matron. All the grown ups, staff etc, would have unseen faces and bodies in the foreground. I designed a school badge based on the Charterhouse coat of arms with a bend sinister instead of a chevron.

We found the Royal Masonic School, which had just closed down. In the few weeks before it was taken over by an American college, we made it our own. The opening and closing sequences were the only ones we shot at Charterhouse. They were simple shots of Denholm and Michael walking towards the entrance. Of course we could not ask permission. I almost panicked in the middle of the shoot. I expected an enraged beak to pop out and say:
'CELLAN JONES? WHAT THE HELL DO YOU THINK YOU ARE DOING?'

In the film, one of the boys is seduced by the housekeeper, or vice versa, played by Jenny Agutter, after being beaten by the head monitor. This mirrored an incident which actually happened. The play caused some fuss, I am pleased to say. One critic, TC Worsley who had been a Headmaster slammed it. Later I met the wife of a man who, when he was about to take over the Headmastership of Charterhouse, saw the film.
'God, was it as bad as that?' she said.
I said, 'It was worse.'

Much later, in 1985, Fred telephoned me. As an Oscar winning screen writer (for *Darling*) he was given a lot of work by producers who couldn't raise the money to make a film but could afford to commission an Oscar winning writer. Fred was quite rich but never saw his work on the screen; could I help?

We chose seven stories from *Sleep Six* and *Oxbridge Blues* and took them to the BBC. I was, for once, in a position of some power. We offered them a deal. Fred would write the scripts and they would be of varying lengths, anything from twenty minutes to two hours. Some would be on film, some on video. We would call the series *Oxbridge Blues*. Keith Williams, the new Head of Plays agreed and commissioned the series. Thus started one of the happiest engagements ever. I produced and directed several of them and Richard Stroud and Fred were the other directors.

Fred had a reputation, people were frightened to criticise his work. I thought I knew him better. When the script for the first play, *Oxbridge Blues*, came in I thought it was a mess, full of smart arse gags and unfeeling. I took a deep breath. I sent it back and said,
'Would you please re-write on the following lines .......?'
In three days I had a beautiful totally re-written script.
'I only wanted to be told,' he said.

We broke lots of rules. Actors appeared in different parts in different plays. Running times varied enormously. We had very little money in the budget, so we shared locations between films and treated the schedule for two films, *Sleep Six* and *Oxbridge Blues* as one. We had a superb cast: Ben Kingsley, Ian Charleson, Jeremy Child, Amanda Redman, Alfred Marks and many others. Fred cast Susan Sarandon in the one he was directing. We had to apply for a labour permit for her. The Home Office always used to consult Equity and abide by their decisions. The North American committee of Equity agreed that we could employ her but said that it had to go to the general committee. They took their time. Susan became fractious: 'It's not as if you're paying me anything much for this job.'

At the last moment Equity refused permission. I went over their heads to the Home Office. They said they would give me the decision on Friday. Susan was due to fly over on the Monday. When I rang at twelve o'clock on Friday, the official that was dealing with the case had left for the week-end leaving the papers in the safe.
'Let me talk to her superior,' I said.
I did.
He immediately agreed they had to give us the licence and she flew over on the Monday. Sucks to Equity.

We had arranged to get a Rolls Royce from the makers for nothing. Ben Kingsley, who played a film producer was to drive it. We needed it on location in the South of France. Rolls said we could not possibly take it abroad.
'The new Mercedes looks nice,' I said.
'Right' they said. 'But you'll have to pay for the driver's overnights.'

In France where we were shooting the films in a glorious muddle I talked to the cast. 'There are no caravans or cars,' I said.
'Everyone goes to work on the bus, same as me, I hope you don't mind.'
Very sportingly, they didn't.
The hotels were clean but basic. The meal allowance wasn't great but every now and then I would take them out for a nice dinner. Amazing! They threw themselves into the films whole-heartedly and enjoyed themselves accepting the financial situation totally. In contrast, down the coast, the BBC were shooting *Tender Is The Night*. There were rumblings of discontent and rumours of strikes. We were told that the director was being paid less than the leading lady's child's nanny.

At Nice Airport we had a difficult scene to shoot. Jeremy Childs who played Ben's agent was supposed to arrive on the plane with a load of tourists whom he had drunkenly insulted and vomited over and continued to do so loudly as they came into the Terminal. We couldn't afford any extras and lighting was minimal. John Hooper shot on fast stock.

We heard that the Lord's Taverners were arriving on the next flight. Without asking for permission, we infiltrated Jeremy into the crowd walking down the ramp which included many celebrities including Terry Wogan and Omar Sharif. Jeremy ad libbed brilliantly. He attached himself to Omar Sharif and insulted him outrageously. Omar behaved beautifully, not looking at the camera once. When they went out of shot. I said, 'Mr Sharif do you mind going back for take two?'

He obliged. I ventured to write a Latin piece for the opening of *Oxbridge Blues*. It went like this:

*Vivant! Vivant! Universitas oxoniensis*
*Universitasque Cantabrigiensis*
*Victoris Wendeque*
*Matres gentilissimae!*

Long live the Universities of Oxford and Cambridge, most Gentle Mothers to Victor and Wendy - as if some pompous music don had written to the couple for a present. It was beautifully sung by Cantabile.

I yielded to temptation and wrote a very pretentious piece for the end, translating into Latin all the names of the actors and technicians. It ended:

*Vivat! Vivat! Collegium Sanctis Iohanni Evangelistae apud Universitatem Cantabrigiensem*
*Frederici Jacobique alma mater tolerantissima. Vivat!*

Spot the grammatical mistake.

Long live the College of St John in the University of Cambridge, most tolerant foster mother of Fred and Jim.

Once again Cantabile sang Dick Holmes' music beautifully. Almost nobody got the joke except one commentator in a book about television, bless him.

The series was quite successful and got several BAFTA nominations. We owed great thanks to BBC Enterprises who had got us some money from America by selling it to a cable company. We were awarded three Ace awards for production, script and Susan Sarandon. We were an idyllically happy company and Fred's brilliant work was deservedly brought to light. One of the films, *Sleep Six* was shown at the London Film Festival.

By now my son Simon was twenty-two and he married a clever and attractive girl called Sarah O'Brien. She was a film producer, though later proved she could turn her hand to anything, They had a daughter, Kate, who at the time of writing is grown up and very beautiful. Their second child died tragically young at seven months old. Sadly, the marriage didn't last and they divorced. Sarah remains a close friend and we see a lot of her.

# Chapter Nineteen
# **Shaviana**

George Bernard Shaw was a cousin of my mother, or so she said.
'Bernie? He was a vegetarian, dear. We didn't get on very well with him.'
Like all the Anglo Irish she reckoned she was related to every famous Irish man of the last two centuries. She said her mother, who was called Anna Gray, was the origin of Thomas Moore's poem, but I think the dates didn't match by about fifty years.

Nonetheless I was brought up on Shaw and had read all his plays, including *Back To Methuselah*, before I was twelve. They were mostly sharply written but easy to read and I loved them. I've already talked about *Saint Joan*. In 1977, when I was Head of Plays and could choose more or less anything that I wanted to do I decided to do *You Never Can Tell*. It is a delightfully funny play with Valentine, an impecunious five shilling dentist, for a hero and a brilliantly conceived scene in the second act where a party of six are served a three course meal with varying drinks in the space of about ten minutes. The role of the waiter, William, who orchestrates this is spectacular.

I got Cyril Cusack to play him and he was even better than Ralph Richardson in the stage production. Kika Markham played Gloria; she was ravishingly beautiful and had a fiery temperament not unconnected with her very left wing politics. Robert Powell, fresh from playing Jesus, played Valentine and portrayed him with a slim intensity which still managed to convey all the comedy of the part. The key to the luncheon scene is a non speaking character referred to only once as Jo. It is he, in fact, that does most of the hard work of serving, while William the waiter has the sparkling dialogue. Jo was played with very quiet and unobtrusive skill by Neville Phillips.

The last act of the play, when William's father is first mentioned always pleased me. The rather pompous lawyer, Finch M'Comas, asks the waiter what his father does.
He replies, 'He's at the bar sir.'
M'Comas says patronisingly, 'A potman eh?'
'No sir, a Q.C. sir, your profession sir.'
M'Comas is little put out. The waiter says, 'Please don't apologise, Sir, I sometimes wish he were a potman, I had to keep him until he was forty; now it's never less than 200 guineas a brief. Refreshers too I'm told.'

I used to quote this incessantly to my son Din, the barrister, who quickly tired of it.

The end of the play is extraordinarily complicated. There is a ball with a band and everybody in fancy dress. It has to be staged in such a way that people dancing by appear at a window at just the right moment. The last line of the play is when William goes up to Valentine and says, 'Ah well sir, you never can tell, you never can tell.'

The first take worked beautifully until the end when Cyril Cusack said, 'Ah well sir, you never, you never … you never know.' I'm afraid I shouted at Cyril but he looked back at me with that sweet St Thomas of Canterbury smile and got it right the next time.

*The Daily Express* described it as a production of real style beautifully presented and acted with complete precision. *The Daily Telegraph* said it had the pace and gaiety of a Mozart opera. I always seemed to get better notices when I was Head of Plays.

*Arms And The Man*, which I did in 1989 was the next Shaw play. I determined that the part should be played by actors of the right age. It is a great temptation to get big stars who are twenty years too old for the part. Olivier and Richardson had played the parts in the West End.

Kika Markham was twelve years older in *Arms And The Man*, but still looked absolutely ravishing and played Catherine the mother superbly. Bluntschli and Sergius were played by Pip Torrens and Patrick Ryecart. Patsy Kensit who has still a terrible and unjustified relationship with the popular press played Louka. We had quite a struggle over the casting of Raina. I wanted Helena Bonham Carter who I knew could play the part beautifully and was the right age. I had quite frenzied opposition all round from people who said she couldn't act. I knew she could act very well having seen her play Eliza at Westminster School when she was seventeen. She played the part with great spirit, getting all the humour into the lines.

It was one of the last productions done in the old way with beautiful studio sets and a crew of six cameras. They were beginning to lose the knack of how to do it and they just managed to shoot it in the time. I managed to do a little trick shot where we inlaid Helena into a doorway of a tiny house and faked up a cloudy night sky glistening with stars, even making the stars vanish as they passed behind the clouds.

Actors are supposed to be frightened to work with dogs or children. I had it in mind to do an experiment disproving this. We had several dogs in the play. Sergius's bull terrier which is mentioned in the script and several others including two Bulgarian retrievers and a pair of deer hounds. They were all extremely affectionate. We were going to play a long scene all in one take and I said to the actors: 'I'd like to introduce the dogs into this scene, if it doesn't work we can scrap it at once and do without them.'

They agreed to try it. Helena picked up the bull terrier, sat in the window seat and used him as a pillow. The other dogs wandered about between the actors asking to be petted and crying a little. Amazingly it all worked beautifully and the scene was quite charming.

I adored Helena and thought she was wonderful. Her father, Raymond, who has recently died, was quite severely disabled. He wrote me a long letter in an agonised spidery script saying that it was probably the best thing that she had ever done. He had played Sergius at school and knew the play well. I was profoundly moved knowing what effort he had had to make in writing the letter, which I shall always treasure.

## Chapter Twenty

# Horace

A friend of mine used to quarrel with actors and also with producers which was a mistake, as he hardly ever worked again. You can afford to quarrel with one but not both. I never had any trouble relating to actors but I suppose I had a bit of a reputation with producers.

I quarrelled with Keith Williams which was very foolish as he was a good producer and didn't deserve my bad manners. I was going to direct six short films about a young man with learning difficulties (he would have been called backward a few years ago and an idiot before that). Barry Jackson had played Horace in a *Play For Today* two years before and Roy Minton who had done the original was to write the scripts. Roy had a reputation for furious lunacy, but I had got to know him well as Head of Plays and he behaved beautifully. Barry Davies had directed the original play, so I had a big act to follow.

Roy wrote these scripts with great delicacy and charm. Keith and I originally fell out because I said I wanted to use Dick Holmes to write the music. He telephoned him and asked him to submit a tape with a theme tune on it. Dick, who had recently won an Ivor Novello award rang me and said, 'Look, I'm sorry but I don't do auditions any more, do you want me to write the music or not?'

I became angry and instead of using sweet reason with Keith shouted at him and our relationship never really recovered; I blame myself entirely for this. It wasn't that long after I had finished being Head of Plays, and I suppose I had a bit of an imperious attitude. Barry played the part beautifully but Yorkshire Television didn't seem to know how to market the films. Barry lent great dignity to the part and made one sympathise enormously with someone who, though he was of very low intelligence, had a sort of purity and dignity. On one occasion when one of the films was broadcast, the announcer, who obviously knew nothing of what was coming said, 'And now here's another chance to meet that crazy character *Horace*.'

Yorkshire had a bad situation with the unions, even worse than that of Thames. On one occasion we were shooting a scene with an old lady in bed and one of the electricians was lying on the floor very drunk and trying to put a plug and socket together, failing dismally and giggling the while. I was about to expostulate when the floor manager said, 'Please don't, they will all go out on strike.' So I bit back the retort.

Yorkshire had a very aggressive shop steward who caused immense trouble. They conceived the idea of sending him to Ruskin College Oxford for a course, but he came back twice as militant. I wonder what's happened to those six little films? They were really quite good.[15]

---

[15] They still survive in the archive at Leeds

## Chapter Twenty-One

# Bill The Bard x4

I've only ever directed four Shakespeare plays and, curiously, they were all comedies. I've mentioned *A Midsummer Night's Dream* already. It had a remarkable cast, so strong in fact that Edward Fox didn't even get billing. Although we had to shoot it at enormous speed I managed to introduce a few amusing touches. I had Hippolyta and Theseus (Eleanor Bron and Michael Gambon) riding across the countryside on two enormous horses. They entered with a pack of basset hounds. Theseus gives a very accurate description of these in the text:

> *My hounds are bred out of the Spartan kind*
> *So flew'd, so sanded and their heads are hung*
> *With ears that sweep away the morning dew,*
> *Crook kneed and dew-lapped like Thessalian bulls,*
> *Slow in pursuit, but matched in mouth like bells,*
> *Each under each.*

I got one of the very few basset packs in England; they are not very fast but they bark beautifully and are very affectionate. In the scene where they arrive and chance upon the young lovers asleep, they licked them in the face and peed all over them. The actors were very good about it.

Lynn Redgrave was a marvellous rider and longed to get on the back of Gambon's horse which measured nineteen and a half hands. She was wearing a long dress and her hair was in curlers in preparation for the next scene. She jumped on the horse, galloped uphill, jumped over a five-barred gate, turned round, jumped back over again and galloped down hill.
'Quite a nice old animal,' she said.

Later I had a go on the horse. It wasn't quite as amenable to me and at full gallop it turned around and tried to bite me on the leg. I fell off very hard.

The next day I became very impatient with the closing scene. I had all the musicians and the cast in a number of punts with swans' heads on the front. They didn't seem to know how to manage the punts, so, furiously I leapt into the water, grabbed the pole from one of them and showed them how to do it: such arrogance.

There are very good things in this production though Peter Fiddick gave it a lousy notice in *The Guardian*. I think John Laurie played the best Quince I have ever seen.

In 1973 I was asked by the Royal Lyceum Theatre in Edinburgh to do their ninetieth birthday production. It was to be *Much Ado About Nothing* which Ellen Terry had played there in 1883.

It was very short notice; I had less than three weeks to get the whole thing together before starting rehearsal. Of course, I was second, or possibly third choice, the director having walked out. I was shown the model of a set and having looked at it said, 'There is no way I can direct that play using this set.'

The designer said, 'Right, I'm leaving,' and departed carrying the model with him. Fortunately there was a brilliant designer called Geoffrey Scott, who was about to be employed by the National Theatre but agreed to put it off to design our set. He and I worked out a very successful plan that afternoon, including all the necessary Shakespearian bits; a bridge for a balcony and three doors.

I then had to go into the Albery Theatre in London, to use it as a basis for auditions. If you offer someone a part in a provincial rep in a few months time they refuse, thinking they might pick up a film. It's quite different saying, 'How would you like to play this part starting next week?' I had to ask Clive Perry, the theatre's director, if I could have full control of the money; it would have taken too long to keep referring decisions back to Edinburgh. He very sweetly agreed, and I kept strictly within budget.

We got a very good cast together, with Bill Fraser as Dogberry, a fiendishly difficult part. It helps enormously if the character wears a recognisable uniform and, because I was setting it in 1919, we were able to dress him like a copper. I got Keith Baxter and Zena Walker to play Benedick and Beatrice. David Rintoul played Claudio and Leonato was played by Fulton Mackay.

Many of the other parts were played by Scottish actors who were encouraged to use their accents. The lady in waiting, Margaret, was played by Jan Wilson whose parents owned a private hotel in Royal Circus in the New Town. We all stayed there and they were wonderfully hospitable and cheap because none of us was earning very much. Every now and then, if they got overcrowded, they would put up a bed for you in the corridor and charge you even less. It was a very happy company and John Westbrook who played Don Pedro was a sort of avuncular figure who led the company. David Collings played Don John (whom I was afterwards to work with several times.)

The second last line of the play is when a messenger comes on and says:
'My lord, your brother John is ta'en in flight and brought with armed men to Messina.'
I persuaded the actor who played the messenger to lend me his costume and I took his part on the last night. As I burst through the door the whole cast corpsed and just managed to recover themselves in time to start the eightsome reel with which we ended the play.

We used to have an old age pensioners' matinee which cost them ten pence. Being a glutton for punishment, I would hang around waiting for the audience to come out. Two old ladies came out of the auditorium moaning a lot about the production. I said to them, 'Didn't you like it?'
'No I thought it was a load of old rubbish,' said one of them.
'Well here's your money back,' I said and offered them 10p.
'Thank you very much,' they said, and took it.

A couple of years later I went up to Edinburgh again to do *The Taming Of The Shrew*, a very difficult play. As usual I spent a week doing research, especially using that wonderful multi-volumed Sources of Shakespeare in Richmond Reference Library. I discovered that although *The Taming Of The Shrew* was written and first performed in 1594, there was a previous play called *The Taming Of A Shrew*. It was written by an unknown hand. The body of the play was not really very good compared to Shakespeare's version but the opening and closing with Christopher Sly were absolutely brilliant, some of the verse reminding one of Marlowe. I think Shakespeare had got bored with Sly and practically written him out.

You know what happens in the play: a Lord and his train come across an old drunk man and while he is asleep take him away and pretend that he is a prince and that they are going to feed him with delicious food and do a play for him.

I enthusiastically used the beginning and end scenes of the earlier *Shrew* and the body text of the later *Shrew* and they seemed to my rather self regarding opinion as an extraordinarily good mix. There was also a very important scene where Christopher Sly interrupts the play in the middle and changes the plot.

Dan Massey played Petruchio and the Lord, and Penelope Wilton played Kate. Again we had a lot of very good local actors including JG Devlin as Christopher Sly and Leonard Maguire as Gremio. There was an important part of a servant in which the young actor playing him seemed to have no interest in the play. He would not learn his lines, he would read novels during the rehearsal and he would be generally idle antagonizing the rest of the cast. After much thought, I decided to fire him, though I dreaded having to do so. I took him into the boardroom at the Kings Theatre where we were rehearsing, and what followed I describe in another chapter.

Dermot Crowley, a fine Irish actor took over, with whom I was to work again. Dan Massey was a superb Petruchio but would go home and analyse the part and stay up all night worrying. Each day he would establish a piece of the play brilliantly and come back in the morning having torn it to pieces. With a great deal of agony we got through the rehearsals and the performance was very successful.

After it had played in Edinburgh for some while, the management decided to take it on tour, but only to one theatre, the Adam Smith Institute, Kirkcaldy; not a very seriously luxurious place. I was a little worried about the lighting and I was told that the lighting man Andre Tammes would certainly come and supervise the get-in.

A week before we were due to open, he said he would send his chief electrician instead, and then, three days before the opening he said he would send another electrician with a lighting plot. When he arrived the electrician had a few notes written on the back of an envelope and nothing else,so I decided to light it myself, never having done it before.

Amazingly with the co-operation of the actors, who edged their way into spotlights, we managed to make a fairly decent job of it. As a production it looked beautiful with the beginning and end all in silver and black and the middle in strong violent Mediterranean colours.

# Forsyte and Hindsight

The difficulty of the play of course is that it is very politically incorrect and quite hard to accept for a modern audience. Penelope Wilton did the last speech, 'A woman moved is like a fountain troubled etc,' with great intensity and passion which absolutely captivated the audience. In the epilogue Christopher Sly described what he has seen as a dream: 'The best dream that I have ever had in my life,' but of course it remains firmly a dream. That's my excuse, anyway, when accused of political incorrectness!

*The Comedy Of Errors* is certainly Shakespeare's shortest comedy and may even be his shortest play. It was designed not to be produced in the Globe Theatre but as a Christmas entertainment for the students at the Middle Temple. Any well educated lad at the time would know the story very well so its complication is not important. The students were probably all drunk anyway.

The description of entrances and exits make it almost certain that Shakespeare envisaged it as a Commedia del Arte piece and I resolved to follow that. Ephesus, one of the two main towns in the story had a reputation for being a haunt of jugglers, conjurors and acrobats so I filled out the set with those people collected by Nick Chagrin, who was billed as Master of the Mime.

If you read the stage directions, the set divides easily into three: the house, the convent and the market. I determined to fill the biggest studio in the BBC with a circular set, the floor being painted to look like a map of the known world at the time, with Syracuse on the left and Ephesus on the right. The three buildings formed the three points of an equilateral triangle. In a rather lordly fashion I had laid down these strictures. Don Homfray saw at once that he had to design something interesting in each of the three gaps and constructed some beautiful views with false perspectives of the sea, the countryside and the town.

I was lucky enough to get Cyril Cusack and Dame Wendy Hiller for the old people. The plot, as I am sure you know, is wildly improbable. Two sets of twins become separated in a ship wreck. One twin is a master, the other his servant in each case and the comedy consists of all the ludicrous mistakes the rest of the cast make in confusing the twins. I believe that Shakespeare intended each pair of twins to be played by one actor and the structure right through the play makes this possible. There is a short scene at the end where all four appear together, but I believe that the audience would have accepted stand-ins for this one scene. It's also much more interesting for the actors, as one of the Antipholuses (Antipholi?) is naïve and innocent and the other is wordly and cynical. The same goes for the Dromios.

I auditioned one or two people for the Dromios and then I got in touch with Roger Daltrey of The Who, whom I thought would be an extraordinarily good actor. He read a speech for me quite well, but he had obviously been studying it all night and when I gave him a passage to read unseen he collapsed. However I knew he could play the parts and his natural sense of rhythm made him appreciate the rhythm of Shakespeare's verse. As rehearsals continued, he made the two Dromios into two entirely different people, and it was a joy to watch. Michael Kitchen played the Antipholi. He, also, managed to separate the two parts brilliantly. For the whore, I interviewed Mandy Rice Davies who, it was immediately apparent, couldn't really act at all. I got Ingrid Pitt to play the part with great strength and intensity.

In the middle of the shoot it looked as though we were not going to finish and the studio was booked for another production. We would have to take up the set and rebuild it several weeks later. Shaun Sutton, who was producing, was worried sick although he kept it from me, but there is a still picture of him looking very woebegone. It made me appreciate what a really good producer he was. We finished on time and I did some trick shots of the two actors talking to themselves which were hugely amusing.

## Chapter Twenty-Two
# Mr And Mrs W

Michael Williams was a fine actor. I was approached about producing and directing a sitcom, probably with Michael in it.

I was a bit dubious, not of the half hour performance in front of an audience because I had a lot of experience of live television, but because I was a bit of a snob. Still, the scripts by Bob Larbey were very good and I noticed at once that they had plenty of opportunity for pauses which I love and I knew I could seduce an audience into laughing at them rather than have to fill the show with quickfire gags.

I still had not made up my mind when Humphrey Barclay of LWT tentatively asked 'What about Judi?' Michael was married to Judi Dench. My ears pricked up. This was an entirely different kettle of fish. We asked her agent. Yes, she was interested if Michael was to be in it. We all three settled and signed our contracts at the same time. For the neighbours, we cast Richard Warwick and Susan Penhaligon.

There was still a great deal of snobbery in the business. I met Jacqui Davis a well known producer in the street. She said, 'What a tragedy, actors like that involving themselves in a grubby sitcom.' I smiled and said nothing. Months later I met her again and she cringed with apology.

When you start working with an actor you can feel that there is a tension between you. Sometimes it lasts right until the first cut and when they see the film they say 'Now I see what you are getting at.'

The first few hours with Judi were seriously awkward. I felt she was uncertain about the job and about me. Halfway through the afternoon everything suddenly clicked and I knew it was going to be all right. We launched into seven episodes, each to be recorded in front of a live audience. Someone - not me, I said firmly - had to warm the audience up before each recording. Humphrey volunteered to take it on. I thought him a bit mimsy but he did the trick. Part of the ritual was the introduction to the audience of cast and director. I foolishly ventured to imitate Judi's bow to the audience. She responded in kind, imitating me and it was so devastatingly accurate that I never imitated her again.

We began to build an audience. The long silences between Michael and Judi worked beautifully with lots of laughs. If anyone dried or if there was a technical mistake we had to do re-takes. Richard Warwick dried on a particularly difficult speech. He got muddled and went to four re-takes. When he finally got it right the audience applauded. I had to go down and say please,

please laugh if you think it is funny and only if you think it is funny, but don't clap. They were usually very good natured audiences and they responded well.

This leads me to the subject of canned laughter. The editors had a collection of laughs on tape which they were keen to use. I forbade it. The only compromise we allowed was that if a line got a laugh on take one and we were using, say, take four we could use the take one laugh. It worked pretty well.

Judi and Michael behaved beautifully when we threw difficult things at them. One night a group of American students came to see the show. One of them asked Judi, 'Do you ever get to play any serious roles?' She smiled self-deprecatingly and left it to the rest of us to explain.

LWT wanted to do another series to make up thirteen shows. We all agreed. We rehearsed in St John's Waterloo where my parents were married. One day the Sacristan brought out the register for me to see.

We were in the middle of a success, money was available, I had thought long and hard about the presentation, the typeface and the pictorial impact. The publicity chief of LWT said that they were going to have huge billboards all over London advertising the show and that an agency was working out the details of the campaign.
'Right,' I said, 'Could you put me in touch with them? It would be a good idea if we were to collaborate on typefaces etcetera.'
'You don't understand,' she said. 'They are sensitive creative people who must be left alone and unsupervised and not interfered with.'
I snarled back at her that we on the production team were no strangers to creativity. The agency eventually came up with a rather banal image of a grinning putto which probably did no harm. I reminded her of the conversation later and she had the grace to blush.

Peter Fiddick, who was now Arts Editor of *The Guardian*, asked if he could come and cover us for a week. I was delighted, he was quiet and modest, wrote beautifully and got on well with the cast. Unfortunately during this week one of the scenes did not work. It wasn't funny and said nothing. We sent it back to Bob Larbey for a re-write. Peter duly reported this - we didn't want to interfere with any of his reports and Bob got the needle. Relations were never quite the same again.

Peter and Jane Fiddick became great friends with the cast. We arranged a day trip to Calais with our families, it was very cheap at the time. We had a delicious lunch. My daughter Vinny who was eight polished off a dozen oysters. I noticed only the word canard on the menu and found myself eating ducks' feet. I don't recommend them, they're a bit rubbery.

We treated the trip partly as a recce. I thought we could do an episode with Mike and Laura having a day trip to France and having a lot of comic adventures there. We had enough money in the budget. If all went well, we could go further afield and perhaps make contacts in countries where the show could be sold.

Bob and John couldn't bring themselves to write it. Finally, after a lot of agonising, they wrote an episode where Mike and Laura planned a trip to France, everything went wrong and eventually they had to go home after missing the boat and never getting near France. It was sad, it could have been such fun.

We had now done thirteen episodes. We had won a British Press Guild Award, though not a BAFTA. for which we had been nominated twice. We were well regarded by viewers and critics and we should have retired gracefully. LWT wanted another thirteen. I bowed out. At this time, there was plenty of work around. Michael and Judi said they would do it, but 'Jim would have to approve the director.' This caused grinding of teeth in LWT. They suggested a lot of unsuitable names which I turned down.
'Well your Lordship,' said Humphrey Barclay petulantly.
'Who is good enough for you?'
'I'll let you know,' I said.
What was needed was a good experienced craftsman who would start where we had finished and gradually make the show his own. It also needed a bright, talented and unselfish person. I recommended Don Leaver, who made an excellent job of it. Thank heavens, after twenty-six episodes the cast drew the line at any more. A long time later, there was a party at La Barca in Waterloo where an enormous cake was cut with both mine and Don's name on it.

Poor Michael died of cancer some years later. He was able to carry on working in radio which he did superbly well until nearly the end. Richard Warwick was slowly dying of Aids. I saw him just before he died, a pale shadow suffering dreadfully from the cold. He was a fine actor. I told him I would never forget his performance in If'. 'Not bad,' he said, 'Not bad at all'
In a few days he was dead.

There was a sad postscript to this story. I had plenty of offers of work and didn't need to do any of the sitcoms I was predictably offered. Later, in the nineties, Humphrey Barclay who now had his own company, was asked to produce an Anglicised version of an American sitcom[16] which was an immensely successful series about older ladies in sexual situations. It was very popular with the gay lobby. Our series was to be called *Brighton Belles* and the scripts were based on the American ones. From the start it didn't work and we should have known. The sexual antics were embarrassing and the Anglicisation didn't work. Now there was less work about, I agreed to direct it and we could get a distinguished cast of women. We did a pilot which was not unsuccessful. When eventually we went into a series of six, the figures went down and down and down and Carlton Television quite properly pulled it. I don't think the show did any of us any good.

[16] *The Golden Girls*

## Chapter Twenty-Three
# Reginald And Wendy

Rex Harrison was born in Liverpool and christened Reginald. He was married many times, the sign of an incurable romantic. Anglia Television offered me *The Kingfisher* by William Douglas Home, a gentle comedy with three main roles: a seventy year old novelist, his former lady friend from way back and his butler. It sounds a bit like a 1930s play to be watched to the sound of matinee teacups, but it was much better than that.

Rex and Wendy Hiller came with the job though we had a nasty hiccup when Rex took against her. I cast Cyril Cusack as the butler whom I encouraged to be at his most mischievous. William Douglas-Home had been a junior staff officer in 1944 after D-Day. He was told to pass on a message that Calais was to be shelled. No warning was to be given to the civilian population as, of course, the Germans would also be warned. He refused. He was court martialled, cashiered and sent to serve a year's imprisonment in Wormwood Scrubs. It was a very savage punishment. I couldn't help thinking that he must have been a thorn in the flesh of the general staff for some time.

He served his sentence with aristocratic insouciance and managed to make a play out of it called *Now Barabbas* which was an immediate success. He and his wife tried to get the sentence reviewed for some years, but it would have meant the government paying him a fortune in back pay and heavy compensation, so it came to nothing. I liked him very much.

After a couple of days' rehearsal Rex started attacking Wendy Hiller: I remonstrated with him. He turned on me and, again, sure enough said, 'Mind your own business; and furthermore don't tell me how to act, you little shit.' I took a deep breath, it was now or never. I said, 'It's no good you going on like that; we shall never get the thing together.'
He shuffled his feet like an embarrassed childish seventy year old and we began to get on quite well. I encouraged Cyril to upstage him at every step. As they were going through a doorway Cyril would do one of his famous trips which were brilliantly funny.
'What's he doing behind my back?' Rex said.
'Nothing Rex, nothing.'
He grumbled, but got on with the rehearsal. I realised we were working well together when he garbled his way through a long speech and I said, 'Rex, that was dreadful.'
'Yes,' he said. 'I'll do it again, shall I?'

When we were about to move to Norfolk he said, 'Will you share a house with me?'
'Certainly not,' I said. 'I'll find my own digs. You're the last person I want to see after a day's work.' He laughed and we continued to get on well.

One small tragedy happened. I needed some shots of a kingfisher going into and out of its nest. I got Oxford Scientific Films to research it for me. They found a nest where the kingfishers were bringing up five babies and set up a hide. They were ready to photograph it when some boys shot the bird with an air rifle and it died stuck in the entrance to the nest. All the babies starved to death.We managed to get some library film, but I will never forget the hurt in the voice of the man from Oxford Scientific Films as he told me the sad story.

We had one little problem; the rushes for some reason had to be printed in toto including all the bad takes. This caused the producer John Rosenberg to say:
'What are we going to do. It's a crisis?' I said
'I don't know what you're going to do I'm going to cut it together and it's going to be very good.'
The executive producer Sir John Woolf, a wise old buffer kept quiet, waiting till the rough cut before giving me some invaluable advice.

We were all having a fairly jolly time in Norfolk. One evening Willie Douglas Home was trying to get a bridge four together. His wife Rachel was there and a General whose name I forget. I said, 'I'm not partnering the General, he'll shout at me.'
'No I won't, I promise,' he said.
William and I were partners. I had wondered how William would feel about the general considering his past but he was perfectly polite. I soon saw that I had an amazing hand with a count of twenty-four and all four aces. I felt a bit shy about bidding but William pushed me up to a grand slam in spades. As I started to take trick after trick murmuring modestly about how lucky I was Willie chortled and laughed and said, 'That'll teach you, General.' The General became more and more red faced and William positively crowed with delight as I made the grand slam. It was a small revenge against the military at last.

Wendy never quite mended her fences with Rex. They were both very good but Cyril stole the show with a series of merciless upstagings.

Later, Rex said, 'We've taken a house in Barbados why don't you come out and stay?'
'No' I said, 'I've got my family to think of.'
'Bring them all,' he said.
I still politely refused. His wife Mercia wrote to Maggie and said we had to come or she would have no-one to play Scrabble with. We went, and in spite of being royally entertained by the Harrisons it cost a fortune. Maggie and my children, Din and Vinny came. Din learnt to water ski very fast. I felt clumsy and incompetent so I learnt to scuba dive which was easier and became an obsession for several years.

# Chapter Twenty-Four

# In The Footsteps Of Ernest

It sounded like the ideal job. I was to be paid £250,000 for a year's work. I would stay abroad for a year to save tax and I would put at least £100,000 into the very small pension fund I had started a few years before. The film was a six-part life of Ernest Hemingway to be shot all over the world. The producers were Danny Wilson in New York and Bodo Scriba in Munich. They seemed to have the will and the money.

I was wary of the character of Ernest. I hated the caricature of himself that he had become late in middle age. He never reached old age but shot himself at fifty-nine. I read some of the early short stories and saw a quite different Hemingway who wrote spare, elegant and economical prose. There were some brilliant scripts written by Arthur Hopcraft. Everything would be plain sailing, I thought. I managed to get Tony Waye an immensely distinguished first assistant who had done a lot of Bond films and was now an associate producer as Assistant Director.

Then began a frenzied round of casting, location scouting and hiring of crew. We seemed to spend most of the time in the air flying between New York, Munich and Rome. Billy Wilder's associate producer Willie Egger came to join us. He must have had a premonition as he kept saying: 'Wer pagt das kaffee?' (Who's going to pay for the coffee?)

We went to Rome, Venice and Torcello. We took a flat bottomed boat out into the lagoon and steered miles through reeds to find mediaeval fish houses. We had an aristocrat down on his luck who would hire us his palazzo on the Grand Canal. We went all over Northern France and, right in the middle of Paris, we found a superb location totally enclosed which was the subject of endless litigation with the city council and very available. We went to the Clos de Lilas the Café Flore and in Normandy found sites where we could stage battles. We went all over Spain, looked at several civil war sites which were incredibly moving and we went to America, New York, Chicago, Miami and Salt Lake City which I found seriously weird. A Mormon dissident had recently published a book that the angel Moroni who dictated the book of Mormon to Joseph Smith appeared to him in the form of a white salamander. This would have been no problem for the early Christian fathers. It would be seen as a manifestation of the Paraclete. Not so the Mormon church, the head of which, the Reverend David O McKay, was called God's Prophet Here On Earth. When we recce'd a cabin with attached swimming pool outside Salt Lake City, the owner, shaking with fear pointed at something and said, 'Get that thing out of here.'

I was amazed to find a white salamander which was dying of chlorine poisoning in the pool. I gently lifted it and put it in the bushes. I don't know whether it survived.

# Forsyte and Hindsight

In Miami which I adored and which we used as a staging post for Key West, we went for lunch at a smart hotel. The waiter said, 'Hi, I'm Alvin your waiter for today and I'd like to tell you about some of our specials.'

Tony who was glancing at the menu said, 'Oh the Sea Bass looks very nice.'

Alvin said, 'Would you mind not speaking until I've finished?'

We remained silent, duly chastened.

We hired a boat to take us round the bay. Miami was like a big hi-tech Venice. The bird life was wonderful. Ospreys rested on every telegraph pole. Turkey buzzards wheeled overhead and I said to the Captain of the boat: 'What a lot of Cormorants you have.'

'We call 'em Nigger Geese here,' he said.

Wet liberal that I am, I fumbled for a reply. I didn't need one. The Bird God spoke and the engine died. The captain suffered the ultimate humiliation of being swum back to shore by Tony and me at the end of ropes to the raucous jeers of his fellow captains.

All Italian make-up artists are called Fava or Bean. Stefano Fava was to do a ruthless job on Treat Williams who played Hemingway. His head was shaved, his eye lashes dyed and he began to look like the old Ernest Hemingway. He was to be made up as the young Ernest with wig and mascara. I had private doubts about this but sat and watched the process in the Favas' vast workshop off the Piazza Navona in Rome.

By now we were fully cast, we had done a long and very detailed recce all over Spain and especially on the bull run at Pamplona establishing eight different camera positions. We had a fortnight to go before the start. I flew in from NY on the red eye to Rome, and was taken to a coffee stand near the Vatican where I was given an espresso which coursed through my veins like whisky.

At the office Bodo Scriba said to me: 'We are going to postpone the film.'

I knew what this meant. It was being put off for the foreseeable future. I went for a blub in the lav and when I returned I said, 'Who's going to tell the actors?'

'We thought you might like to,' said Bodo.

I sat down with the telephone and rang as many of the actors and their agents that I could. 'Get the money!' I said.

Jimmy Villiers and Joanna Lumley were among the English actors who didn't get a cent. Treat had immediately gone home in disgust, looking to say the least of it, a bit weird. All the American actors got paid. I, amazingly, because I was with William Morris at the time, who said that none of their people would ever work for Danny again unless I was properly paid, got a very good deal. I was to be paid half (£125,000) and have an option to direct the film if it were revived. It wasn't quite as good as it looked. I had already spent £100,000 on the pension fund and had been living it up for six months on my expectations. I had a whole lot of tax to pay and no future employment but it could have been much, much worse.

# Chapter Twenty-Five

# Ken And Emma I:
# The Illyrian Shore

*Fortunes Of War* is the omnibus title of two trilogies written by Olivia Manning. *The Balkan Trilogy* takes place in Romania and Greece and *The Levant Trilogy* in Egypt and Syria. The BBC had been trying for years to mount them. The books were a bit close to home for them. They were very autobiographical. Olivia's husband, Reggie Smith, was a much loved radio producer who, during the war, had worked for the British Council in Romania and Egypt. Fay Weldon wrote a couple of scripts. I disliked them intensely and they were abandoned.

In 1987 the BBC decided to make the films and Betty Willingale was now to produce them. It was an enormous undertaking and would need a budget of over £6,000,000. The BBC had some co-funding from the Richard Price organisation which was trying to put pressure on the brilliant Alan Plater who was writing the script and, more importantly, they were expecting money from an oil company through WGBH in Boston. Suddenly the oil money disappeared. Either Mobil or Exxon, I can't remember, who decided not to invest. We then started chasing the other company Exxon or Mobil, who were very reluctant. The BBC, probably for nearly the last time in its history, behaved well over the contract.

'We can't offer you a full engagement of eighteen months' they said, 'because we don't know where we're going to get the money. Will you accept a three month contract while you try to get it underway? You can't spend any money, of course and but you can do the recces and talk about casting but don't actually cast anybody.' All this was to be a secret. The world was meant to think that we were going ahead anyway. I agreed.

Betty was on the staff, so the BBC could say come and she cometh and go and she goeth. I begged her to resign and take a freelance contract. She would have got more money and residuals.
'Oh no,' she said, 'The BBC will look after me.'

Ha ha I thought. Betty had been with the BBC since she joined as a typist at fifteen years old. Her father and his father before him had been a Thames lighterman.[17] She had been brought up by the river and had a natural feeling for it. She worked her way up through the BBC eventually becoming a script editor and then a producer. She understood writers more than anybody else I have known. They trusted her and she was able to put her finger on anything that would not work.

Betty and I went on a series of recces. Romania itself simply would not do; it was tired, oppressed, poverty stricken and crawling with secret policemen as we found during a short recce, but we needed to go there to see what we had to reproduce. We found that Ljubljana in Slovenia and Zagreb in Croatia could be made to look very like the old Bucharest.

---

[17] The Captain of a riverboat

# Forsyte and Hindsight

Every few days we telephoned America and said, 'If you don't give us the money now you will find yourselves paying double for the show when it's made.'

There were some serious shooting problems to be solved. Guy and Harriet lived in a flat high up overlooking the Royal Palace. There was a good exterior and the University of Zagreb made a passable royal palace, but they were miles apart. We decided to build a shell on the roof of a block of flats near the university. Most of the flat interiors would be shot in Ealing Studios.

By the third month we had got the money. We went home to carry on casting. I already had Ken Branagh in mind and we offered him the part. I saw Juliet Stevenson, Joanne Whalley-Kilmer and half a dozen other actresses for the part of Harriet. None of them were right. We decided on James Villiers for Inchcape and Ronald Pickup for Yaki. Then disaster struck. We were having a casting session in my house with Betty and Ken and some actresses and I suddenly fell to the floor in agony. I had a burst appendix and while I was waiting for the ambulance I saw the hook nosed face of a prominent Irish actress leaning over me and I said mentally: 'Oh no, not her.'

I lay on a trolley in Queen Mary's hospital for three hours until Maggie threatened the nursing staff with a screaming temperament and I went into theatre. All went well. When I woke I remembered that we were due to fly to Egypt on a recce the next day and there was no prospect of it now. Betty came into see me and said, 'I brought the scripts, you can have a look at them and we can talk about casting.' What she thought but didn't say was: 'I wonder who else is available?'

They got me up on the second day and I staggered through the ward pushing a saline drip on one hand and carrying a sort of suitcase with tubes leading into my abdomen in the other.

I was out of hospital surprisingly quickly and we carried on casting. Emma Thompson came to see us. I knew she was talented, having see her in *Me And My Girl*. Her hair was dyed a disgusting shade of red for *Tutti Frutti* and she looked awful. I knew at once that she was the girl I wanted to play Harriet. I didn't even bother to audition her. When she had left I talked to Betty. 'If your instinct really tells you she's right, go for her,' She said.
I did and she was.

Slovenia and Croatia are not the merriest places to spend the winter months and were even less so in those days. There were few restaurants and food was rather ordinary though I did have smoked bear's leg which was delicious. We tried to get the ping pong room in the hotel opened but they were not authorised to give us the key, an argument I was to discover in other communist countries.

Romanian is an elegant Romance language, probably closer to its Latin roots than any other European language. I learnt a little and used to send postcards to Ken Branagh in Romanian in the hope that he would learn some, as he was playing a renowned linguist. He didn't play.

What was more difficult was the Yugoslav cast; very fine actors, they responded well and spoke good English but despised the language of any other country of the former Austro-Hungarian empire. They learnt, grudgingly, a few words of Romanian.

We worked hard and although night fell early, by dint of clever scheduling by the Assistant Director, Jeremy Woolf, we were able to fill the daylight and night hours.

The cameraman was David Feig. This was his first big job. Early in the schedule, we were shooting an open-air night club scene with 500 extras and a cimbalon band. It was partially lit by several hundred small light bulbs. David wanted them all changed for a lower voltage causing a delay of several hours. The electricians set to work. Three hours later, all the extras were drunk and we had to put off shooting until the next night at great expense. There was a move afoot to sack David, which I fought strongly against and won.

When we went into the mountains to shoot a love scene between Ken and Emma I was captivated by Lake Bled. I chose a camera position in a little Belvedere high above the lake which had an island with a church in the middle of it. It was breathtakingly beautiful and I had got the actors excited about it. When we came to shoot, a mist descended and we could see nothing. I quickly had to decide to change the location to a court yard with pleasingly honey coloured stone and grab every red flower in the area to give it some bright colour. They played the scene beautifully.

The opening of the film, showing the Orient Express belting through the Balkan countryside, needed a locomotive and seven coaches and a helicopter. We managed to get the train assembled. One of the coaches was the wrong colour and I saw a Yugoslav painter languidly painting it with a one and a half inch brush. Somehow the train was put together. When we came to do the aerial shots the police helicopter pilot who was taking us and the camera up was, to my eyes, not quite sober. We flew up and skeetered about the sky. I had seen him drink at least one slivovitz just before we took off.

We were trying to do a following shot of the train. The pilot didn't seem to know what he was doing and we were darting about incontinently. I made a decision, 'Land, NOW!' I said. We made a rather crunchy return to earth.

We had to put the shot off for a couple of days to get a new pilot. This meant that the train had to be disassembled and then reassembled at enormous cost. Another black mark. Next time the shot worked beautifully the first time and it was goodbye train.

We caught up and were half way through the schedule and were due to move to Zagreb. The Slovenian Minister of Culture came to dinner.
'I hear tomorrow you go to Croatia,' he said. 'Why?' I explained about urban locations and such. 'The Croatians are liars and sheets and filthy traitors,' he said, 'They collaborated with the Germans in the war. You must stay here and finish your film.'
I mumbled some sort of confused answer. We moved next day and he didn't come to see us off.

It sounds a bit pretentious but during the long winter evenings with little to do we used to sit around the dinner table and read Shakespeare plays. We sent away for the copies and illegally duplicated a few. We had two rules 1) play as cast and 2) absolutely no one to look at the text before starting.

With *Twelfth Night* I heard the wheezing voice of a fat man coming from my right. Ronnie Pickup was playing Sir Toby Belch and this voice was coming from a thin nervy actor who normally had a reedy tenor. It was a remarkable performance. Alan Bennett was the best Feste I have ever heard and Emma a delightful Olivia. In *A Midsummer Night's Dream*, I played Bottom with a Welsh accent and the cast were too polite to barrack me.

Yaki (Ronald Pickup's) car was a beautifully reconstructed Hispano Suiza which he drove with great panache double-declutching as to the manor born. We shot a scene where they ploughed through a fascist march. It was fraught with danger but we managed to avoid injuries except for a few scratches and sprained ankles.

We shot a scene in the theatre in Zagreb. Guy, Harriet and Professor Pinkrose played by Alan Bennett, walked out of the theatre when the German national anthem started - Pinkrose under protest. The cloakroom attendant, a Yugoslav actor, handed him a tiny pink matinee jacket. It looked so ludicrous that the whole cast collapsed into gales of laughter and couldn't stop. We shot take after take but no one could stop laughing; both actors and crew. Eventually we got a clean take but the editor kept all the others and glued them together with my performance as a sergeant in Egypt and it looked as though they were laughing at me. It made a very funny joke tape which pleased our simple minds.

The climax of the first third of the story came when Guy (Ken Branagh) had mounted an amateur production of *Troilus And Cressida* at the theatre. James Villiers played Achilles and I shall always remember his wonderful voice.
'Time hath, my lord, a wallet at his back wherein he keeps alms for oblivion.'

The performance coincided with the fall of Paris to the Germans. Jeremy Woolf researched some striking black and white stock footage of the actual event and we intercut it with the play.

Bucharest was often described as the Paris of the East and the Romanians felt its capture very keenly. In our film Jimmy Villiers made the announcement in his clear strong voice. Ronnie said very quietly, 'Ah, such times we had in Paris.' It was very moving and affected the rest of the cast greatly.

The last shot of the Yugoslav sequences was of Harriet, much against her will, boarding a Lufthansa plane for Athens. Guy stayed behind and it was doubtful if they would ever meet again. The pilot refused to take off with actors on board as no one would insure us. We did a low angle shot of Harriet with a window in the background and the light burning out the background which was shot on the ground.

Lufthansa were furious that the plane bore their 1930s logo and a large swastika. They insisted that we remove one or the other. From our research we knew that the planes did carry the swastika on their tails and we insisted that they did on our plane.

After two months, we went back to the UK for several weeks shooting at Ealing and a proper Christmas week off, clever scheduling which avoided overtime. Soon we would be ready to board the Air Egypt plane for Cairo.

# Chapter Twenty-Six

# Ken And Emma II: Carry On Up The Pyramids

Filming in Egypt seemed fraught with difficulty. Fortunately most of the problems disappeared after a few days. Censorship was a bugbear. The censors who stayed with us every day and had to initial the rushes before they were sent off, started by having a stormy meeting with Betty. They wanted no sex, nothing detrimental about Egypt ('What is this? A boy says to the soldier 'You like my sister? An Egyptian boy would never offer his sister in prostitution.'
'Oh yeah??' we thought.)

What was more sinister, they wanted to present Egypt as a modern law abiding country where nobody smoked pot or rioted in the streets, where many of the professional people in the film were women and where the old customs had disappeared. Betty protested that in the original book all the doctors and teachers were men, all to no avail. Alan Urwick, the British Ambassador, who was a fluent and elegant Arabic speaker and had been to school with me became very fierce: 'If you don't give these people what they want they'll go and shoot the pyramids elsewhere.' They capitulated on nearly everything and where they didn't we were able to shoot in England.

We had an enormous crew swollen by many Egyptian technicians. Most had not worked since *Death Of A Princess* when the all powerful Saudi Government forced Egypt to blacklist them. They were enthusiastic and a joy to work with. The caterers would erect, in what seemed minutes, a twenty-foot high tent in all the colours of the rainbow to keep the sun off.

We had two production managers.
'Why?' I asked.
'One of them gets a little upset sometimes,' I was told.
I saw an example of this when we went on a recce. I had a panama hat which I had lost, probably at one of the previous locations. I wouldn't have worried, but it had been given to me by my sons. I asked Ahmed to look for it. He burst into tears and had to be comforted. The other P.M.[18] took over. Ahmed was okay in an hour or so. That's why they needed two of them.

Our Egypt trip consisted of three locations. The pyramids and Cairo, Luxor and Alexandria, the latter much loved by my father during the war and now horribly spoilt by road development. There are three large pyramids at Gizeh. We filmed on the third, smallest one but it was a breathless climb to the top. I went up one morning and just as I got to the summit a camel driver popped up and said, 'You like Coca-Cola?'

---

[18] Production Manager

Ken, Emma and Rupert Graves became very good at climbing the pyramid at great speed unaided by the lifts that had been built for *Death On The Nile*.

The last shot of the whole series showed Ken, Emma and Rupert Graves sitting on the top. We used a twenty to one zoom and pulled out to a very wide shot with three tiny figures. We were irritated to read in the *Daily Mail* that the whole pyramid sequence had been shot at Ealing Studios, on plaster rocks.

Jack Watling was over seventy, but still looked fifty. I offered him the very small part of a father whose son is horribly killed by an exploding grenade.
'Not much of a part is it?' he said.
I said, 'We are shooting it in Egypt.'
'Ah' he said and flew out to join us.
As it turned out the schedule exploded on us and we had to send him back to London and bring him out again a fortnight later. It was a brilliant and enormously well paid performance.

We built a soukh in Cairo. It was much too difficult shooting in the real soukh, the Khan al Khalil. Our soukh was full of furnaces with blacksmiths and craftsmen hammering away with copper and brass, and jewellers and tent makers. Tim Harvey designed it wonderfully and the Egyptian carpenters built us a camera tower for the high shots. It swayed gently back and forth with six of us on top. We had to stand very very still when the camera turned over. In England we would have made a fuss, but here it seemed natural.

We were doing a very long tracking shot, the length of the soukh, with little boys crowding around saying, 'You like my sister?' The Egyptian censors having forbidden it, we dubbed the lines in England. Greg Hicks played Aidan, a character thought to have been based on Stephen Haggard, Piers's father. It needed great subtlety. Aidan was in love with Guy but had to approach the seduction subtly. There could be no overt approach.

The tracking shot, 300 feet long included the whole scene, ended as Greg got into a garry. The craftsmen had momentarily to stop hammering as they passed, for the dialogue to be heard. Just before we turned over, Greg said, 'I think the whole business of acting, not acting well you understand, but acting at all is so difficult that I can't see how anyone, least of all I, can do it.' My heart sank, how should I deal with this? I said, 'It's not too late to get someone else you know. We don't even need to get a new uniform. We can shoot you and overlay the face and voice of a proper actor.' He laughed so much that I thought we would never get started. He and Ken did the whole shot in one take and it was brilliant.

Esmond Knight was a distinguished eighty-three year old actor who had been blinded in the Navy early in the war. He had been at the Old Vic as a young man and after he left the service he was kept working by his old friends. He played Fluellen in Olivier's *Henry V* and a Gestapo officer in *The Silver Fleet* with Ralph Richardson. Later, he met an ophthalmic surgeon, who said, 'I think I might be able to do something with that eye of yours.'

He operated and gave him a little window of sight, so he could just read a script with a magnifying glass. It lasted a few years and then he became blind again.

I had known, admired and worked with him for many years. I cast him to play Mr Liversage, a potty old gentleman who went everywhere with a toy dog on a string. We managed to hide his blindness by pretending he was lame and Michael Cochrane and Emma had to help him into and out of cars. He was loved by all the company. He taught Rupert Graves how to dive backwards into the swimming pool. He could behave outrageously and had a fund of risque, slightly dated jokes. One went: 'There was a pianist in a cocktail bar who had a pet monkey, which was ill behaved. There was a fellow sitting nearby nursing a dry martini. The monkey leapt over and squatted over his glass. The man said, 'I say, do you know your monkey's dipping its balls in my martini?' The pianist said, 'No, but if you hum the tune I'll vamp it'.'

When Diana Hardcastle was telling us, 'I've got one of these new bikinis and, do you know, it's so embarrassing I have to shave down there.' Esmond was passing, he said,
'What do you do with the clippings?'

Esmond did everything in Egypt that we did, he rode a camel with great style and when his part was finished we saw him off. Two days later he was dead of a heart attack. I rang his wife in some distress, she said, 'It was wonderful, he adored being with you and he loved playing the part, then he went out like a shooting star, I couldn't think of a better way to go.'

I have one of his paintings which his daughter Rosalind gave me. It is of Corporal Nym shooting a bird for dinner on the night before embarking for Harfleur. It was painted after he was quite blind and I treasure it.

Emma bore the brunt of the Egyptian episodes, she was supposed to be struck down with cholera or something like it. Ciaran Madden, so brilliant when mourning her son who had been blown up, had a new lover, Castlebar played by Robert Stephens. He was pursued by a vengeful wife, played by his real wife, Patricia Quinn, and died horribly and brilliantly of some appalling disease. Sam Dastor played the doctor who looked after Harriet.

When we moved to Luxor my wife Maggie and Vinny flew out. We stayed in Luxor for a short time at the Old Cataract Hotel made famous by *Death On The Nile*. It was wonderfully imperial and graceful. The only trouble was we had to eat at the New Cataract Hotel which was disgusting. We all went to the Valley of the Kings. They ended up seeing much more than I, as work beckoned. I did see something which was right off the tourist trail. I persuaded the guide at Karnak to open the door to a little temple. Inside was a statue in black granite of Bast, the panther goddess, lit only by a tiny hole in the roof. The atmosphere was tangible and terrifying. We shot Greg Hicks there, playing a long scene to Emma about his experience in a shipwreck. It was quite spooky and marvellous at the same time.

One of the strongest memories I have is of Esmond and Alan Bennett on camels racing each other. Alan's pompous and hated character was assassinated during a lecture. We filled the place with 400 extras and used two cameras to shoot scenes of indescribable chaos - easier in Egypt.

Ken played a scene in which he thought his wife had died. He climbed the stairs to give a lecture to his students who adored him; they had clubbed together to buy an enormous wreath. I asked one of them: 'What would you say in Arabic as a message of sympathy.' He told me.

I said, 'Now quickly translate it into English.'
He said, 'We share your sads.' 'Perfect,' I said and we put it on the wreath.
The censor interfered. She said, 'This makes Egyptian people look illiterate.'
'No it doesn't,' I said. 'It's a quotation from *Romeo And Juliet*.'
I left her doggedly thumbing through Shakespeare as we shot the scene!

In Alexandria we heard that Alasdair Milne had been fired as Director General of the BBC. Mike Checkland, a good man, was to take over for six months and then the appalling John Birt was to be given the job. I wrote to *The Times*, dateline Alexandria and said I had heard the news while spending six and a half million pounds of the BBC's money, and I said that Alasdair had taught me more about the splendours and miseries of office than anyone else could have, and that the BBC was now being run by time-servers and sycophants. *The Times* telephoned me in Alex and asked me to confirm it. I did. I don't think it did me much good with the BBC. I see Alasdair from time to time. Mrs Thatcher vindictively prevented him getting many of the jobs he was offered but typically he never complains nor looks backward.

Three pictures of our time in Egypt will always remain with me. We drove out into the desert to film a sunset. I found that the sun takes four minutes to fall below the horizon. It was breathtakingly quiet and there was no green flash that I could see. We had brought three Muezzin callers with us to record the voices in the evening desert air. We couldn't use the real thing, as in the middle of Cairo the calls to prayer were all amplified and distorted. One after another the men took their turns and gave the call. The last one was blind. He filled his lungs cupped his hand around his mouth and gave rise to an amazingly beautiful sound. 'ALLAHU AKBAR!' The sound reverberated through the empty desert. When he had finished, we all stood for a little, not speaking. It was quite different from the others and we recorded it and used it all through the Egyptian episodes.

On another day Ken, Emma, Rupert and I went out riding. The ponies were poor starved things so thin you expected your knees to meet. We were trotting around the pyramids when suddenly a desert fox ran across our path followed by all the pi-dogs in the area. We galloped after him into the desert for what seemed a couple of miles and watched as he disappeared over the horizon, trailing his light brown furry tail behind him. It was beautiful.

The great pyramid of Cheops is the biggest of the three at Gizeh. Although it was illegal, we were determined to climb it. It is a really hard climb, as it is made of five feet cubes of granite. We bribed the tourist police and started to climb at four o'clock in the morning.

Luckily the full moon was behind the pyramid, so while we had just enough light to see what we were doing, we weren't too obvious to the casual observer. It took us over an hour to get to the top and and we sat for awhile in the moonlight, till the sun gradually rose, suffusing everything with a golden glow, and an early camel train walked slowly across the wind-blown sands. One day I will return to Egypt, Inshallah.

It was time to leave, we had loved our time in Egypt and liked the Egyptians greatly. We were excited to be going to Greece, which was to be the summit of our experience. It didn't turn out quite as well as we expected.

## Chapter Twenty-Seven

# Ken And Emma III: Et Dona Ferentes

We knew there was trouble as soon as we landed. First, the Egyptian customs had impounded our explosives, so the battle scenes were put in jeopardy. Second, the Greek union said we weren't employing enough Greeks and that their members would stand in front of the camera so that we couldn't shoot. Since the first shot was a vast battle scene with 200 extras, a lot of guns firing and an exploding house lovingly made by Tim Harvey, we were in trouble. Betty telephoned Merlina Mercouri the arts minister. She said, 'Dollenk there's nothing I can do.'
So we took on quite a lot of Greeks, mostly make-up artists.

At five o'clock the next morning we assembled. There were six Greeks there. 'Look,' said Jeremy. 'We didn't want you at all, let alone at five o'clock.'
'We need the overtime,' said their leader.

Fortunately, the ruinously expensive thirty second battle shot went well, in spite of the lack of explosives.

The little town of Nafplion was very probably the port where Agamemnon landed after the Trojan war, bringing Cassandra home as a slave. (If you believe all that stuff, and I rather do.) It seemed to me enormously atmospheric and we chose it as a location for the sequence of the escape from Piraeus. I ventured to write a little sonnet about the harbour:

> *Not dark as wine but green as green can be*
> *The water laps against the harbour wall*
> *Here Agamemnon took leave of the sea*
> *Here stepped Cassandra, gyved and vacant eyed.*
> *But not for me Mycenae's blood soaked house,*
> *Where both would feel the Queen's avenging knife.*
> *I seek the groves of Aesculapius*
> *Bringer of dreams and quickener of life*
>
> *And thence to Delphi with its holy spring*
> *I climbed Parnassus hill with shaded eyes*
> *No souvenir from Grecian lands I bring*
> *But on my desk a little pine cone lies*
> *I gathered it on high Parnassus' slope*
> *It speaks to me of calm and peace and hope*

A very fanciful digression! We managed to shoot the escape from Piraeus not quite as we had planned, again because of the lack of explosives, but satisfactorily nonetheless.

Over a year before I had gone out in a small boat in the bay of Salamis just before dark to find a ship. The bay was a huge graveyard of massive cruise and merchant ships, usually bound together in threes with a single watchman on board. I saw a nice looking ship with three funnels. 'How much is that?' I asked.
'You can have it for nothing,' they said. But it would cost £20,000 to get up steam. We rowed home in the gloaming through the mist; I could see Eleusis where Theseus had wrestled King Kerkyon to death and is now dominated by a cement factory, and as night fell, the rowlocks sounded to my fancy like the squeak and gibber of long dead Greeks and Persians. The boat we eventually found was an infinitely sad old rust-bucket tanker. It was perfect. When did we want it they asked? I knew that if I said in a year's time they wouldn't believe me. The ship might be dead in Salamis bay so I said, 'Soon, soon,' and the team kept in touch.

When we came to shoot the scene a year later with Ken, Emma, Alan Bennett and Charles Kay we found the crew painting over the rust. They didn't want their ship to look bad. Tim Harvey had to go in with a squad of painters and rustify it. We filled the boat with actors and Greek extras playing refugees, ignoring the strict rules of the Greek maritime ministry, with the shrill cries of the Harbour Master echoing in our ears. Ken recited *Death Be Not Proud* by John Donne. As the scene was about a submarine warning, we shot in an eerie silence. All the actors were a bit overawed and I think we felt ourselves not in the second world war, but in Homeric Greece.

Shooting in Athens was sometimes wonderful, sometimes not. We couldn't shoot in the Acropolis after 10.30 in the morning because the smog was so thick. We had a young man attached to us who was a director at the Greek National Theatre. He was rather sulky. Why he said, did the British think we could perform Greek Tragedy? Greeks would not attempt to dramatise Lancelot and Guinevere.
'Why not?' I said rather pompously, 'It would probably shed a new light on the legend. Literature of all countries is a part of the world heritage.'
He remained unconvinced. Four centuries of Turkish occupation warps the soul. Later on I met his father, a businessman, who was fairly contemptuous when he found that I had forgotten nearly all my Classical Greek.

Emma and her boyfriend were supposed to take refuge in an air raid shelter. We re-wrote the script and had them take shelter in the temple of Theseus, inserting a line about how it had stood here for two and a half thousand years and would still be here when the Germans were long gone.

When we shot in the Acropolis there was a very old photographer with a primitive camera which developed film on the spot. We wrote him into the script and had our pictures taken by him.

At Sounion, in the Temple of Poseidon, we were to film several sequences. Tim had painted a beautiful ship on glass which would appear to be sailing the ocean with the temple of Poseidon in the foreground. I saw where Lord Byron had crudely carved his name in the column.

'I must get this in the film,' I said. And I used it in the shot. It looked unredeemedly pretentious in the rushes, so I cut it out. The first day at Sounion was cloudy. I prayed to Apollo and as the sun came out a school of dolphins leapt from the water and played in the shallows.
'There you are, you see,' I said.
'You're nothing but an old pagan,' said Maggie.

On a day off, many of us decided to visit Epidauros, the most beautifully preserved Greek theatre which I was told could seat 50,000. I rather think they meant 15,000 but it was very impressive. We walked through the groves of Aesculapius and came to the theatre which was packed with French and Spanish school kids, some with ghetto blasters playing distorted pop music. Many were chewing gum and spitting it out on the steps. After a few minutes they vanished into their buses and we were left alone in a perfect silence.

I suggested that we all try to perform something. Alan Bennett demurred but went right to the top into the pine trees to see if he could hear. There is a spot where, if you stand on it and speak with a normal voice, you can be heard anywhere in the theatre. I did 'O for a muse of fire' and everybody else did a piece. Alan could hear every word from what looked like miles away.

We left and went to Delphi though we did not drink from the Pierean spring (a little learning is a dangerous thing). We climbed up to Parnassus where I picked up my pine cone. I keep worrying that it will be thrown away but I don't really like to attach a label to it. When we got back to Athens, poor Jeremy caught his leg on the tramline and suffered a compound fracture of the tibia and fibula. We took him to a Greek hospital, then hurriedly removed him and sent him home. He was very talented. I haven't heard of him since but I hope he is doing well.

*Fortunes Of War* got ten BAFTA nominations but only three awards for design, costume design and sound. At the ceremony I was sitting with Emma, Betty and Bill Cotton when *Tutti Frutti* was announced as the winner. I smiled, as one does, and showed no disappointment. Bill Cotton kindly bought me a cigar.

# Chapter Twenty-Eight

# Miami

Until 1990 I had always refused a job unless I had a good script in my hand. Murray Smith was a good craftsman writer with a strong romantic streak. He had been in the SAS and longed to make intelligent but adventurous films. He collaborated with Frederick Forsyth on a series of short stories which would be introduced by Frederick on film and then published. They offered me one of these films and were very evasive when I asked about the script. I said there was no way I could do it without seeing a script.

'We are shooting on location in the Bahamas,' said Murray.

'Ah,' I said and we went rambling on for a few days not really knowing what was what. They said would I like to go on a recce to the Bahamas?

'What the hell am I going to recce?' I said. 'We haven't got a script.'

'Well,' said Murray, 'it's about drug running on an island in the Caribbean and we need to find the island.'

'What's it like?' I said. 'Is it big or small, has it got sandy beaches, is it hilly?'

They were remarkably unforthcoming. Finally they sent me a simple line drawing and said, 'The island looks like this.' The picture seemed familiar.

Suddenly I asked, 'Has anyone got a copy of *Treasure Island*?'

Someone had. I looked at it and the drawing they had sent me had obviously been traced from the book, right down to the naming of places like Spy Glass Hill. I shut up and took a plane to Miami.

It was odd doing a recce for a non-existent script, but we found various nice places and indeed a few islands, none of them looking a bit like the *Treasure Island* one. What we did find was a wonderful little airline called Chalkies which is one of the oldest existing airlines in the world, being founded in 1936 and still using flying boats. The planes land on the water then race towards the beach. At the crucial moment the wheels come down and they drive up the beach and come to a halt.

Finally we got a script and started casting. Alan Howard had been in a number of other stories by Fred, and so he was already cast. As the Detective Superintendent from London (this was rather a chauvinistic film, it took place in a British colony and eventually had a lightning raid by British commandos) we cast Larry Lamb, an old friend. His counterpart in the Miami police force was Chris Cooper, a mild and quiet actor who has since done very well. I was persuaded into employing Philip Michael Thomas, lately of *Hawaii Five-O*, as the chief gangster and gun runner. Rather childishly I made the gangster obsessed with heraldry and had a big Charterhouse coat of arms built above the fireplace in his house with the motto Deo Dante Dedi.

# Forsyte and Hindsight

Kitty Aldridge was the love interest and a local black actor called Clarence Thomas was the crooked island chief of police. We were just going out to lunch when the production manager said, 'We have talked very vaguely to Lauren Bacall and she is interested. Would you like to ring her in Paris?' I was quite hungry but went to the restaurant telephone and dialled her number. She was delightful and amusing and had been given a strong recommendation about me by Lee Remick. We talked for about half an hour about the part, the clothes and everything. I now had the script at last and so did she.

There was an important role, the Miami Chief of Police; I cast the real Chief of Police who liked acting and didn't have very much to say, but had to be discovered as a dead body in a car which was dragged up by a crane from the harbour. He got very wet and had to hold his breath for rather a long time.

We started shooting. The island we had chosen was called Bimini which was one of the northernmost of the Bahamas. It was less than a mile long and only about 200 yards wide so any real storm would flood it entirely. It was full of interesting people, many of whom I suspected had a background in drug smuggling. On the mainland, we had to find a luxurious house and grounds leading down to the sea for the head crook, Philip Michael Thomas. It was important to be able to take aerial shots of this for a chase sequence near the end of the film.

Here is a little bit of advice. If you are hiring a helicopter with its pilot and, I should say, it is much cheaper in America than in England, ask him to fly you around the area of what you think is going to be the shot. While he is doing it, keep a close eye on the compass and then ask him to do it again and if the compass bearings match exactly at the right places, you know he is a good pilot. Ours was.

While we were filming on Bimini I fell over and bruised my leg very badly so that it swelled up. When we got to the mainland I was taken to hospital and was not able to see anyone at all for a quarter of an hour. Then I met a rather junior nurse and fifteen minutes later a senior nurse. The first question she asked was, 'How are you going to pay for this treatment?'
'I'm not,' I said and walked out, fed up with waiting. Since then requests for payment of fifty dollars have followed me all around the world.

Chris Cooper was astonishingly modest; he was playing a scene with Larry when Larry had come into his office and he was looking at things on his desk.
'Why aren't you being more angry with him?' I asked Chris.
'I don't know,' he said.
'Do you like the English?' I asked.
'Well yes, I do, rather' he said.
'Well you shouldn't like this one, he's behaving like a real bastard, shout at him!' He did.

'Betty' Bacall was a delight to work with. She was very impatient with incompetents and quite ruthless. The costume designer was shaking like a jelly and said, 'She insists on having everything designed by Armani and we haven't got enough money.' I went to Betty's room and said, 'I bet you've brought a lot of clothes with you, can I look in the wardrobe?'

She smouldered a little, then opened the doors, she had a perfect set of clothes for the whole film, elegantly designed but not too flashy.

I said, 'These will do nicely except for this one and this one. They're a bit too flashy.'

'You bastard,' she said, but she smiled.

When we came to shoot with her, she was incredibly nervous: she was playing a very bright woman who was a skilled painter and I wanted to do a scene with her sitting in the top of a lighthouse with an easel painting a red kite. She was shaking a lot so I said, 'Don't worry we'll start on a close up of your hands.'

'Oh God, my hands,' she said and fussed around with the make-up for quite some while. As soon as we had done a couple of shots, she calmed down and enjoyed herself immensely.

Philip Michael Thomas was a little bit of an outsider and very status conscious. We each had a caravan (or trailer as the Americans call them) though I very rarely got to sit in mine. Philip had an assistant; he was lying in his trailer and he sent her into mine to cook him some sort of macrobiotic food. I found her there and said, 'Why can't he use his own trailer?'

She became very upset and left and wrote me a long letter saying, 'I'm sorry I invaded your space.' What a carry on!

Our American production manager was called Linda McGowan who was very funny and was a part time cop which made life very easy, arranging traffic and so on. We were shooting in a little fenced off part of the coast where the only entrance was in the wire fence that was very close to a tree. Stretched out in the tree looking quite somnolent was an eight foot yellow snake, I found myself nervously sidling around and getting through the gate as fast as possible. I had forgotten how much amazing wildlife lived around Miami and in the sea. We saw manatees. They are charming gentle mammals who live on seaweed but more and more of them are getting killed by motor boats driving too fast.

We found a village on a little island off Miami and were able to shoot a lot there. One thing happened which made me very ashamed. I wanted a shot of an old rattly bus arriving with a cloud of dust and scattering chickens as it came to a halt. We got half a dozen chickens and put some corn on the road. The bus came through, they took no notice and were all crushed. I felt awful.

We had hired a couple of helicopters, painted them black and put royal naval markings on them. At the climax of the film men dressed as commandos would slide down ropes and attack the house. A tremendous gun battle would then take place. Later, the baddies would run out and get into a cigarette boat and drive away. They were to be followed by our heroes played by Alan, Chris and Larry in a helicopter. I explained to the actors that I would take a shot of them getting on to the helicopter and then I would cut and we would put the stunt men in. They got hold of me by the throat and said, 'Don't you dare, we're going to do the shot ourselves.' There was a certain amount of murmuring about the insurance from the production management but I agreed.

I explained that they would take off in one helicopter and I and the camera crew would be in the other one flying parallel. We took the doors off both helicopters. They acted up astonishingly, leaning out of the doors to the full extent of their safety belts and pretending to shoot a motor boat. I think they really enjoyed it.

For the climax of the sequence the cigarette boat had to explode having been shot by Alan with some weird gun. The special effects guy arranged a boat to be towed by another boat with a cable under water. We covered the explosion with three cameras shooting at different speeds. The special effects man said, 'Now, Jim when you want the explosion to happen just say JB Fire!' So we turned over and the boat gathered speed. We were just approaching the ideal position when for some reason I forgot his initials, stammered a little and said, 'Fire!'

I have never seen such an enormous explosion, even in the army. The sky was full of black smoke and wreckage kept on hurtling to the ground. Murray Smith was incensed. What he had originally written was that Larry would climb down a rope onto the boat and have a hand to hand struggle arresting the baddies. I thought this was a bit silly and so wrote in the explosion. Murray came around to it in the end.

I learnt from this film how important it is to communicate with the property department. In England there is much more conversation about props but in America they tend to read the prop lists and follow them slavishly. The props man said to me, 'I'm very worried, I can't find the exact 1965 Transam car that you need.'
I said, 'It doesn't mean that we need that particular car. What we need is something that looks really interesting and it doesn't matter what.'
They found a Bristol 405 which looked lovely, but didn't actually work and while Betty sat in it regally we pulled it along on ropes. It looked OK.

We had a serious crisis when my briefcase disappeared containing my passport, all my credit cards and a lot else. To fly from Miami to Bimini we were actually leaving the United States so I needed my passport. We enquired about getting a replacement one in a hurry but were told it would cost £750. When the props men were unpacking the skips there was my briefcase and probably a whole lot of other stuff. It was a great relief.

The cast and I took Betty Bacall out to a Japanese dinner near the end. She was a really nice woman, and a laugh a second.

# Chapter Twenty-Nine
# **The Council**

The British Council is one of those organisations which everybody has heard of and nobody much knows what it does. It represents British art and writing all over the world and works on a very low budget. Like the BBC World Service it is a constant target for governments who want to save a few pennies.

I first came across them when they had a headquarters in Pont Street. I wanted a location for a night club for *Roads To Freedom* and they charmingly came up with one of their offices. They shortly afterwards were pushed out of there by a government who put them in less pleasant and certainly less expensive premises.

When I went on a recce to Romania they were enormously helpful. The embassy in Bucharest is quite small and in the garden there is a sort of superannuated Nissen hut where the British Council people work. When we went there, it was just before the revolution and the two British Council people had to be given diplomatic status and called Cultural Attaches. Very often there was a queue, which went right around the block, of Romanians desperately wanting to borrow British books and videos. I remember seeing one rather tired worn out looking old man going in and saying, 'Pliss have you the poemss of Ted Hughessss?'

When, in 1991 the Council asked me to go and teach in Israel, I was delighted to do so. I was supposed to run a short course in directing for people who worked in educational television in Tel Aviv and I started preparing a series of lectures. I had a letter from one of the students which said, 'I understand that you are taking two days at the beginning of your stay in Israel to look at the country. This is a waste of time. I suggest you start at once on the course and that work should be from eight-thirty in the morning until six o'clock in the evening with half an hour for lunch.' I wrote back and said, 'I think that you seriously mistake the purpose of my visit: the course must be quite gentle and give people time to think.' In the end we did work very hard and I had about twenty-five students most of whom were fairly pugnacious.

It is fashionable, because of the present situation in Israel, for people to castigate the Israelis for the way they are behaving and this very often conceals a latent anti-Semitism. I have to confess that I like the Sabras, whose name derives from the prickly cactus which grows everywhere in Israel. I got to know the students quite well and we would argue strongly about all sorts of things, not least about their treatment of the Arabs.

I was very struck by the fact that there was a certain tension between the Ashkenazis and the Sephardis on the course. The rather more sophisticated Ashkenazis tended to patronise the

Sephardis and treat them a little bit like peasants. One of the Sephardis, who had been born in Morocco, had made a musical programme about his traditional native music. I praised this extravagantly as it was probably the best thing I had seen so far, which shut the Ashkenazis up a bit.

About half way through the course I managed to get hold of half a dozen hand-held video cameras. I divided the class into groups of five and said: 'Now go away and make a film.' There was consternation.
'What do you want us to make a film about?' they said.
'Look,' I said, 'You're supposed to be directors, so think up something, and just to show you, I and the lady from the British Council will also improvise a film and shoot it.'
This prodded them into action, while they watched us play a married couple who couldn't stop shouting at each other.

At the end, when all the students had signed a book about Israel and presented it to me, one or two of them shyly asking if I was going to make Aliyah, I took some of them out to an Arab restaurant in Haifa. I told the student who had written to me that I was going to introduce him to prawns. He looked horrified. I said, 'Yes I know that it is an animal that divides the hoof and does not chew the cud, but it is delicious.' He found them so, though I think the sinful breaking of the dietary laws added an extra savour.

I spent a couple of days in Jerusalem at the American Colony Hotel which was beautiful and unlike many of the hotels where you are not allowed to cook toast on the Sabbath. I went to the Dead Sea and was covered in black mud and washed it off in the very salty water. A wind got up and some Australians were trying to surf on the water. Jerusalem, although it was destroyed in AD65 and nothing is left of the Biblical city, was terribly moving and I was able to go to Temple Mount which is now forbidden to most Israelis.

When it was time to leave I was interrogated by a security man for over an hour and I was very thankful that they took such care. My last memory of Israel is of a Chinese Restaurant with a green tiled roof by the banks of the sea of Galilee bearing an inscription:

*This is the only Glatt Kosher Chinese Restaurant in Israel.*

The Council haven't asked me to do anything since, but I would go like a shot if they did.

# Chapter Thirty
# The Wide Blue Yonder

They say directing a film is like having a giant Meccano set to play with. Imagine having three Spitfires, a Messerschmidt 109 and a Grumman Avenger in the air and directing three cameras from the mid gunners pod of the Avenger. It was wildly expensive and we didn't really have enough money. Each aeroplane cost £2,200 an hour plus fuel, so we had to get the full worth out of them.

But the flying was only a part of *A Perfect Hero* adapted by Allan Prior from Christopher Matthews' book. It tells the story of a pilot hideously burned in battle and his journey back to the air under the healing hands of a brilliant plastic surgeon. Obviously the story is loosely based on Richard Hillary's *The Last Enemy* and the surgeon on Archibald McIndoe but we kept firmly away from trying to portray the real people. It made life easier as McIndoe's wife was very much alive and showed great interest in the film.

I was producing and directing. Michael Whitehall, the agent, was executive producer and we had splendid offices in the LWT tower looking out over the Thames. We were next door to *The South Bank Show* offices and swiftly learnt their code number so that we could get all our duplicating done for free.

We came badly unstuck over make-up, it wasn't nearly horrific enough. Nigel Havers is a very good looking man and seeing a hideously scarred face in close up after close up is quite different from reading it on the page.

We got a wonderful collection of young actors to play the pilots. Nigel of course, Nick Palliser, Nick Pritchard, Pat Ryecart and Harry Burton. Actors can do almost anything under pressure. A lot of the scenes were set in Cambridge before the war; I approached the Lady Margaret Boat Club and asked for their help. I wanted the actors to row an eight convincingly with some members of the LMBC crew. They had two afternoons of practice. When we came to shoot, they rowed elegantly and beautifully, if not very fast, and did all the skilled things, like lifting the boat out of the water, perfectly.

Geoffrey Page had fought in the Battle of Britain had a DSO and two DFCs and had been badly burnt, though his hands were worse than his face. He became our greatly valued adviser. One of my most poignant memories is of a group of us waiting on an airfield in Norfolk for the arrival of the aeroplanes from Duxford. I explained to Geoffrey that we had three Spitfires and an ME 109. We waited quietly then began to hear in the far distance the wonderful throaty roar of Merlin engines 'Four spitfires,' said Geoffrey.

'No,' I explained, 'Three.'
They appeared circled gracefully around and came into land.
'There you are you see, Geoffrey, three Spitfires and an ME 109.'
He said nothing but walked over to the Messerschmidt and pulled back the nacelles. 'There you are,' he said, 'A Merlin engine. It's been rebuilt.'

We had to make three Spitfires look like nine which involved running out and changing the matriculation letters nearly every shot. We had to make the Messerschmidt look like twelve. Digital enhancement was in its infancy at the time, but we just about managed it. For the aerial shots I sat in the Avenger, an elegant three-engined fighter bomber which acted as the camera ship. The spitfire pilots were immensely skilled and keen ex-RAF people apart from one rich man who flew his as a hobby. It was daunting to be asked by the chief pilot to give them a full scale briefing but I think I managed it. We staged a very dangerous near collision on which we eventually superimposed an explosion to make it look like a real collision. I think it looked rather good.

We had been forced by Nick Elliott of LWT to use video tape rather than film. It was a long argument which we lost. It had one advantage, however. We attached a video camera the size of a pencil to the wing of an Me 109 and passed the connecting cable invisibly through to a recorder on which the pilot sat. The pilot then did several loops and rolls in and out of the sun. I don't think anyone has done it before, or since for that matter.

James Fox played the plastic surgeon with great presence, deliberately not impersonating McIndoe. Joanna Lumley played an actress who seduced our hero; the rumour was that the character was based on Merle Oberon. Later in the series Joanna sang a little French song for the benefit of the wounded airmen. I had written it myself and was rather proud of it. She looked ravishing but her voice was not really up to scratch. She showed immense professionalism by saying, 'Why don't you shoot me doing it and then find a proper singer who can dub my voice?' And that's what we did.

The song was one of the best I have written; although it was in French, it was intended to show wounded airmen they were still loved and respected, even though they were hideously burnt. It went like this:

*Madame ma mere, car je fus sage,*
*M'a donnee un oiseau chanteur*
*Qui chantait dans sa p'tite cage*
*Un chanson que ravit mon coeur.*

*Chorus:*
*Mon p'tit oiseau aux ailes dorees*
*Tu chante clair, tu chante long.*
*Je veux le dire - personne ne sait*
*Comme je t'adore, mon oisillon.*

*Il s'est passe, une triste nuit*
*Quand je sommeillais dans mon lit*
*Le tresor de mon coeur s'enfuit*
*Et laissa vide son petit nid.*

*(Chorus)*

*Melancolique et malheureuse*
*Pleurant la mort de mon ami*
*J'ai vue en elevant mes yeux*
*Deux oiseau chanteurs dans un nid.*

The last verse, in English was spoken by Jo Lumley, not the singer:

*My little bird with golden wings*
*He flies so swift, he flies so free*
*It breaks my heart the song he sings*
*O little bird, fly home to me.*

Perhaps Jo couldn't sing perfectly, but she could certainly act. The English lines were heart-breaking.

One day we were filming in Central London by the Embankment and we got a little ahead of schedule. 'Nigel,' I said, 'You know that scene, we were going to shoot on Friday?'
'Were?' he said suspiciously.
'Do you think we could do it this afternoon?' I said, 'You could learn it in the lunch hour.' The scene was five pages long and he went pale.
'OK,' he said and went to get his lunch.
He was word-perfect in the afternoon. He was, and is, a true professional. Like all really good comedy actors, he is underestimated by the public. He makes it look so easy when, in fact, blood and tears have gone into the performance.

We had a very distinguished Oscar winning costume designer, Julie Harris. I told her I was playing a small part in the film of a middle aged former World War I pilot, now grounded, who fired the Very lights calling for a scramble and then sadly watched the planes taking off. I asked Julie to supply the uniform.
'You won't need to supply trousers,' I said, 'It's a medium close shot.'
She took me at my word and we shot the scene with me in shorts and sandals and service dress jacket and cap. There was a certain amount of raucous laughter from the crew.

# Chapter Thirty-One
# Carry On Up The Danube

I have a long and affectionate relationship with Hungary. It started like this.

In 1967, which was only ten years after the revolution when Imre Nagy was shot, I had, for some reason, a great desire to go to Hungary. Thomas Cook and Ibusz, the Hungarian State Travel Agency, were anxious to get tourists to come to their country. They advertised a scheme which cost £70 for adults and £35 for children. You could drive through France, Belgium, Germany and Austria and eventually into Hungary. It would take three days and they would pre-book the hotels which you had to stay at.

Then in Hungary you would have four days in Budapest and ten days on Lake Balaton and then home along the same route. All hotels and meals were paid for. Even in those days it was pretty cheap so Maggie and I decided to go taking the Bristol 405 and the two boys (Vinny was too young). It was quite an eventful trip. When we got to Germany for the first night's stopover, we went to this very pleasant hotel and I ordered a bottle of wine. The waiter said curtly, 'You are Thomas Cook; for you no wine!' Maggie looked at me expectantly. I found myself becoming very British and said, 'Ein flasche Nummer Vier Und Vierzig. Schnell!'

I remember reading that Doctor Johnson said that he had seen a salamander in the fire when he was young and his father clouted him so that he would remember. The Black Forest was really quite spooky and the children were affected by it. I found myself saying, 'Look, a wolf!' Simon, for many years afterwards, was convinced that he had seen one.

When we crossed the border into Austria and reached Salzburg we stayed in a marvellous hotel with a room the size of a tennis court. Maggie unaccountably began to cry. I said, 'What is it? Is it something I said?' She continued to cry, and she is not a weepy person. The waiter was beginning to look a bit suspicious and American tourists in the dining room were whispering behind their hands.
I said, 'Look, you must eat your nice schweinfleisch und kartoffel.'
She carried on blubbering, though she ate her dinner. Afterwards I said, 'What would you like to do now? We could go and see Mozart's birthplace?' so we wandered around the town with her weeping copiously and later, she cried herself to sleep. In the morning she got up quite cheerfully and I said, 'What was all that about?' She said, 'I have no idea. I've never done anything like it before.'

Later on when we were staying in Massachussets with Chris Plummer, he wasn't in the least surprised, 'Everybody cries in Salzburg,' he said, 'It's the Foehn.' He was talking about the mysterious southern wind which drives people insane and apparently had laid low most of the cast of *The Sound Of Music*.

When we got to the Hungarian border it was quite frightening to see giant barbed wire fences with the killing ground in the middle. There was a soldier on a tower training a machine gun on us from the moment we arrived though the effect was somewhat mitigated by the fact that he had a flower in his mouth. We were the only tourists to go in to Hungary through that gate that day.

Before we left, I had been called in by an administrator at the BBC who said I should be very careful, as we were liable to be closely watched by the secret police; and in fact it had taken three applications for us to get our visas. We had also been told that the great big European motorway E1 led into Hungary. It did, but only for two or three hundred yards and the road reverted to an ill maintained track.

We stayed for four days at the Astoria in Budapest, a delightful Fin de Siecle Hotel full of dusty palm trees and old waiters. We became certain that our room was bugged; when we came downstairs after Maggie had been saying she wanted to visit the mountains. As we passed the telephone exchange, where the door was always kept open, one of the telephonists said, 'Hello, I believe you want to see some mountains. I can arrange it.'

There was a cimbalon band in the dining room with violins and a cello which the kids found enchanting. The violinist leant over our table and insisted on playing numbers from *My Fair Lady* until I handed him a discreet banknote and he played some Liszt.

We enjoyed Budapest. There was hardly any traffic except the trams, but occasionally a large black car with a licence number starting with A would come up behind us and honk impatiently. This belonged to a senior civil servant. We always refused to get out of the way.

On the last day, we were leaving the dining room when the band stopped. We turned around to see what had happened and found the boys embracing the band who were becoming very emotional and were crying a lot. It was then that I first thought of using the cimbalon as a lead instrument for some film music.

The next day we drove to Lake Balaton which is twenty-three miles long and quite narrow. We moved into a hotel at Szeged on the South Bank. It was seriously ghastly; it was made of rough concrete lit by fluorescent tubes which kept flickering and was full of Russian factory workers who had fulfilled their norm. The food was not too unpleasant; it was the usual cherry soup, stew and the wine, which, at the end of the communist period in Hungary was quite good, including Tokay Szamorodny which tastes fine in Hungary but doesn't travel. The atmosphere was ghastly and there was no beach. Maggie said, 'You've got to get us out of here.' I said it was really difficult because it was all planned in advance. She said, 'Never mind that, just do it.'

I went to see the manager and told him we wanted to leave. He burst into floods of tears and said it was beyond his powers to do anything. I would have to go to Ibusz, the state tourist agency in the next town, so I did. When I started to explain myself, suddenly nobody could speak English and I used my far from fluent German and said, 'Unser Hotel ist nicht gemutlich.' They all got together and whispered for a while. Finally they came up with a typically Hungarian solution. They would move us to a nice hotel on the north bank at Tihany and we would have pleasant rooms and all our food paid for but we would not exist officially and if anybody asked we were to say we were just passing through.

The hotel at Tihany was quite beautiful with a sandy beach which must have been imported. Most of the other guests were Germans. Hungarians were not usually allowed to stay in hotels. The food was more than adequate and at meal times a pop group played a series of rather old numbers. Their favourite was *Red Roses For A Blue Lady* which we must have heard thirty or forty times during the week. The boys immediately went up to the bandstand, grabbed hold of the group and said you must meet my mummy and daddy. They were very quiet and well behaved. They were very resentful of the fact that they had to have short hair. It was cut on the orders of the issuers of identity cards and they were told 'no hair cut, no identity card'. They had all spent three years at the state pop Conservatorium and felt lucky to have been posted to Tihany. We told them about Szeged on the other side and they shuddered.

From then on the holiday was quite idyllic. The soft, slightly milky waters of the lake were unpolluted and full of a local fish called fogas, a sort of pike-perch unique to Hungary. We swam all day and met the only two Hungarians who were staying at the hotel. She was a model and he was a doctor. They were never allowed out of the country together and she would be sent to model clothes in Egypt and Libya. Her father had been a general in the Hungarian army with a big estate. When the war ended the communist government took over his estate and made it into a school. He asked if he could have the job of gardener and a small cottage on his old property. They laughed and agreed. He spent the rest of his live blissfully happy tending the garden and not missing the grandeur of the big house.

The couple appeared to want to talk to us confidentially but were very hesitant to do so. They said, 'Shall we take a walk down to the fishing lodge. It's a couple of miles away?'
We agreed and having put the children to bed where they were looked after by a nice old lady, we set off. The man in charge of the fishing lodge was an old friend of theirs who paid us the compliment of covering one of the rough wooden tables outside with a cloth and serving us wine. They told us that they were planning to escape to Germany and the real difficulty was their little girl who could be held as a hostage by the government. I think they wanted us to smuggle her out; as it turned out it was a very good thing we regretfully refused, but we wished them well. We heard later through friends, they had escaped and gone to live in Munich.

The days went by in the blaze of sunlight. A lot of the Germans would go riding every morning and would leave their boots outside their rooms to be cleaned. It gave us a little frisson to see whole lines of jackboots. The boys very naughtily muddled them all up one night causing a lot of chaos.

One thing about the communist government was that there was more or less full employment. There were too many waiters all of whom were beautifully mannered and who loved to serve the children. All the lifts had operators even though they were fully automatic. We met almost no other English people during the stay. On our way back we met an English engineer who was completing a big contract. He wanted to go home but they would not give him an exit visa, nor would they give him the steel to finish the job. He was beginning to get very worried.

We started the journey home and when we got to the frontier post at Hevgyeshalom, suddenly things started to turn a little bit funny. The frontier police made us get out of the car and almost took it to pieces. They opened all the luggage and spread the contents on the floor. It took three hours before they finally and reluctantly let us go. We realised that what they were looking for was another child. We had our two boys and Vinny on my passport and they thought we were trying to smuggle another one through. It was a good job we hadn't tried any such thing. We drove back to Salzburg and this time there were no tears and, I suspect, probably no foehn.

As we raced through Germany on the Autobahn at ninety miles per hour being constantly overtaken by nearly everything else, we realised how much we liked Hungarian people and hoped that one day we would be back.

Slow dissolve.

Twenty-five years later Malcolm Bradbury was writing a sequel to *The Gravy Train* and he rang me up. He said, 'I think it's very important that you direct this and you will see why when you read it.' It was about a little European country emerging into freedom from years of communist rule. The country was Slaka, which had featured strongly in *Rates Of Exchange* which, you may remember, I had adapted but was never produced. He said I was the world expert on the Slakan language and it was essential that I be involved. Malcolm had in fact invented the language for the novel and published another little book called *Why Come To Slaka* expanding our knowledge of the language. In my adaptation I had expanded it further and written a national anthem in Slakan.

I think Channel 4 were a little dubious about me, because I was not thought to be biddable and they were very worried about money. Malcolm's original book was based on Bulgaria where he had been as a young man. He had since been to Hungary and we both agreed that that country was the best place to shoot the new series which I suggested we call *The Gravy Train Goes East*. On our recce we found some amazing locations, including a little square in the suburbs of Budapest which looked like the Place Nationale of a small country.

We found Hungary extraordinarily changed. The streets were full of cars. Everyone was much more prosperous and restaurants of all sorts: American, French, Italian and Hungarian could be found in the city and were not too expensive. We stayed not at the Astoria but at a rather grand hotel on the Margitinsel in the middle of the Danube. We had two producers who complemented each other very well. Ian Warren was well over seventy but full of energy and spoke beautiful German which was useful as mine was not very good. Philip Hinchcliffe was young and also very energetic and totally committed. On one occasion he went off into the country to shoot some oxen and came back with about twenty minutes of very good footage. I said, 'I only wanted twenty seconds' and he said, 'I know but they do look lovely don't they?'

Many of the cast featured in *Rates Of Exchange* were in *The Gravy Train*, including Katya Princip, who at the beginning of our story was elected President of the newly emerging democracy. We cast Francesca Annis whom I had known since she was fifteen and was ravishingly beautiful.

It was a strong international cast. Jacques Sereys was under contract with the Comedie Francaise and had enormously long speeches in English which must have been very difficult to learn. Anna Zagaria was a very distinguished Italian Actress and Christoph Waltz was an Austrian actor who came from a distinguished family of thirty-two quarterings and who had married a New York Jewish girl who belonged to some very exclusive sect. They got on terribly well and had marvellous children. When they came to supper with us we had to think very carefully what to give them to eat, because of their strict dietary laws. They were charmingly insouciant although I am sure they were breaking all sorts of interdictions.

Christoph was fond of all things English. His very favourite joke was one that had, I think, appeared in Punch in the 1880s.
Waiter: 'What will you have, sir?'
Diner: 'I'll have some kiddleys.'
Waiter: 'You mean kidneys, don't you?'
Diner: 'I said kiddleys, diddle I?'
Christoph would go into paraoxysms of laughter whenever he heard it.

I very much wanted to direct this show, not least because of going back to Hungary. Ian Richardson said he would do it if his part was heavily written up and Malcolm agreed to do this. We got a very good English cast: Judy Parfitt played his wife, Henry Goodman from the National Theatre, later to play Shylock, favoured us by playing the villainous Minister of the Interior and Jeremy Child played a lunatic British Ambassador with a stammer. The crew was nearly all Hungarian.

The costume designer, Emma Porteous, was very forthright. She, Francesca and I went shopping for clothes around Bond Street and left with some quite beautiful costumes.

We still hadn't got the script right at the beginning. We needed a spectacular event to represent the revolution and I was trying to write new scenes in the car and giving them to Dickie Bamber, the associate producer, who was desperate to get things settled. Finally we got the go ahead to do a lavish opening scene where the President and his wife, which I based on Mr and Mrs Ceausescu were watching a march past of soldiers and police. We couldn't really afford enough extras so I got the lorries and tanks and soldiers into a tight circle and they marched past the saluting base and dashed around the back of the camera to come around again. I had an idea that we should have an enormous Slakan flag with a red star in the centre and that two men should abseil down from the roof and cut the star out. This worked spectacularly and it worked even better when Elemer Ragaly, the cameraman, insisted on having hundreds of fireworks lighting up the sky. The climax came when all the soldiers threw down their rifles and the people gave them blue flowers. Blue became the symbol of the revolution and I had everybody from the president downwards wearing little light blue bows in their button holes.

We had an enormous unit; after all, the Hungarians were used to full employment and many of them had not worked very much recently. So when we went on a recce which would normally include five or six people we would find that we had thirty or forty, I would point to someone and say: 'Who's he?'

One of the guys said, 'He's my cousin, he's interested in film.'

They were there really for the fun of it and to get a square meal.

We had a long and very difficult scene to shoot in an opera house. We couldn't find a space in the schedule of the state opera but decided to go to Kecskamet, (it means Goat City) about forty miles away where they had a beautiful little opera house. The resident company said they had a performance on Sunday afternoon, after which they would rehearse with us and would we like to come and see the performance? We weren't very keen but for politeness sake we went and it was a wonderfully enthusiastic performance. They were doing an operetta which took place in a night club, the second floor of the Eiffel Tower and the Algerian Desert as the hero had run away to join the Foreign Legion. They played it with such brio that we felt enormously refreshed and although we were tired from working so hard, we were able to throw ourselves into the rehearsal.

I had written the Slakan National Anthem which the opera company learnt incredibly quickly and sang beautifully. On this occasion Elemer and I fell out a little. We had 300 extras who were all amateurs and we were about to shoot this long scene in which they had to applaud frenziedly. I thought that the sensible thing to do was to shoot the audience first because amateurs get tired very quickly and would find it difficult to keep up the enthusiasm through the day. Elemer said, 'Yes we could do that or we could do this other shot concentrating on the boxes.' While I was rehearsing with the actors I noticed him lighting the other shot so I stopped and said, 'No, I want to shoot the audience first.'

Elemer looked a bit sulky and his crew, which was very large, looked at me with fury as someone who had dared to question the master. We soon made friends again and shot a powerful scene in the theatre with all our cast and extras and the opera company. Francesca gave a wonderful performance as she was elected President by acclamation.

I always wear sandals; I'm not sure why, I just took it up twenty-five years ago and they seemed more comfortable, even in cold weather. We did a recce to an Austrian schloss which was on a very steep hill. I knew that there was an excellent shot from low down and the recce involved going right round the schloss to find the shot. There was snow on the ground and it got progressively deeper as we walked round. Soon, I was up to my knees in snow and my feet were beginning to get rather cold. I said to the crew, 'Do you mind if we run the rest of the way?' We did and finally got around to a very good low angle shot only a few yards from where we had started. If we had got the other way around we could have ended dry shod.

One of the important scenes was a supremely silly shot of Christoph Waltz in a solar topi on the top of an elephant. An Indian bearer got a message on his mobile phone which was in his loin cloth and he tossed it up to Christoph who caught it. It wasn't very easy finding an elephant in Hungary. The only one we found was apparently rather delicate and its owner would not let it stay outside in the cold weather for more than an hour. We got behind schedule and the trainer sulked and refused to allow his elephant to be used. We had to wait until we got back to England to shoot the scene. There, the trainer had a splendid elephant called Janey and when he went

200 yards away and called out 'JANEY!!', the animal would lumber forward slowly. She was an extremely nice elephant and I had my picture taken with her.

One of Elemer's crew was a Turk. He was rather silent and forbidding but would pick little bunches of wild flowers and give them to various actresses in the cast. There was a beautiful wooden statue of a woman in a medieval castle where we were shooting. I asked him if he would gather some wild flowers to put in the statue's hands.
'No' he said.
Elemer said to me quietly, 'It's because he's a Turk.'

I had written some rather charming scenes for Katya Princip in the adaptation of *Rates Of Exchange*. I inserted them into our schedule; in one of them Francesca Annis had to drive a tram which she did with great style and a commentary in Slakan. The Channel 4 Commissioning Editors said I was interfering with the script. I had already discussed it with Malcolm and told them to get lost.

It was an extremely happy shoot, we edited more or less as we went and we had a very successful showing for the crew in Budapest. When I left there were tears all around and we promised to keep in touch though we thought we'd never meet again.

Quick dissolve to two days later.

I was telephoned by Granada Television who said, 'Can you shoot Paris in Budapest?'
'Yes,' I said, 'But only the old Paris of the 1950s before the buildings were cleaned.'
'Right,' they said, 'Would you like to be Lead Director on the new series of *Maigret*?'
I agreed to do it, especially as the first episode was written by Alan Plater who had done *Fortunes Of War*. It was to be a very different experience. Michael Gambon, a very old friend was playing Maigret and I immediately started casting. I cast Ciaran Madden as Madame Maigret. She was slightly posh but, unlike many of the production staff, I had read the books and knew that her father was a high up civil servant in the Ministere De Ponts et Chaussees who thought that when she teamed up with a policeman she was marrying beneath her.

John Moffat played the Chief Examining Magistrate. He was an actor of great skill who always wanted, from reasons of humility, to put something between himself and the audience. Could he wear a pince-nez, he asked? I knew that this would mean that he would be fiddling with it all the time, so I persuaded him out of it by saying, 'You have such expressive eyes. I don't want anything coming between them and the audience.' Without props he gave a very still and funny performance.

Henry Goodman agreed to accept a small part as a concierge and Maigret's assistants were James Galloway and James Lawton. Cheryl Campbell played the villainess brilliantly and Greg Hicks played the young murderer with great style. Trevor Peacock, who had been playing a drunken catholic priest in the last Hungarian trip, came in and played a sad wise old person.

I was so pleased to be working with Gambon. We were all staying at the Ramada Hotel on the Margitinsel which I thought was quite idyllic. Previously I had fallen out with Jonathan Alwyn the producer. I said that although I knew Paris well, I needed to spend a day there photographing the important locations such as the law courts, Maigret's flat and the headquarters of the Police Judiciaire. Jonathan refused absolutely. He said there wasn't enough money. We argued for some time and I said, 'Well whatever you say I'm going to fly over, take a lot of photographs and fly back on the same day. If I have to, I'll pay for it all myself although if you don't reimburse me you should be ashamed.'

I then flew over and shot two reels of film which I gave to the designer and also took copious notes of movie shots that we could take to cut into the film if we could eventually afford to give a cinematographer half a day in Paris. Eventually I was reimbursed. The stills, about fifty in number, were incedibly useful both to me and the designer and eventually we shot half a day on film in Paris.

I had seen Ann Todd, David Lean's first wife, in London who was prepared to play a tiny part. I remembered her vividly from *The Seventh Veil* when James Mason hit her across her hands with his walking stick and said, 'If you won't play the piano for me Jessica, you won't play it for anyone.' She was now very much older but still had a star quality about her. I offered her a small part of a mad lady who was surrounded by parrots and domestic birds of all sorts. She had just the one scene with Maigret. It was a charming digression and not very important to the plot, but it looked good at the end. Not long aftwards Ann died and this was her last professional engagement.

We continued to shoot all around Budapest. We had built enormously realistic metro entrances as designed by Mucha and placed them at street corners. When we shot the extras going into the metro they were supposed to be descending stairs that we could not see, so to complete the illusion, they had gradually to decrease in height until they were on their knees.

In one of the episodes, the script was very exigent about the exact relationship between various houses, schools and the police station. It was soon obvious that we were never going to find an exactly correct location, so we had to synthesise one by shooting in various different places. In this way we managed to persuade the audience that one side of the street faced another by doing tracking shots of the two leading actors in two different villages and inter-cutting. It was an interesting exercise.

In another, we had to do a scene looking out to sea. Lake Balaton made quite a good sea, but you may remember that the lake is not very wide so we had to wait for a mist to come down. We were trying to set up a shot full of imported lobster pots and nets hung up to dry but there was a lamp standard in the way. I couldn't seem to manage to get the right shot whichever way I put the camera. Elemer Rogaly snapped his fingers and someone immediately cut it down with a chain saw which I thought was rather bold. After it was over they welded it back together again.

One of the saddest moments happened when a man who had been hired to bring a parrot to the location failed to notice that the window was open and this beautiful multicoloured animal which had never lived in the wild before flew out of the window and was never seen again.

The series was not an unqualified success although I recently bought a copy of the video which said this 'award-winning show' was made entirely in Paris. John Glenister, the other director, was not too happy either. When they came to do a second series they got together a rag-bag of directors and a new producer who summarily fired Ciaran, presumably because she talked too posh and he hadn't read the books. I gathered that it wasn't a very happy experience for anybody and I don't think the second series looked very good. My mind goes back to Birmingham Rep, and to the Algarve, with Gambon saying, 'Then, old age and experience, hand in hand ....'

When we finally went home from Budapest, Elemer and the crew gave me an enormous bottle of Apricot Liqueur (known as Hungarian rocket fuel). It was the size of about ten ordinary bottles. I put it in the rack above my seat in the aeroplane and unfortunately, it leaked onto the person next to me who became very angry. When I came to go through customs I said, 'There is no way I am going to pay duty on this, even though its classed as a spirit and is sixty per cent proof. If you want you can all have it and share it amongst yourselves.'
'Thank you kindly for the offer,' they said, 'but we'd rather drink Lysol. We'll treat it as a single bottle of wine, good luck with it.'

So I took it home, leaking copiously, and it hung around the house for sometime until I finally used it to ignite a bonfire.

Serena Scott Thomas
in *Harnessing Peacocks*

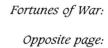

*Fortunes of War:*

*Opposite page:*
Emma Thompson, Rupert Graves
and JCJ at the top of a pyramid.

*Left:*
JCJ with Emma Thompson
and Ken Branagh.

*Below:*
Emma Thompson, JCJ,
Esmond Knight and
Michael Cochrane.

*A Fine Romance:*

*Above:* The author obscures the view of a promotional billboard.

*Left:* With Michael Williams and Judi Dench.

*The Comedy Of Errors:*
*Clockwise from top left:* Dame Wendy Hiller, Cyril Cusack,
Roger Daltrey, Michael Kitchen.

*The Vacillations Of Poppy Carew:*

Script extracts and storyboards.

WILLY AND POPPY DRIVE ..

WILLY'S POV

FOG SWIRLS AROUND THEM

CAN YOU SEE OUT YOUR SIDE ?

12 . Police car around        114
                              185

114. EXT. COUNTRY ROAD/INT. WILLY'S CAR. EVE/NIGHT.    114.

WILLY driving, POPPY next to him.  A relaxed silence.

                    WILLY

          What are you thinking ?

                    POPPY

          What am I thinking ?..... Actually, I
          was  thinking  the  last  time  I  was
          kidnapped  from  Dad's  house  was  by
          Edmund.

WILLY glances round from the wheel.

          Sorry !  Won't mention his name again !

More silence as WILLY drives.  Fog suddenly swirls around
them.

                    WILLY

          Oh no.

                    POPPY

          What is it ?

                    WILLY

          Fog..... Bloody hell I hate fog....

                    POPPY

          Don't say that.  You're meant to be the
          strong and capable one, able to deal
          with anything.

                    WILLY

          I am and I can.  Except for fog.

It's engulfing them now.  WILLY can barely see ahead.  He
switches on the lights but they have little effect.

                    WILLY

          Can you see out your side at all ?

                    POPPY

          No.

WHAT WAS THAT ?

ITS A WHOLE HERD

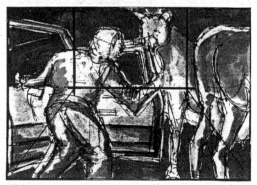

I'LL GET THEM BACK INTO THE FIELD

                    WILLY
        Great.  That makes two of us.
                    POPPY
        Don't joke.
                    WILLY
        Sorry.

But he's not joking.  He slows down to a crawl.  Peering
out of the window as he drives.  POPPY sitting bolt
upright, hating it.

        Are you all right ?
                    POPPY
        No of course I'm not all right.

He manages to give her a reassuring smile.
                    WILLY
        We'll be fine.  It'll clear up in a
        minutes.  Probably just a patch....

POPPY screams as a vast shape bumps into her side of the
car.
                    POPPY
        What's that ?!

Enormous shapes loom all round them.

        Willy - what is it ?!

Even more alarmed as he stops.    sensy I thrik.
                    WILLY
        It's a cow. - a whole herd of
        cows. /....some bloody fool must have let
        them out.

He gets out.

        Just stay there.  I'll get them back in the
        field.

*A Bequest To The Nation:*

*Opposite page:*

*Top:* Peter Finch as Nelson briefs his captains before the battle.
*Bottom*: On location in Windsor with Simon and Maggie.

*This page:* Nelson's body, preserved in brandy, is brought home.

*Oxbridge Blues: Sleeps Six:*
JCJ with Ben Kingsley and Diane Keen.

*Opposite page:*

*Top:* With the pilots during the making of
*A Perfect Hero*. Nigel Havers is on JCJ's right.

*Bottom:* Simon, Maggie and JCJ
in New York for *The Adams Chronicles*.

Alec Guinness

Meeting HRH Princess Anne
at BAFTA.

*Above:*
Maggie Smith in *Mrs Silly*.

*Opposite:*
Barbara Parkins and Lee Remick
in *Jennie, Lady Randolph Churchill*.

With Sir John Mills, *Harnessing Peacocks*.

## Chapter Thirty-Two
# Friday And After

In happier days, when the Independent Broadcasting Authority[19] was a power in the land, ITV companies needed to review their contracts every few years. This meant that a company that was worth millions could lose its licence overnight and there was always a queue of applicants to fill the gap. Such were we. Georgina Abrahams was a bright, go-getting woman married to an estate agent. Tim Emanuel was a bright, amusing self-mocking Jewish Catholic. The rest were a varied group of producers and teachers.

We were bidding for the South South-East region which at the time was held by Southern TV who had produced *Caesar And Cleopatra* (qv) and whose days were numbered. I thought we should call ourselves CRESSET after the fire bearing baskets that were put up around the coast to warn the people of the approach of the Armada, and the letters SSE would be in capitals. We worked out a detailed plan of how we would run the station. We made one crucial mistake. We should have designated a managing director. Actually we wanted to use the incumbent who was very good, though it would have put him in an awkward position. In our address to the board we had to show our seriousness and commitment to the arts.

Edward Lord Montagu came and spoke for us, promising to continue to encourage opera on television. I did several television interviews putting our case. On one I was doing reasonably well until I saw over the interviewer's shoulder a monitor with a big close up of me. It put me right off my stride and I started stammering. Fortunately they allowed me to go for a second take. We didn't get the franchise; nearly but not quite.

There had been a lot of creative effort put into the application which could be wasted. Georgina moved decisively. We formed a company eventually known as Friday Productions which lived in the basement of her house. She, Tim and I were directors.

I had had an idea for a children's serial called *The Medway Queen*. I knew that a few Thames Barges were still under sail and that a hundred years ago there were over 6,000 of them on the East Coast. They were enormous and so cleverly constructed that they could be sailed by a man and a boy. I envisaged two rival boats, one sailed by a man and his son and the other by a woman and her daughter.; there were many records of women skippers. I worked out a story and a treatment twenty pages long. It eventually became our first production. We had to change the title as there was already a famous boat of that name. We decided to call the show *The December Rose*, after the name of a ship. Georgina found a distinguished children's writer, Leon Garfield, who adapted it into a six part serial. He did it well, though I worried a little that it was derivative of Charles Kingley's *The Water Babies*. Georgina offered me the chance to direct it. I

---

[19] Subsequently superseded by OfCom

was unfortunately busy, so we got Renny Rye, one of the bright young men I had encouraged while Head of Plays. It was eventually made and sold to the BBC.

Later on, if one wanted to sell a show abroad, one had to go through a distributor who took 30% of the profits. Georgina sold *The December Rose* all over the world, we pooled our knowledge of foreign broadcasters and she telephoned them direct, it was as simple as that.

Running the company was hard work. It was easier for me as I was directing other things most of the time. Georgina organised a concert to be held in Buckingham Palace and broadcast on the BBC. Not enough money, but a lot of prestige. She offered me the chance to direct it. I knew I wasn't good enough; directing a music Outside Broadcast is a very particular skill. I recommended the best in England, Humphrey Burton, who made a superb job of it.

The culture of vicious and cynical competition, now almost universal, was spreading. We bought the rights of a very successful book by a lady novelist. Because it was such a difficult undertaking, we needed a co-producer, and we chose one of the big ITV companies, Anglia Television. They, quite cynically, waited until the option ran out and persuaded the writer to dump us. The second-rate ex-BBC administrator who was involved sneered, saying: 'You should have been there, instead of away directing.' The show ended up an artistic and financial disaster.

Seven years had nearly gone by. The company running the SSE franchise were ready to pack it in. We had had many ups and downs in the intervening years and some disasters. As I mentioned earlier, I adapted with Malcolm Bradbury's help *Rates Of Exchange*, one of his best novels. David Rose of Channel 4, hated the adaptation and because the iron curtain had now fallen, thought the book to be irrelevant.

We had wanted for some time to appoint a Chairman of the board. We had various attempts which had not worked. In spite of my instinctive mistrust of the aristocracy we settled on Norton Romsey, Mountbatten's grandson, who had been an assistant director and production manager and who seemed to be professional in spite of his rarified ancestry.

We had been in contact with Mary Wesley, a very agreeable old person and a very successful novelist who had not been published until she was seventy. I fell in love with a book of hers called *Harnessing Peacocks*. We got Andrew Davies to adapt it. I had known Andrew for many years and had been involved in *Tussy*, his first adaptation for the BBC.

We had a slightly unfortunate history. I had a book of Daphne Du Maurier's called *The Parasites* which I thought would make a wonderful television film. Richard Price, a well known independent producer, became very enthusiastic and suggested that we produce it in partnership sharing the expenses. I naively agreed. We got Andrew to write a treatment; it turned out to be absolutely brilliant and contained the lyrics of a lot of the songs which would be used in the show.

We couldn't seem to sell it anywhere,. People didn't like the title; they thought it sounded like a scientific book. A few weeks later, I found I had lost £2,500 and the thing was abandoned. I don't know whether Andrew ever got paid but I suspect not. Whether it was to do with that piece of history or not I do not know, but Andrew could easily turn sulky and while we were waiting for the script, his agent telephoned us to say he wanted out. We were in crisis. I had to telephone Andrew and beg him to stay with it. Eventually the script turned out well. We tried to sell it as a cinema film without success. Eventually we picked on Meridian, the prime contenders for the new SSE region. Colin Rogers was then Head of Drama. They agreed to produce the film if they won the franchise at a budget of 1.25 million pounds. They won the franchise and immediately cut £200,000 off the budget.

At this stage things began to go sour. I found out from Colin Rogers that Norton had offered to get rid of me and find another director if that would seal the contract. I found this unpleasant and disloyal. Fortunately they turned him down.

Eventually we went into production. We hired a production manager called Brian True-May. He was very insistent that we have our offices at Elstree. Why, I wondered when they were much cheaper at Shepperton? He avoided the question. We agreed after he offered me a car to work every day. Later we discovered that he had been employed by a company in Elstree and he had left under acrimonious circumstances. He wanted to walk back into the building, and he did.

Brian had a genius for saving money without much damage to the production. He obtained savagely reduced room rates for the hotels and arranged that when we finished early that the hotels would give each of the crew a free drink. When they squealed, he explained how little it would cost and how good it would be for morale. It was a brilliant idea and worked well.

For some reason Colin and Meridian absolutely vetoed our choice of Tara Fitzgerald for the part of Hebe, the lead. After a lot of argument we offered the part to Serena Scott-Thomas, the sister of the more famous Kristin. She was very intelligent, totally inexperienced and luminously beautiful. We had to teach her to act in a couple of weeks. She couldn't at first speak or move, let alone do both at the same time, but she picked it up incredibly quickly and was a joy to work with.

John Mills and Renee Asherson played two delightful old buffers. Peter Davison, Nick Le Prevost, Jeremy Child and Richard Huw were also cast. John especially was unexpectedly thin, sharp and intelligent. He said, 'I'm half blind, so I learn the lines from a little machine.' He did and never dried. The character he played had been based by Mary on an old homosexual friend. John had to tread a careful line. In the film he was manifestly heterosexual but loved beauty and in the scene where he dressed Silas, Hebe's son, in jewellery it could have been embarrassing and ugly. As it was it seemed natural and charming. He portrayed a sort of hearty aesthete, a wholly sympathetic character.

One day the camera operator turned to me in great embarrassment. We were doing an over the shoulder shot of John. 'His hearing aid is very prominent. I can't hide it,' he said. No one had mentioned deafness, but it could have got very embarrassing. I said without thinking: 'Let's lose the deaf aid for this shot, John.'
'Right you are, boy,' he said and put it in his pocket. 'Now I can't hear a thing.'
But he heard my 'Action' and did the shot in one take.

Renee's clear cut glass voice held depth of wit and humour which made her character deeply sympathetic.

Nick Le Prevost had a genius for comedy which to my mind had been underused over the years. He had played a young leading part for me in *Slip Up* (qv) and I was very lucky to get him to play Mungo. Dilys Hamlett, Casper Wrede's widow, whom I hadn't met for nearly thirty years played Mungo's mother. Richard Huw played Rory the nervy hat designer. There was a scene where Rory came into the room and Serena as Hebe was wearing nothing but a hat. He was dumbstruck. 'I say,' she said, 'Do you know you've got an erection?' 'Yes,' he said, 'it must be the hat.' It could have been gross or sentimental, or sickly or pornographic. As it was, it was quite charming.

Tom Beasley played Hebe's son, Silas, with an innocence stronger because it was true and real. Child actors are cynically supposed to be arrogant, smug and unpleasant. Tom and the other boys played the scenes with great enthusiasm. They were a joy to work with including Tommy Manderson, the make-up artist's grandson Ben Keyworth who gave a cameo performance which should have set his career up as a young actor. He now works in editing.

We had hired a forty foot yacht for a scene where Silas is horribly sick and the other boys laugh at him. We put to sea in a very fresh wind. The tutors and chaperones who were supposed to stick like leeches to their charges were left behind bleating on the quay. As we moved out into the bay the sea began to get very rough, then typically in film, the unexpected happened. Silas, who was supposed to be very ill was totally unfazed, even when ingesting the tinned minestrone we gave him to represent vomit. The other boys were very sea sick indeed and I had to say: 'Now, you boys, stop vomiting and start acting at once!'
They managed to do so, even when confronted by Silas spewing out great jets of minestrone.

When we got back to shore, Brian True-May was waiting with packs of fish and chips. He had been pacifying the chaperones all this time. It was brilliant. It hit the spot with the kids and saved money on catering.

David Harewood played a musician who happened to be black and whom Hebe had taught to make love. He afterwards played Romeo at the National Theatre. Abigail McKern, Leo's daughter, played Serena's friend and Brenda Bruce a wicked old lady who lived up the street.

The budget was quite restricting, we could mostly afford only to go within a thirty mile radius of Elstree, but if you look hard it is amazing what you can find in that small area and we did. We needed a few days in a seaside town and some time in the Scilly Isles; we also had a very complicated carnival scene in Sicily which another production manager had estimated at £200,000 at least.

For the town we chose Lyme Regis, it was just the right size but we were very restricted in the time we could spend there. Likewise with the Scilly Isles.

St Mary's Island is a magical place, it has a formidably dangerous coast line which many years ago accounted for the loss of Sir Cloudesley Shovell's fleet with appalling loss of life. We could afford to spend just one day there, flying from Elstree and shooting on the plane all the way. We should really have shot a lot of the scenes in the harbour. Luckily we discovered that Lyme Harbour is almost a perfect mirror image of St Mary's. We were brought up short at Lyme when we looked at the fishing boats, all bearing the wrong identity numbers. We had to row around hurriedly and beg the owners to cover their identity numbers with ones we had made up. Everyone was very co-operative, thank goodness.

Jeremy Child showed his skill in one of these sequences; he was playing a bad tempered father who shouted at his children. As the boat pulled out he ad-libbed a whole scene where he shouted at the kids and argued with them; he was very real and very funny.

The scene which might have given us the greatest problem, the carnival in Sicily, was shot in one night on the church steps and around the graveyard using the local amateur dramatic society in fancy dress and grotesque masks. I had heard someone playing a hurdy-gurdy earlier in the year. It was a weird evocative mediaeval sound. Dick Holmes found a player with a beautiful instrument whom we dressed in a sinister mask and he wrote a spine chilling piece for him which we used several times in the film for memory-flashbacks. The whole sequence cost a few hundred pounds.

Tariq Anwar, who had edited *Fortunes Of War* and went on to edit *The Madness Of King George*, used a new system: the Avid system of electronic editing. It was a great labour saving device but at this stage, apt to go seriously wrong. Avid kindly sent an engineer down to us day after day. The sadness is that if we had been editing on film we would have had eight or nine people in the cutting room while Tariq was working practically single handed. All this was inevitably the March of Progress. I had to agree with it and had been brought up with video editing but how were people to be trained? The danger was, and is, that the slick operators, would elbow aside those with a good artistic eye.

About this time, Georgina, to my mind, started acting very oddly though I suppose she felt the same about me. She didn't want to let me look at the budget. She had heard somewhere that directors were to be kept ignorant. I, who had produced forty or fifty shows, objected and we fell out. Directors can be the first to save money, they know what can be sacrificed and what can't. Betty Willingale had been brought in as co-producer and stupidly I fell out with her as well. The shooting went smoothly, the film was launched successfully and we wondered what to do next. Norton arranged everything. We were going into our last board meeting when he said, 'You and Georgina aren't getting on. One of you has to go. Because the offices are in her house, it has to be you.' So I resigned from Friday Productions.

The press show for *Harnessing Peacocks* went well, but because Peter Davison and Andrew Davies had worked together before, the press decided that they were the only begetters of the film. Betty, Georgina and I accepted it, gritted our teeth and smiled.

It was well received by the critics and after a few weeks Colin Rogers rang up to say we had been put forward as the British Entry at the Monte Carlo Festival. Were they going to pay for us to fly over I asked?
'Possibly,' he said.

# Forsyte and Hindsight

A few days later we were told we had won the Nymphe D'Or, the top prize of the Festival. Definitely we were to fly over. Georgina and I, very polite to one another, flew to Nice and then by low flying helicopter along the coast to Monte Carlo, a magical trip. We went to a lot of parties dominated, as was to become the fashion, by sales people and other suits.

The Reception at the Palais Royal, was even more glamorous. Prince Rainier was charming and amusing and my old friend Robin Scott was there. We met Ronald Neame, an immensely distinguished director whom I much admired, partly because he, too, had started as a call boy. He said in his autobiography, 'By the time I became a Director nobody could pull the wool over my eyes.' He was now chairman of the Monte Carlo Prize jury.
He said to me: 'You know I liked your film, I liked it very much and I said to myself how can I persuade all these foreigners on the Jury to think as I do? So I began gently to bad mouth the film and said 'Do you really like it?' They got more and more keen on it and eventually I pretended to capitulate and we awarded it the prize.'

At the party afterwards Georgina and I went up to collect the pretty little gold-plated statuette from Prince Rainer. When we got back to the table Colin Rogers said, 'I'll take that on behalf of Meridian,' and we never saw it again.

During the party I spoke to a French Producer called Nellie Kafsky who asked me if I spoke French. 'Je me debrouille,' I said, meaning 'I get by'. The word is so difficult to pronounce that if you can do it well they think your French is perfect. Mine is pretty good but not perfect.
'Would you like to direct a French film?' she said.
'Yes I think I would,' I said.

When Friday Productions broke up - I still think it was unnecessary and did us all harm - Georgina and I each left with a project - the rights to a Mary Wesley novel. Mine was *The Vacillations Of Poppy Carew,* a book I loved, but about which the network seemed luke warm. The choice had narrowed, and as far as the network was concerned, it was to be one or the other - mine or Georgia's.

Eventually they decided on mine and we needed to form a new company. I said to Brian True-May, 'It's time you became a producer. Let's form a company.' We did. It was called Bentley Productions to signify style and wealth, though we did not have much of the latter. We had several board meetings. To my eyes they seemed oddly informal. We got offices very reasonably at Pinewood. Brian hammered out a contract in which he was to get a lot more money than me. We rewrote the contract.
'Wouldn't you rather leave it and get a bigger slice of residuals?' he said.
'No,' I said, 'I'll take the money now.'

We cast Tara Fitzgerald as Poppy and a young unknown actor called Joseph Fiennes as the hero. I knew at once how good he would be. Charlotte Coleman, who not long ago died tragically young, played a soubrette part with great style. Edward Atterton and Sam West played bright young men. The latter's career has now taken off spectacularly.

I had made a sort of fragile peace with Betty Willingale. I shall always regret ever falling out with her at all. She is a wonderful person with an unerring eye for a script. We asked her advice about a writer and she came up with William Humble. Mary did not like his script much.

We had one vitally important part to cast. Poppy's father was very ill in hospital and when she went to visit him and told him that she had just broken off with her long term boyfriend whom he hated, he laughed himself to death on the spot. The next part of the film was about the funeral. The father was a short part but absolutely vital.

Bob Stephens was in the Royal Free Hospital waiting for a liver transplant. I went to see him and put a proposition to him. We would take him by ambulance to the set so he would go straight from bed to bed. He would shoot for one day for quite a lot of money and then go back to the Royal Free. He was hugely amused by the idea, but he had one caveat. If a compatible liver was found, he would have to cancel the whole thing. I agreed. Colin Rogers, the executive producer, and Brian were beside themselves with worry.
'Keep cool,' I said.

On the Friday before we were due to start on the Monday, the hospital telephoned to say a donor had been found and that Bob was already in theatre. I had to think fast. Dan Massey was an old friend. At this short notice I had to be open with him and offered him the part, explaining about Bob. He agreed. Dan wasn't very well himself at the time, but gave a superb performance, dying spectacularly in the middle of peals of laughter. It was the first day of shooting and it went well.

We had the same strictures about travel; a thirty mile radius of Pinewood. We had some amazing locations. One part of the film concerned a sensitive young man who had bought a trout at a fishmongers and found to his horror that it was still alive. He immediately put it in a bucket of water and drove to a river. We realised the story accurately though we had quite a job keeping the fish alive. When he finally released the fish into the water and it swam away to the strains of Mozart's *Die Forelle*, we cheered. It was a one take scene and it worked perfectly.

Strangely a white duck swam up river while we were shooting. It seemed very friendly. I picked it up and it nestled into me. It was thought to be a tame, or even a trained duck and when we had finished, we put it back in the water and it swam quietly home.

The crew were having a wonderful time, Davina Nicholson, a superb first assistant organised a party around the swimming pool with tequila slammers (you pour a shot of tequila into a glass, top it up with lemonade, slam it on the table and toss it back). The atmosphere got more and more frenzied. I was overcome with drunken accidie and threw myself into the pool with all my clothes on. The crew were very sweet and tolerant, pulled me out and dried my clothes and gave me another slammer.

We shot the funeral sequence in Denham, a village only a few miles from London, which was ravishingly pretty. We had a hearse drawn by a pair of black horses with plumes and I added another horse with boots in the stirrups reversed as in the Duke of Wellington's funeral. It was a very touching sequence. Dick Holmes did a very quiet arrangement of *I Do Like To Be Beside The Seaside* to accompany it, which had been sung by Dan on his last appearance.

We went to Tunisia to shoot the North African sequences. They remembered me well from 1979, though there had been a bloodless revolution since and the previously powerful rulers no longer were so.

In Sousse I started to have a few doubts about Bentley Productions. One of the crew said, 'It looks like a good deal that your company's done with…' and here he named a prominent Independent Producer. I must have looked blank. There began to circulate rumours about my position in the company. I faxed Brian with this who said, 'Oh we must have another board meeting and talk about it.'

The shooting went well. David Feig thought it a better film than *Harnessing Peacocks*, though that may have been something to do with the limpid quality of the lighting. Joe Fiennes I thought especially good. He is an even better actor than his brother.

When we got home we had a showing at the RSA. Mary seemed to approve, but her son, a publisher, hated it. I was at this time preparing *Chouchou*, but still had nagging doubts about Bentley. I went to Companies House, feeling very dishonourable and looked up Bentley. I found I was not a director of the company at all. The only Directors were Brian True-May and his wife.

I was naïve, admittedly, but could not believe I had been deceived. A more streetwise director would have put it down to experience and started working with Brian again. Instead, I let him know how I felt. He is now one of the richest producers in England with a great many cars and is in charge of a show called *Midsomer Murders* about a small village where the number of violent deaths per year exceeds that of the United States. Good luck to him.

# Chapter Thirty-Three
# Carry On Up The Nieva

When, in Monte Carlo, Nelly Kafsky asked me to direct a French film, it was an impulsive gesture which she was to regret. Although the European Community theoretically has freedom of employment between countries, the French are violently chauvinistic and when the executive producer of Telfrance, Didier de Coin, found that a Briton was to direct a film about Debussy, he made all sorts of trouble. Nelly was very loyal, but she had an uphill battle to fight, especially as the other film she was making, about Schumann, was written by her boyfriend. I soon found out that although the action of the film took place in Paris and Deauville all the shooting was to take place in St Petersburg which is very beautiful and quite unlike Paris.

On the recces I kept on saying, 'Cette maison est trop jaune.' As house after house that we visited was painted in Romanov yellow, the crew all got a bit fed up. We also had to find a theatre like the Opera Comique to stage Debussy's opera *Pelleas Et Melisande*. This was difficult, as nearly all the theatres had a royal box and parterre which took up most of the circle and did not look like Paris. The script, by Eric Emmanuel Schmitt, was excellent. There were forty-four speaking parts. I asked how many of these could be French.
'Four,' they said, 'The rest must all be Russian.'
'What happens if they don't speak French?' I asked.
'You must on no account allow them to speak French. They will speak too slowly. Let them speak Russian and we'll dub them.'

I cast Therese Liotard and Pascal Rocard as Debussy's two wives. Francois Marthouret as Mr D and Marcel Berman as his friend. Marcel passionately wanted to play Debussy and it took all my powers of persuasion to get him to play the friend.

I had a small connection with St Petersburg. My sister-in-law Ruth had given lodging to Alyosha Soukoussian, a young Russian boy, and when I went on the recce I looked up his mother. 'It's very close to the centre of town,' Alyosha had said. In fact, after the last station on the Metro it was another half hour's walk and the flat was one of a grey heap of ugly buildings, but compared with the way most Russians had to live, it was pure luxury. Marina Soukoussian did not approve of taxis. They were too expensive, but she took me on a conducted walk around the city. We did about fifteen miles. We didn't stop for coffee, it was again too expensive.

One day I saw an ice-cream seller.
'Would you like one?' I asked.
'I will have one not if it is from Moscow, nor from Kiev, but only from St Petersburg.'
My Russian was lousy. I said to the Babushka, 'Pajalsta ice-cream Kievskaya?'
'Niet.'

'E Moskovskya?'
'Niet.'
'E Sankt Peterburgskaya?'
'NIET. LENINGRADSKAYA!' Which, of course, was the name of St Petersburg under Communist rule. The proletariat were still unregenerate I thought as I bought us some ice-cream.

At night in St Petersburg, the cantilever bridges are all raised. The city is built on a series of islands like a sort of Northern Venice and just as beautiful. It becomes rather difficult to get about at night unless you can hail a passing boat. In summer they have white nights, where there is no darkness. It's a bit difficult for night filming.

We went to the Hermitage, St Issac's Cathedral, though not the Church of the Holy Blood which was being mended after decades of ill treatment. St Issac's had a vast pendulum reaching right up to the roof. It had been redesignated as a museum of atheism, though curiously, the pendulum, which was supposed to direct the mind towards the practical rather than the spiritual, gave it a very religious feel. I was able with my Russian identity card and my name rather crudely spelt in Cyrillic letters to get in almost everywhere for nothing. I wonder if I could still use it?

We operated out of the Lenfilm HQ, now sadly deserted and occupied only by us and a little commercial. The canteen was closed. The lavatories were appalling and the walls were lined with pictures of past triumphs. The crew were mostly wonderful but the cameraman, Valery Martinoff, was surly, opinionated and slow. When we started work in the morning, it was later than I would wish, but nobody on the crew had a car; they all arrived by public transport looking immaculate and we knew that they were living hugger mugger in crowded flats and it must have been a real ordeal to keep clean and tidy.

At the beginning of a film it is customary to hold a meeting with all the heads of departments so that the director can talk through the whole film from start to finish and say what he needs for each scene. It can be changed later of course, but it establishes the frame-work to start with. The meeting normally takes about two hours. On this occasion Valery Martinoff argued every point and the meeting began to drag on. After five hours they said,
'Can we break for lunch?'
'No,' I said. 'We'll have lunch when we finish.'
It should be remembered that I was speaking French all the time. The interpreter was translating it into Russian. Martinoff would argue back in Russian and the interpreter would translate for my benefit into French. After ten hours I wound the meeting up and we sent out for roast chicken.

The extraordinary thing about the people in St Petersburg was their musical sophistication. When I interviewed actors and asked them if they sang or played an instrument they would say, 'Of course, doesn't everyone?'
We couldn't afford to hire the Philharmonic Orchestra, so had to recruit a line-up of eighty-five people from a general pool of musicians. It took us only a couple of days and they were all brilliant.

The Professor of Composition at the Conservertoire, who was reputed to have been a pupil of Prokoviev, came to advise us. He argued a great deal. He always called me Jeem and I called him

Professor. One day I got fed up and asked him what his first name was?

'Nikolai,' he said rather sulkily.

'Well if you call me Jim, I'll call you Kolya.' He still looked sulky.

We eventually found some locations. We even made them look a bit like Paris. On the first day of shooting, we did a complicated scene in which Francois Marthouret as Debussy was talking passionately with a number of colleagues. They talked Russian and he talked French. He found it extraordinarily difficult. He felt like saying after every speech: 'As tu fini?'

The rushes weren't very good, partly because of the hesitant acting, and partly because instead of sending away to London for fog filters, Martinoff had made some himself to save money.

The scene was unusable. Fortunately, to the fury of the production people, we could schedule an extra day at the end of the film. When we did so it was much better, except the actor playing Maeterlinck was unaccountably missing. This was unfortunate, as he challenged our hero to a duel in the scene, and I had to do a quick re-write saying, 'Monsieur Maeterlinck vous a envoye une telegramme.'

When we had a party we laid on a buffet and a lot of vodka. At the beginning everybody was rather stiff and polite. I asked,'Why aren't they eating and drinking?'

'They're waiting for you to start,' the production manager said. I obliged and they fell on the food and really hit the vodka.

When we eventually found a theatre that looked not unlike the Comedie Francaise I asked for a crane to do some dramatic shots linking a box with the stage. When I arrived in the morning I found Martinoff on his haunches puzzling over a mass of rusty pieces of equipment on the floor.

'Where's the crane?' I said.

'This is it,' he said.

'I asked for a crane from Moscow and they sent me this. I think it comes from Omsk.'

We built a rostrum instead.

Russian actors were marvellous to work with if not totally reliable. Sometimes they would disappear and we would have to shoot around them. When they finally turned up they would just mutter a very great deal and get on with it.

All the smart hotels and restaurants had security guards who wandered around looking menacing and being rude to the guests. Some of them carried guns and many wore the striped shirts of the Russian Special Forces. Some of the cast and I went to dine in one smart hotel. I was wearing a long jacket, one of the goons affected to regard it as an overcoat and grabbed me by the arm and told me to take it off and put it in the cloakroom. Francois for the first and only time spoke English. He said,

'How dare you speak to my friend like that! The iron curtain has been down for years and you are behaving like a KGB swine.' The astonished thug dropped my arm and we went into dinner.

The French were very choosy over their wine. Russians are in the main vodka drinkers and, except in Georgia, wine is regarded as a slightly effeminate import. In the hotel the price of a bottle of indifferent claret was £40. I suggested we buy some Australian wine at £15.

'Tu rigoles!' they said, 'Il n'est pas possible de boire ce piss de chameau.'
I persuaded them finally; they were still very suspicious though they eventually drank it.

Nadezhda Vasiliewseka was a very young and very brilliant costume designer. She drew half a dozen dresses for Therese Liotard for her first few scenes. They were lovely, but as I gently pointed out Therese was to go into mourning three quarters of the way through the picture when Debussy died and she would continue until the end. So perhaps it would be sensible to give her bright colours for the first few scenes? She looked distraught. She left and came back two days later with six more ravishing and colourful drawings.

It was difficult to find props in St Petersburg, the Lenfilm prop store had been looted so it would always be: 'I know somebody who has one.' We managed to dress the sets quite well nonetheless.

We had to shoot an audition scene. Debussy and his director were trying to cast Melisande; the actress had to have a pure, untrained, not too loud voice and be ravishingly pretty. We shot a montage scene with six sopranos from the Conservatoire, all singing a piece of the jewel song from Faust. We cut in shots of Debussy and the musical director smoking, looking bored and chatting, then we cut the whole thing together. When we came to dub it in France many of the French actors were in tears because the scene was so cruel and so real.

I gave myself a small but vital role. The original opening night of *Pelleas Et Melisande* at the Opera Comique was a fiasco. We shot several scenes with singers from the St Petersburg opera. They were superb and the tenor, especially, who played Pelleas, gave a wonderfully ironic bow to the booing sneering audience as he took his curtain call. As Melisande was saying, 'Je ne t'entend pas,' I, as a moustachioed brute in a box shouted: 'Nous non plus!' which set the whole audience roaring.

Sergei Zamourev played Debussy's friend Erik Satie. He was the only Russian actor who could speak perfect French, though with a slight accent. He played the piano beautifully and his rendition of *Gymnopedie* was superb. When we got to Paris the management would simply not have a foreigner speaking French. He was dubbed, albeit excellently, by a French actor.

I had an opportunity to see the skill of French actors at dubbing during a bedroom scene with Francois and Pascal Rocard. I had wanted a rain effect, as if sheets of water were slowly running down the windows and back-lit. The scene lasted five minutes; the effect looked very good but made a terrible noise, so we had to dub the whole scene. We started, as usual, doing it sentence by sentence. Then the actors said, 'Screw it let's try to do the whole scene in one.'
It was a complicated scene; much of it was in close-up where she is trying to get him to make love to her and he says: 'I don't feel like it.' (Je n'ai pas l'envie)
Amazingly they did it all in one take. I don't know any English actors who could do that.

We shot a scene by the sea which was supposed to be Deauville. On the day it was pouring with rain and blowing up a tempest. It was a languid scene with them all talking about how hot it was. I had to do a total re-write to match the weather. I felt very nervous. Fortunately the actors accepted my words gracefully, only occasionally correcting them. I described the Atlantic ocean ironically as 'un etang' (a pond) Francois changed it to 'une marre' (also a pond). The soft light filtered by the rain made the shots look like Impressionist paintings.

We had a contretemps between the cameraman or 'chef-op' Valery Martinoff and Therese Liotard which was partly my fault. He had stopped using fog filters on her as she grew older - typical Russian gritty realism - and certainly made her look much less attractive. She almost fainted when she saw the rushes and complained to Nelly. We had to re-shoot a whole scene between her and Marcel. Marcel hated her and refused to do it. I managed to persuade him and we shot much of the scene. Then Marcel left. For her close ups she had to play the scene with me. She was quite right actually. Martinoff was a miserable curmudgeon.

When we shot the long scene in the Philharmonic Hall which was supposed to be the Wigmore Hall in which, at the climax of the piece, Debussy collapses on the rostrum with a heart attack, it was uphill work. I may not be Humphrey Burton but I knew how to shoot an orchestra on film. Martinoff was slow and boringly painstaking. We needed a cameraman who would take risks and grab unexpected shots. He behaved as though it was the 1930s and he was shooting with heavy old-fashioned equipment.

The sequence was covered - just - after we had shot all night, but it could have been so much better.

We had a vodka soaked farewell party and the unit presented me with the carved wooden frog which Debussy had stolen during the film.

In Paris the Post Production went on for a long time. The company was good about expenses and I stayed in Paris for three or four days a week until we had finished.

One unexpected benefit: I had had a medical card when in Paris. I bethought myself of the generosity of the French social security system.
'Could I be due for a pension?' I asked.
Yes I was.

I now have a pension from the French Government of about £14.50 a month and all I have to do is once a year go to Richmond council and get them to stamp a form certifying that I am still alive. It pays for a bottle of Vodka every month and is very welcome.

# Chapter Thirty-Four
# **Bread On The Waters**

Cast your bread upon the waters and it will return after many days; or alternatively: Be nice to the people on the way up as you might meet them on the way down. In the 1980s, Graham Benson who was now a very distinguished producer, offered me one of the best scripts I had ever read. It was called *Slip Up*. It concerned Ronnie Biggs, one of the Great Train Robbers who escaped to Brazil and was tracked there by a group of free-wheeling jolly journalists who all joined in the chase and thought it was a tremendous lark. Or rather, most of them did.

The story which, was based on fact, was first told in a book by Anthony Delano. It was very patiently researched but didn't really come to life. The ideal person to do the film script was a journalist who was also a playwright; Keith Waterhouse wrote a wonderfully affectionate and foolish script which I fell in love with. The two protagonists were Biggs, who was subtly played by Larry Lamb, and Detective Chief Superintendent Slipper of the Flying Squad who was brilliantly brought to life by Jeremy Kemp.

The story was basically like this. A young reporter called Colin MacKenzie had information which he thought would lead him to where Ronald Biggs, the train robber was hiding. He confided in his superior, Vine and they both went to the editor of the *Daily Express* where they worked, asking to be allowed to follow the story up. The wily old Editor, played by Fulton Mackay, allowed them to carry on with it. MacKenzie found out that Biggs was in Brazil and wanted to give himself up. Biggs thought it would look better if he came back voluntarily to serve the rest of his sentence, and MacKenzie thought that he could get a book out of it, at least, and make his name as a journalist. The editor insisted upon calling in Scotland Yard and Jack Slipper was to accompany them to Brazil. Thus making MacKenzie betray him. The story broke and all Fleet Street followed them to Brazil. Journalists like Desmond Purgavie and Tony Delano were part of the pack. The *Express* sent one of their best photographers, Bill Lovelace, who had much more experience than MacKenzie and steered him along.

Everything went pear shaped in Brazil. Slipper arrested Biggs and took him to the police station. He, in fact, took him to the wrong police force: the local instead of the federal. Just as it seemed that he would be carried home in triumph by Slipper, Biggs discovered that if you were to have a child by a Brazilian citizen you could not be extradited, and his girlfriend immediately got pregnant.

Biggs was released and Slipper had to go home without his prey. Although Bill Lovelace had taken marvellous pictures throughout, it was Brennan of the *Daily Mail* who got the scoop picture. Slipper and his assistant were sitting in the aeroplane and when Jones, his assistant, left to go to the lavatory, Brennan snapped a shot of Slipper with an empty seat beside him which was spread all over the front page of the Mail with a caption.

*SLIPPER RETURNS WITHOUT HIS MAN*

All the actors became very excited by the film as did most of the real people. The real Colin MacKenzie was not best pleased nor was his boss Brian Vine. MacKenzie's career, which had seemed so promising had not turned out as well as expected. The real Bill Lovelace, who was played in the film brilliantly by Desmond McNamara came on location with us and took some splendid photographs.

The beginning of the film had a shot of Biggs running along the seashore. Biggs was quite a poet and had written a piece which we used:

*Well, charged I was and printed*
*My soul suffused with pain*
*I'd gone from rags to riches*
*And back to rags again*

*Then swiftly off to Bedford Nick*
*Into the flowery dells*
*Late night sombre silence*
*And foul familiar smells*

I felt the need of another verse so without asking permission from Ronnie Biggs I wrote one:

*But when I climbed that ladder*
*And skipped across the sea*
*I thought I'd done with birdlime*
*But it hadn't done with me.*

We were at tremendous pains to be as real as possible. At the time, the *Express* was still in Fleet Street in that black glass building known as the Ljubianka and we needed permission to shoot not only the exterior but the newsroom. Finally, they grudgingly gave us permission but said we could only use the newsroom on Sunday morning between 4.00 and 6.00 a.m. We had to work very, very fast and just managed to do the interiors before the real reporters came in and sat in their usual places. At the time of the Biggs incident the *Express* had just lost its pre-eminent position as biggest daily seller and they had to take the sign down from the front of the building. I was shooting this when suddenly they panicked, and said, 'If you do that we'll withdraw our permission.' But, generally speaking, the relationship worked very well.

During the preparation period we consulted with all the real people. As I said, Colin MacKenzie was not happy, but Slipper was less so. I had a lot of meetings with him and on one occasion he said, 'I can't get on the square with this script, Jim,' and did strange things with his feet. 'I'm sorry Jack I'm not one of the Brotherhood,' I said. Poor Jack certainly looked a little bit silly in the film but he looked even more silly in the actual case and, as brilliantly portrayed by Jeremy Kemp, seemed like a dogged, committed but not over intelligent officer.

We made enquiries about going to shoot in Brazil where over a third of the film took place. We were advised that the police would confiscate all our camera equipment and that we would have to bribe them heavily to get it back, so we abandoned the idea. Instead we decided to go to Portugal, where at least all the street signs were in the right language and the people, as I had found before, immensely enthusiastic. We got a local Rumba band called Roda Pe (which means skirting board) who went right through the film. We made Lisbon, look like Rio and we found some very good locations for Brasilia, the capital.

I had a scene where John Humphrys interviewed Slipper. It was a brilliant piece of reporting and he managed to doorstep him before any of the other reporters could find him. The scene was one of the few that really didn't work, partly because Humphrys was so well known. I asked the real John Humphrys if we could use a bit of the real film or alternatively whether he could do a little piece to camera for us. He said he would be delighted. This was vetoed by the Head of News, so I quietly got hold of a piece of news film from the library with Humphrys standing in front of the sugar loaf mountain and used that.

We started having serious legal trouble. Jack Slipper kept on saying he would sue us and the BBC. I felt the BBC didn't stand up to him. Colin MacKenzie persuaded Nigel Dempster to write a vicious piece about us in the *Mail* where he described the film as 'deeply flawed' and said it would have to be altered because of libel considerations by the bungling BBC at a cost of £200,000. We did in fact cut a couple of small scenes. The editing costs were about £150.

Dempster went on to say that the film was deeply insulting to Colin MacKenzie who was 'a former head boy of top public school Malvern,' though what that had to do with the matter, I had no idea. When the film went out the title was changed to *The Great Paper Chase* and it was much liked. Slipper eventually sued and the BBC agreed not to repeat it and to repay his costs.

There was at the time an absolute prohibition on using the word 'fuck' which made the confrontation scene between Biggs and Slipper a little bit awkward. The dialogue in real life and in the film went as follows:

Slipper: Hello Ronnie, long time no see.
Biggs:   Fuck me, how did you get here?

The film had to be agreed by Michael Grade. I had always believed that he watched two programmes at a time while answering the telephone and writing letters. Anyway he didn't seem to notice any four letter words in our film, and they remained as they were. I hope, eventually, this film which was brilliantly played by a cast who seemed to be having the time of their lives will be shown again. It would, I am sure, be well received.

# Chapter Thirty-Five

# Bread On The Waters Part II

By 1997, Graham Benson had set up a really nice little production company called Blue Heaven in Portsmouth with an enthusiastic crew and a strong line of supply to Meridian Television. They did the Inspector Wexford books and quite a lot of other short stories by Ruth Rendell. It should have gone on forever. Graham was intelligent and highly adaptable but a new Head of Drama was appointed at Meridian, who had been my AFM many years before and didn't seem to know how to deal with him, or anyone else for that matter.

Eventually in disgust Graham sold up. He had been a producer of great distinction and the fact that he is not working in television reflects very badly on television rather than on him. In 1997 he offered me a Ruth Rendell story called *May And June* which was only four pages long but had been beautifully adapted into a ninety minute film by Ken Blakeson.

I stayed in a house by the water's edge which was quite idyllic though I had to get my own meals. It was mid winter and the central heating had gone wrong. After a couple of days wearing my overcoat I managed to get it fixed. The office was full of young, attractive and keen people who were a pleasure to work with. Ken Blakeson's script was remarkable in that he had created real characters which only existed as two dimensional people in the short story. He had used a song from the 1950s which started as charming and innocent and became towards the end extraordinarily sinister:

*I see the moon, the moon sees me*
*Down by the shade of the old oak tree.*

We cast, as the more successful younger sister, Christine Kavanagh. Everybody congratulated her on being the voice of Babe in the film of that name. You may recall that Babe was a small and attractive pig. Of course we had got it wrong. The voice of Babe was recorded by Christine Cavanagh. There was much merriment about this.

The slightly suspect young composer who fell for both sisters, was to be played by Julian Wadham to whom I had offered a large part in *Fortunes Of War*. He turned it down, I think because he had a strong social conscience and preferred to do a Caryl Churchill play which was more relevant. The lead, a sister who had spent her life being put upon and turned out to be a scheming murderess was played by Phoebe Nicholls who was married to Charles Sturridge, another director. She was violently opinionated and awkward and questioned everything. She could be a pain, but was a magnificent actress who played the part superbly and should have had an even more successful career than she has had. Graham later said to me:

'She's a bit difficult, but you would work with her again wouldn't you?'
I said, 'You bet I would.'

We had some difficulty in finding a house in which June, the rich sister, lived. One in the village of West Meon was perfect inside, the other had a perfect front elevation. We combined the two to make them look like one house although they were two miles apart.

There was a stream running down the main street of the village. I thought it would be amusing to have a lot of playful white ducks swimming there, but the level was too low for the camera so eventually we dammed the stream and brought it up to the right level. When we introduced the ducks, who were charming, into the water they started looking a little bit unhappy. I asked the handler: 'What's the matter?'
She said, 'They're not used to swimming and I think they're going to sink.'
We had to shoot quickly before they drowned.

I always liked to introduce dogs into a film, as I'm sure will be apparent to my readers. We managed to get the local Beagles to have a meet in the main street with the huntsmen who I think were mostly stockbrokers and city gents rather self consciously blowing their horns. They were charming and slightly ill behaved (the dogs, I mean) and brought the whole street to life.

One of the locations we used in the village was owned by the managing director of Monsoon the chain of fashion stores. It was an act of kindness letting us use the house as he obviously didn't need the money. His wife was a vegetarian and had several Labrador retrievers whom she had also turned into vegetarians. We set up a party in the house with a lot of delicious sausage rolls and small meat pies. The hunger of the dogs for a meaty dish was more than our sentimental hearts could bear and we fed them with sausage rolls all evening.

The story was of two sisters. May, although she was the elder, had been continually put down by her family; she had met a young man who fell for her but immediately he met June he fell for her. They did not meet for some years. When the young man whom June had married, died, June tried to make amends with May and asked her to visit her. As they got to know each other better, June said she would leave her money to May when she died. This was obviously a difficult scene to play. It could come out as flagrant plot-laying or melodramatic nonsense. We did it as they were walking together. June let the news out casually and May fell about laughing. It was a very skilled performance by them both which made the scene real.

June then fell in love with the young composer and May worked hard to steal him from her and eventually succeeded. She cleverly gave herself alibis and worked out a scheme where she could shoot the composer and then her sister; it could be blamed on burglars. Melodrama it certainly was, and it took all of Phoebe's skill to make it appear real. The last scene happened in the graveyard in the pouring rain (supplied by the local fire brigade in vast quantities). Phoebe was standing there under an umbrella looking at the gravestone which bore the name of the man who had married June and deserted her. The scene was especially poignant for me, as William Douglas Home was buried in the same churchyard with a very simple stone saying William Douglas Home - playwright. Over a close up of Phoebe in the rain we played the song which had featured earlier in the film: 'I see the moon, the moon sees me, down by the shade by the shade of the old oak tree. Please let the light that shines on me, shine on the one I love.'

It was extremely eerie; we recorded Phoebe singing the song unaccompanied in the dubbing theatre. It was obviously quite a difficult job and I asked whether she would like me to give her the opening note.

'No,' she said and sang it perfectly in one take.

*May And June* was well received with quite a lot of publicity and repeated later on Channel Five for which of course I got no residuals. I use it very often when teaching students about the nature of adaptation from the short story.

# Chapter Thirty-Six
# **Mr Chairman**

No; not Mr Chair or Brother Chair or even Chair. I am not a piece of furniture. When I became Chairman of the Directors' Guild, Sue Dunderdale - a member of the council - said, 'You can't be Mr Chairman, it's gender-specific.'
'Wanna bet?' I said.

But all that happened much later. At the beginning of the 1980s I was elected to the council of BAFTA. You may remember how disappointed I was that there was no surprise in the announcement of awards in the 1960s and part of my reason for joining was this. In those days BAFTA was a much more relaxed place than it is now. The council consisted of mainly directors and producers with the occasional administrator and even one or two actors. We had quite recently moved into very sumptuous premises, formerly the Royal Watercolour Society in Piccadilly which we could barely afford. We used to invite people to dinner in the Run Run Shaw Theatre endowed by the Hong Kong millionaire who sold Tigerbalm. They were pleasant and useful occasions and we got quite interesting people to come and have dinner and talk including film producers, politicians, princesses and once a Prime Minister of which more later. It was run rather like an army mess and very relaxed.

Gradually, I made my way higher up the council and became elected Vice Chairman, Television. This meant I had to accompany Princess Anne at the craft awards and take some part in the proceedings of the main awards. At the time, the awards took place in the Wembley Conference Centre where no-one had anything to drink and the ceremony was followed by a dinner, which was felt by many to be unsatisfactory. One year we had what seemed like pork chops although they were alleged to be veal. With the large number of Jewish people in our profession, if they were pork chops it showed considerable lack of intelligence on the part of the management.

Many of us wanted to move the awards ceremony, which was, of course, at this time a combined film and television occasion away from the Wembley Conference Centre. Reginald Collin, a distinguished former actor, director and producer was the administrator of BAFTA. He had a pleasant but totally windowless office which began after a while to give him the symptoms of claustrophobia, an unexpected effect on someone so down to earth and together. The symptoms disappeared instantly when he moved out. He agreed that we should move the awards ceremony from Wembley. The only location big enough in central London to contain the 1,200 people whom we expected to attend, giving them dinner first and then a ceremony, was the Grosvenor House Hotel in Park Lane. Wembley squawked a great deal and there were rumours of lawsuits, but we left anyway.

Later, I was elected Chairman of BAFTA. It made a certain difference to my professional life. I had to turn down jobs which necessitated me being abroad for a long time. At the awards, the Chairman at the time had a very big role. He had to sit next to Princess Anne and have a table full of other distinguished guests, and when the awards started, make a spectacular entrance with the Princess down a set of rather awkward golden steps. Princess Anne managed this, no problem, I tripped once or twice. Before we went on, we sat back stage with Terry Wogan who afterwards appeared unexpectedly in *Sleep Six*. (qv)

I found Princess Anne not only impressive but extraordinarily attractive. I couldn't take my eyes off the insides of her elbows. She was also very amusing. When the coffee came around she said, 'A friend of mine was at one of these functions and the waiter who came around with the coffee was a very good looking black man; when he asked her how she liked her coffee she said "I like my coffee as I like my waiter, big, hot, strong and black." He said, "I'm sorry Ma'am we don't serve gay coffee."'

In 1985 the beginning of the evening had become a very pleasant social occasion and lots of people used to table hop. Sting's first wife, Frances Tomelty, whom I had worked with in the theatre, brought him over and said, 'I'd like you to meet my husband, Sting.' It seemed so ridiculous that I couldn't help laughing and to his great credit he laughed also.

One year Dame Anna Neagle came to sit at the table. She was absolutely charming and had beautiful manners which many of the smart and arrogant people who joined us did not have. I remembered that her name was Marjorie Robertson and that she had been one of Mr Cochrane's Young Ladies. She was delighted that I should remember this and I think she was the only person among the guests who wrote a charming bread and butter letter afterwards.

I never got a BAFTA award, unlike my son Simon, though I may have the record number of nominations, eleven in three categories.

During the second year that I was chairman we had Margaret Thatcher to dinner. I begged the council to go easy on her and let her get some dinner down her throat before pestering her with accusatory questions. 'If we want money from her, and we do, for God's sake go easy on her to start with,' I said. They all looked a bit truculent and said nothing. When she came in, she sat next to me and we chatted quite amiably but the trouble soon started. The council all whinged on and talked about how they had belonged to the Hampstead Labour Party and seemed to forget why we had asked her. She remained perfectly polite but left rather early. When she had gone I said, 'What bloody fools you all are, we could have got money out of her for the industry, or at least tax relief.' They mumbled on about retaining their own integrity. It was years later that Dickie Attenborough managed to glean some tax concessions from her. Much as I disliked her politics I thought we behaved insufferably rudely.

It had become the custom for each Chairman to leave a gift for the council to grace the dinner table. People had given decanters and various other items. Sydney Silverman, always generous, had given several objects including a chain of office for the Chairman which had been immensely expensive to produce and which we all refused to wear. I decided to give them an Irish Potato Ring which had belonged to my mother and which I had lined with blue glass and made into a salt cellar. I had engraved on it Laetus fui in academia. When I made the speech presenting it I rather oversagely said it was the salt below which ex-Chairmen and such would sit. Perhaps their wisdom would be useful and they could speak independently, being below the salt. Until recently it used to be displayed in the showcase at the top of the stairs at BAFTA. I asked plaintively where it was and it was produced for me to see. I notice it hasn't been cleaned in years!

One year after the awards I had begun the traditional walkaround to introduce the Princess to all the award winners when I suddenly needed to pee very badly. I had not taken the opportunity earlier in the evening but preferred to chat with people. It was agony, as the presentation went on for over forty minutes. I was so distressed I stopped remembering people's names and before she got to them, I sometimes had to whisper, 'Who are you?' Michael Buerk was extremely incensed at this and snapped his name back at me. The lead singer of Claddagh in contrast was absolutely charming and said, 'Please don't worry, we're Claddagh,'
'Of course you are,' I said, 'I knew that all the time really,' and smiled at her. Michael Caine whose name I didn't forget, surprised me a little. Princess Anne asked him, 'Where do you live?' He said, 'I live abroad because of the taxes, they're outrageous and I can't afford to live here.'
'Cheeky thing,' I thought to myself.

We decided to take Princess Anne over to Hollywood to promote British films. Three or four of us were to accompany her. We travelled on the late much lamented British Caledonian Airlines. We sat in business class while the Princess and her Equerry sat in First. After a few drinks we decided to send a small gift forward to the Princess. Knowing she never drank alcohol we sent her a can of Coca-Cola with a note saying 'A respectful gift from your council.' It obviously got a bit damp on the way forward due to condensation. Her Equerry sent us back a note which read, 'The Princess thanks you for your gin-sodden note and hopes you will sober up by the time we get to Los Angeles.'

While we settled in to the Beverley Hilton Hotel, Princess Anne was performing another engagement with a ballet company. The place was awash with security staff, all of whom were looking steely eyed and grim, apart from our own inspector from the Royal Protection Squad. He was wearing a little badge marked F in his lapel. I asked him what it was.
'It's for firearm,' he said, 'The Americans make me wear it.'
'Have you got a gun?' I asked.
He winked and flashed his coat back for a fifth of a second to show me the automatic in its holster.

We had been given a choice of films to take with us for the gala performance. One was *Superwoman* which had been produced by Tim Burrill, a former chairman of the academy, and the other was a very splendidly amusing story about the Glasgow ice cream wars, called *Comfort And Joy*. This was the one we chose. We had a very grand reception at the American Academy and I had to introduce Princess Anne to a whole host of British expatriates including Stewart Granger and Elizabeth Taylor. Elizabeth Taylor had been a little bit awkward about coming; she said she would only come if I would escort her.(Not because it was me, she didn't know me from Adam, it was the office not the man) It was explained gently that I couldn't do that, as I was escorting Princess Anne but eventually we got around it and someone else escorted her. She behaved beautifully when introduced and afterwards Princess Anne said, 'What an amazing front' which I took to be royalspeak for bosom. As I went around the line introducing people, all the photographers kept on shouting 'Sir, sir' meaning get out of the way of my shot. Of course the trouble was that when I moved one way I would be in someone else's shot so with great difficulty I dodged around as much as I could.

The showing of the film went really quite well considering most of the audience couldn't understand the Scots accents. The Princess could and she clapped with pleasure when a piper came on.

Earlier in the day I had an object lesson in security. When a VIP gets into the first or second car of a line of cars all the car doors are closed at once. This is because it is thought that getting into and out of cars is the most dangerous time when snipers can pick off a VIP. I was travelling in the third car with the British Consul-General. As the door was closed on me I fell headlong at his feet. He smiled in that usual sinister foreign office way.

At the dinner after the film I had to make a long speech and it would not have looked good if I had been reading it. I was able to keep it in my cupped hand and not be noticed. When I escorted Princess Anne outside the restaurant there was a lot of spontaneous cheering. The Americans love royalty.

At another big reception I had to find as many interesting people as possible to present to the Princess, which was quite difficult: her lady in waiting kept hissing in my ear. I got hold of a very well known and heavily made up alleged actress and her young man and brought them over. There was a short wait as Sydney Silverman was introducing his accountant and he was droning quietly on. The lady said to me, 'Do you expect me to hang around here all night?'
I suddenly found myself becoming very angry and said, 'I don't give a damn whether you stay or go, but, if you are going to stay, just shut up.' She did. When I finally introduced her to Anne she started making remarks about how dreadful the press were. We all knew the *Daily Mirror* was going to break a story that day about Anne and her husband Mark. They had not much evidence to go on except that they were staying in different hotels. She was very persistent and said, 'I do think The Daily Mirror is the worst paper of the lot don't you?'

The Princess was way ahead of her. She said, 'Yes they're supposed to be breaking a story today about me and Mark, I don't know where they get the information from, but it's a lot of nonsense really,' and she gave a little nod and the removal of eye contact which Royalty does so well meaning Bugger Off, I want to talk to someone else.

We flew home the next day. We all, quite unashamedly, were very fond of Princess Anne and wanted to show our appreciation. We said we would like to give her a gift and that we would like her to come to dinner and we would present it to her. What she really wanted was an ice cream maker which was really very cheap. We had a very pleasantly riotous dinner and she left with the ice cream machine.

She is an extraordinary woman. She has connections with so many organisations that you would expect her to be a little bit tongue-tied, but she knew all about our Academy and quite a lot about the British Film Industry. When we had two different ceremonies, which were the craft awards and the main awards, she chose very often to come only to the craft awards feeling that they were more important. It certainly pleased all the technicians who were there to receive their awards. Dickie Attenborough is a splendid president, but I will never forget Princess Anne.

After two years as Chairman, I stood down. During my time there the council meetings had been very relaxed and jolly affairs and anyone who got too serious was immediately crushed. We had one difficult decision. Anthony Thomas had made a film called *Death Of A Princess* about the Saudi Royal Family. There had been a rumour that one of the Saudi Princesses had fallen in love with a young man and committed adultery with him. She was wrapped in a sheet and shot and he had his head cut off in public rather slowly. Anthony made it into a sort of dramatised documentary, which we had decided to show to an invited audience. From the start it caused a lot of trouble and various threats were made by the Saudi government if we continued to show it. The Foreign Office panicked and we were told, though not officially, that if we had our showing it would cause great harm to Saudi-British trade and that the government would be very angry and we would lose our royal patronage. Some of the more pathetic members of council were keen to cancel. I said that if we did cancel, I personally would go public with it and cause much more trouble than we had already. We had the showing followed by a very vigorous discussion. The film had been made in Egypt with an Egyptian crew and, you may remember from an earlier chapter, that the crew had all been blacked and unemployed until we made *Fortunes Of War*.

Some years later my friend Eddie Mirzoeff became Chairman. He was one of the old crew who had joined in Council meetings with enthusiasm but no intensity. On his leaving the Chairman's job he said that he was rather sad that Council meetings had become very intense and humourless. He held a reception at which all the former Chairmen, including me, were made life members and presented to the Queen.

The Directors' Guild was an organisation which had its roots in the Producers' and Directors' Society. It was almost entirely the creation of Piers Haggard who worked tirelessly over the years on behalf of directors and was recently, and deservedly, given life membership of the Guild. I was number eight in the guild membership; in fact one of the founder members. I got elected chairman after a couple of years and did what I could to advance the interests of directors which was very uphill work. The companies and the BBC, once they saw that they had a chance to seize power, rewrote agreement after agreement and treated directors very shabbily. One of the problems was the diversity of unions. ACTT (Association of Cinema and Television Technicians) represented directors with the ITV companies and in feature films. There was no way you could get anywhere without an ACTT ticket and they were very hard to get hold of. My son Simon did nearly six months as a runner on a television series and then on the film, *1984*, where he was given much more responsibility than one would expect. He was then offered a job with the BBC as an AFM. He had been on the verge of getting a ticket because of his film work, but when he joined the BBC they said, 'Start again. You're on two years probation from now.' I found them always a cruel and ruthless union run by politically active and not necessarily very talented people. Alan Sapper in particular, the general secretary, was almost as ruthless as his predecessor George Elvin. There were many cases of people being refused tickets. When the BBC trained a lot of new directors in the 1960s not all of them could be employed there but the ACTT refused to give them tickets even though they had done six months training. The only union recognised by the BBC was the Association of Broadcasting Staff (ABS).

By the 1980s the whole structure was beginning to break down and, as a temporary measure, we formed an organisation called the Directors' Council which consisted of two people from the Directors' Guild, two from ACTT and two from ABS and with a theoretically neutral chairman. We had various meetings over the months and gradually they developed all the characteristics of old fashioned union politics. People would say 'On a point of order, Brother Chair' and there were interminable small nit picking arguments. When we attempted to bring up a point under Any Other Business we were told that because we hadn't given notice in advance that we were bringing up a point, it was not to be permitted.

Alvin Rakoff and I were the DGGB representatives. After a very great deal of fruitless meetings, we decided the time had come for action. We stood up and said, 'We're leaving, we'll resign from this foolish organisation and those of us who are members of both your unions will also resign and we are reporting to our council what has happened and encouraging all our members to resign.' The ACTT representative said, 'You'll be blacked, you'll never work again.'
We said, 'Bollocks,' and left forever.

One of the great strengths of DGGB was Suzan Dormer the administrator. We had all spent a lot of thought on how to get hold of director's residuals which existed in the continent of Europe. There were large sums of money sitting in banks because under European Law royalties belonged to the directors and not the producers even though the producers were doing their best to get their hands on the money. Piers Haggard and Suzan worked very, very hard to establish contact with all the European agencies. They all said they would only release the money to a properly formed and constituted collection agency so the Guild formed one called DPRS - The Directors and Producers Rights Society, modelled on the Performing Rights Society (PRS) which has a turnover of tens of millions a year. When DPRS started, it had to be separated entirely from the Guild due to British Union Law. This was a great pity because it took away the incentive for Directors to join the union. If they had been forced to join before they could get paid any residuals they would have flocked to do so. Suzan moved over to become General Secretary of DPRS which grieved many of us in the Guild. She now runs it superbly, and I am pleased to be on its council. In the first year we distributed a few hundred pounds. By this year we had distributed more than ten million.

Pennant Roberts is the Chairman, who was a director and producer who was prepared to give many hours of his time to the organisation. Gradually contacts are made with collection agencies all over Europe and although many of the sums are not large it is really nice to see distinguished old film directors who are having a hard time suddenly get cheques for a few thousand pounds.

The Guild continues due to the devoted work of a few people, now no longer myself. What we all hope will be the turning point is the establishment of a Directors' Guild Awards Night which in January 2004 was adjudged a great success, and in 2005 even more so.

# Chapter Thirty-Seven
# All The World's A Stage

When I was still quite a young director, an old actor took me to lunch at the Garrick Club and we sat at the centre table.

'Would you like to join this club?' he asked.

'Yes, I think I would,' I said. I wasn't very keen on clubs but I liked this one with its varied membership and rather raffish air.

'We must see what we can do,' he said.

This was in 1968 and I gradually forgot about it.

Sixteen years later, Nigel Havers offered to put me up.

'You can't,' I said, 'X offered to put me up years ago, and I must have been blackballed.'

'If you'd been blackballed, you'd know it,' said Nigel and he put me up.

Old X had evidently forgotten all about it.

It took three years to get in. In the eighteen years I've been a member I've met all sorts and conditions of men: actors, barristers, writers, painters, novelists, judges, publishers, even the occasional businessman.

I got to know Kingsley Amis rather well; he'd been a distant acquaintance before. He helped me very considerably with a lecture I was giving at Swansea University. On the first Thursday of the month, a lot of theatricals appear and behave rather raucously. This funny old place is one of my greatest pleasures; the conversation is intelligent and amusing, and if you choose to sit at the centre table you must have your wits about you; you might find yourself sitting between a former chancellor of the exchequer and an American professor.

Every now and then the Garrick organises what it calls a Library talk. The room is beautiful and I used to work there quietly when I started this book. It has what is probably the world's best collection of playbills and books about the theatre. The library doesn't hold an audience of more than about thirty five, but it is one of the most penetrating and critical in the world, though always rigorously polite. When I was asked to give a talk, I turned up early, sick with nerves and hid in the little room under the stairs. My friend, Peter Sallis, came in and proceeded to mock and insult me in the roundest terms which made me feel a lot better. He then bought me a cup of tea and wished me luck. The talk included quite a chunk of this book and I think it went reasonably well. Afterwards, I felt absurdly pleased to be sat down at the head of the centre table, supposedly Sir Henry Irving's place, and given dinner.

My son Din is a member and asked me there once as his guest, which made me rather proud. When people ask, 'How can you bear to belong to such an old-fashioned institution?' I laugh quietly to myself.

# Chapter Thirty-Eight
# Enforced Leisure

My original idea was to call this book *Screen Directing For Pleasure And Profit* and you will find at the end of the book some sage words of advice to young and old directors.

But as you get older, no matter how skilled you are you will find that fewer and fewer people are seeking to employ you. In feature films it is slightly different. Directors can go on until they are very old indeed, like Fred Zinnemann, a man whom I admired immensely. But much of their time is spent talking about films rather than making them. The vitally important thing is to keep your brain active; presumably you have saved enough money to live fairly frugally for the rest of your life. The problem is not so much lack of money as the possibility that your brain might atrophy. In our business you don't retire, but you can quite often be totally unemployed. There are various ways of keeping your brain active and lively. Teaching is one and arguably you ought to be putting as much as you can into the business in gratitude for what you have taken out of it. Writing is another. It has now become extremely hard to get a novel published or even to get an agent, but this has always been the problem with novelists. One very successful novelist got so dispirited with the number of rejection slips she had had that she threw the manuscript into the dustbin and covered it with potato peelings and other rubbish. Her husband came home and rescued it and the potato stained manuscript was sent to a publisher who accepted it and it became a great success. However many rejection slips you get, you have to remain convinced of your own talent and above all, keep working.

There follows a selection of the things that I have done in the last few years since I stopped working regularly, to keep my brain active.

1. TEACHING IN ENGLAND.

The Actors' Centre is a brave organisation which just manages to keep going because of the devotion of its staff. They run two-day courses for actors. They pay directors reasonably well for extraordinarily hard work. They now have so many directors to choose from that work has become much scarcer. I encourage the actors, of whom I teach a dozen at a time, to prepare a piece, either that they have played before or that they want to play, and I persuade them to offer parts to the other students. Each student has to bring a videotape and for the first day we rehearse the different scenes. Actors are extraordinary people, they will give themselves to a period of instruction as much as they would to a well paid play.

At the end of the first day we bring in a cameraman and start shooting the scenes which they have prepared. It is quite hard work for the instructor. He has to make ten or twelve little films in two days and give the students something to take away with them. Sometimes, you have to shoot a scene twice, so that each of the two people in it has a copy. At the end we play all the scenes back. They learn as much from their own scenes as they would from those of all the other students. I find the whole process immensely stimulating and meet a lot of old friends as well as some very talented new young actors.

## 2. TEACHING ABROAD

Verde Valley School in Sedona, Arizona is a very progressive high school in the desert. It was founded in the 1940s by a group of idealists and the first set of pupils had to build the school. It has since grown enormously. I was asked to come and put on a play with the students. Saul Benjamin was the headmaster and it was a fairly brutal assignment. I had twelve days from start to finish, to cast, get a set ready and rehearse the play. I chose *The Devil's Disciple* by G. B. Shaw which I thought would intrigue the kids. There were more girls than boys at the school and there were some native Americans as Verde Valley had a policy of giving scholarships to a number of kids from a tribe who lived at the bottom of the Grand Canyon. I wrote a new introduction for the play and had made an enormous copy of the 1775 Grand Union flag which acted as a front cloth; at the beginning of the play it was torn from top to bottom.

Several of the kids were very talented. One or two were seriously boring and there is always one in America who is truculent, chews gum and wears a baseball cap on back to front. A lot of the girls did their very best to shock me. I asked the stage manager where Courtney and Amelia were. She said, 'They're having sex in the next room. Oh gosh, I wasn't meant to tell you that.' But so long as I remained cool they worked very well.

I had been told that it was always warm in the desert and I wouldn't need any sweaters or top-coats. As soon as I got to Arizona, it started to snow very heavily.

The school had a splendid plan for getting the kids on horseback out into the country which was very wild and hilly. They lent me a quarter-horse, so called because it has big hind quarters. It had been trained to be controlled with one rein just touching very gently at the side of the neck to make it turn left and right. We rode down a very steep hill covered in mesquite and sagebrush. The horse was very sure footed but slithered a little and I got punctured in the leg by a sharp thorn and bled copiously. I was taken to the local doctor who gave me a local anaesthetic and put a lot of stitches in.

Saul and I, on my one day off, made an expedition to the Grand Canyon. It was still snowing quite heavily and we decided to walk down one of the paths leading to the bottom. We slithered about so much but we only got half way down before it was time to come back up again. I hope one day to see what it looks like from the bottom.

An isolated community like this is always full of quarrels and feuds and provided an outsider can remain apart from them all he can do very well. But once he starts allying himself with one faction - look out! It was a very satisfying eleven days though not at all highly paid.

The next time I went to Sedona, which, by the way, had a sort of holy mountain from which Shirley Maclaine was convinced that she would be drawn up to heaven; it looked fairly ordinary to me. The really spectacular scenery appears in Utah the state next door. I discovered that Saul had left and that the head teacher was now the Chairman of the Board, and when I asked why, everyone was a little bit tight lipped about it. Saul was a brilliant Fulbright scholar who did many jobs including serving in Bill Clinton's government but never seemed to realise his potential.

This time I decided to do a version of *McLibel!* which I had done for Channel 4 as a three hour television play. I had to cut it down to about an hour and a half. The two leading parts were played by a pair of very bright kids who behaved astonishingly badly. The only way I could bring the girl to heel was to say that I had one of the teachers on stand-by to perform if she wasn't able to do so. She threatened at least twice a day to walk out because the part was making her ill. I smiled and said nothing.

I managed to cast the play quite well, but I couldn't find anybody to play the Judge and in the end decided to play it myself. I managed, by a lot of blackmail and cajolery to get a pair of wigs from England for counsel for McDonalds and for me as the judge.

As in the television production, the words had to be dead right, and there was no paraphrasing because they were words actually spoken during the trial. The kids became slightly bored with the show. There was a lot of horrific evidence about how filthy McDonalds restaurants were and how badly the staff were treated and in what monstrous conditions the animals were kept. I found great difficulty in learning the judge's lines and nobody would hear me rehearse my words because they felt too embarrassed. I had a desk covered in briefs and notebooks and all my cues written out on them and just got away with it. When we came to the performance, the kids were very surprised at the reaction of their parents who were all hippies from way back and the performance was punctured by cries of 'Right on!' and 'Give it to them, buster!' It was a really very successful production and I was amazed at how quickly the kids could learn their lines and develop their characters in such a short time.

The school seemed to be flourishing and I hope it still is.

3.  A LECTURE TOUR

With a very great deal of hard work I managed to arrange a lecture tour of four universities, Middlebury College, Vermont, UMass at Amherst, Stonehill and Susquhanna in Pennsylvania. I had prepared the lectures in some detail though there had to be some variation for each college.

The money wasn't terribly good and I suddenly got a commission to do an article for *Harpers And Queen* on New England in the Fall which fitted exactly. I could bring Maggie with me, I was able to hire a car, and many of the hotel expenses were paid for by the magazine. It became slightly difficult, because we had to go to certain specified hotels, many of which were not really very nice and I couldn't exactly say anything vile about them in the article. I think I irritated the editors of the magazine by praising the state of Maine too much, which is my favourite state on the Eastern seaboard. There is a story of an old man in Maine sitting on a stoop on a rocking chair at the junction of two roads. The signpost to one says MILLANAUKET 6 MILES and the sign post to the other says the same. A New Yorker in a fast convertible comes roaring up to the old man and says:

'Does it matter which way I go to Millanauket?'

The old man says, 'Not to me, it don't.'

Middlebury is a very rich college, where my friend John Wilders used to teach. We stayed in one of the only two hotels, which managed to hold the parents up to ransom every graduation day. It was a pretty little town but there was no excuse for most of the rooms opening onto a rather crummy car park. The other hotel was charming and beautifully furnished and unfortunately did not open until the next week. I had to write a report for the magazine telling them what I really thought of the two hotels without being really obvious, I think it worked.

Amherst is a nice little town whose population trebles during term time. It has five colleges in or around it and I was invited there by Jim Leheny who became a great friend and later invited me to do a summer school in Oxford.

We stayed at the Trapp Family Hotel up in the mountains. They were the people who were afterwards dramatised in The Sound of Music. It was charming and astonishingly Austrian in feel. All the waitresses wore dirndl skirts and embroidered blouses. The lavatories had cute representations of Austrian boys and girls on the doors. It had been a small but successful venture until it burnt down a few years ago and was rebuilt as a vast place capable of taking several hundred guests.

Stonehill was a Catholic college and Marlene, my friend, was rather prized as being the only Jew. She would get into furious philosophical fights with all the old priests. When I came to do the lecture, Marlene gave a very embarrassingly complimentary introduction about our history which made me squirm a little.

Roger Bacon wrote that universities were like Horti Conclusi - walled gardens, with all the advantages and disadvantages of enclosure. I remember vividly the fact that at Stonehill the drama students who would have benefited most from the lecture were not permitted to come by their professor. In fact nearly all of them did come in, about five minutes late, and it was obvious that many of the Faculty were not speaking to one another. The technician organising the playback for the lecture was very keen and anxious to help. He gave me a tape of the whole proceeding converted into 625 lines but unfortunately he had forgotten to turn on the microphone during the lecture. I have hesitated to play it back ever since.

It is difficult to know where to pitch your talk: some American students are amazingly naïve and easily shocked, and others as worldly-wise as Oxbridge students. You have to judge your audience as you go, and be prepared to alter it on the hoof. In the next engagement I failed to do this.

Susquhanna was a very small university which was extraordinarily rich and had been a Lutheran seminary. They were charming people and John Bennett had been given an Honorary Doctorate of the university. I couldn't quite imagine why, unless it was because he had played Al Johnson's agent in the eponymous musical. The principal benefactor of the university was the nephew of the real agent. He was determined to reward John and recommended him for a Doctorate. He looked very distinguished in his gown.

Susquhanna, although it was a small liberal arts college with about 1,500 students had three auditoria, the biggest of which, a combined theatre and chapel held 2,000, and I gave a lecture there. I was shown around the music school full of beautiful practice rooms and a small concert hall and remarked upon it. They said this was well out of date and they were going to knock it down and build a new one.

I made a mistake in treating the students like English students. These kids weren't even allowed to drink until they were 21; we had a small reception with only watery orange juice to drink. One of the sequences I showed was a montage from *Oxbridge Blues* which I thought hugely funny but it was very sexy. When it was finished I detected a slightly prim demeanour among the Faculty and even among the students. I had forgotten that it was originally a Lutheran seminary.

The article turned out rather well. I had to take all my own pictures on slides for it and they were reproduced beautifully in the magazine. At the end of the trip we stayed with Marlene in Boston. I do not recommend driving in Boston. It is a bloody nightmare, not only because they are frantically rebuilding the city but because you get lost more than in any other city I have visited.

4. SUMMER SCHOOL

I was asked to do a six week summer school at Trinity College, Oxford for the University of Massachusetts in 2001 and was devastated to have to refuse as I had a job directing *Holby City*. However they brought the kids across to Elstree Studios and I was able to give them a couple of lectures. I also travelled to Oxford to give another lecture for which I was shamefully overpaid.

The next year I was free to do the summer school and it was quite idyllic. I had very comfortable rooms in college, not too many pupils and a very pleasant room in which to teach. There was a carving above the fireplace with two trees, one of which said Arbor Scientiae and the other Arbor Experientae. I pointed these out to the kids and asked for a translation. Not one of them had learnt any Latin so I was obliged to translate it and say I didn't expect them to work too hard in climbing the tree of knowledge but they should leave time for climbing the tree of experience. In fact, like all people who teach subjects connected with the media, I made them work harder than most of the other courses. My course was on writing for the screen.

One thing I was able to give them was individual tutorials which they were not used to and I think appreciated. I spent some thought on what films or television programmes to use. I decided to look only at adaptations, mainly of classics and to concentrate on my own productions even though many of them might probably seem out of date because, knowing the background in detail, I was able to give them an insight into the problems of production. They seemed to appreciate everything they saw and wrote really very good essays. By the end of the course they were supposed to submit a completed film script and those who wished were given a chance to shoot something, as I had got a pair of video cameras for them to play with. What struck me forcibly was how confident kids are with technical equipment nowadays. I had thought to bring in a cameraman but soon abandoned this idea as unnecessary.

I had to grade the kids and this counted towards their degrees. They had all paid a lot of money for the course so I hated the idea of failing any of them. There was one girl who was seriously stupid and incompetent but very beautiful. I was on the verge of failing her and as soon as she saw this I made absolutely sure never to be alone with her and in the end I gave her a D which just allowed her to pass.

It was quite an idyllic six weeks. I made them work quite hard and worked very hard myself. I think they got as much from the atmosphere of Oxford as from the course. I hope they did anyway.

Trinity College is a proper size, only about 250 people, much better than my own which now has about 900. Being interested in heraldry I was fascinated to see a coat of arms above the fireplace in Hall which was of the English Royal Arms quartered with those of Spain. Then of course I remembered the queen who founded the college was Bloody Mary who was married to Philip of Spain. Only 100 yards away they had burnt Latimer and Ridley alive as heretics. In order to hasten his death they had given Latimer a bag of gun powder to hang around his neck and when the flames caught it, it blew his head off right across the road and smashed into the main gates of Balliol College.

## 5. A FILM SCRIPT

I had read many years before Allan Prior's *The One Eyed Monster*. It described to me with extraordinary accuracy what television was like in those early days. I asked him if I could write a screenplay of it and he agreed. Because I remembered vividly a lot of the details of those days I think it was rather good. It was about six months' hard work. He and I and our agents had a little discussion about it. He decided that he wanted the credit to be dramatised by Allan Prior and James Cellan Jones. 'Not on your nelly,' I said, 'It's got to be by James Cellan Jones and Allan Prior.' He went and whispered a little to his agent and agreed. It is the most fiendishly hard thing to sell but we might just manage to do it.

## 6. BATTERY CHICKENS

Shaun Hill, the Ludlow chef, said it only takes a bit of humility to make a good meal out of good ingredients but there is nothing you can do with battery chickens apart from giving them to someone you don't like. *Holby City* is a battery chicken.

I was asked to see Kathleen Hutchison, then the Executive Producer of *Holby City* and for the first time in my life, had an hour's audition. On the face of it I was an ideal candidate, as I had produced and directed many better programmes than *Holby City* and I had a good general knowledge of medicine, having been brought up in a doctor's family and studied medical sciences at university.

I discovered she was called Executive Producer and that each episode had a producer. Overloaded at the top I thought. My producer was called Matt Tombs and it was his first ever production in any medium. We seemed to get on all right. He seemed to be very nervous of anything innovative or unconventional: His inexperience showed strongly and I didn't really know what he was there for. The much feared Mal Young was in the background as another executive producer.

The trouble with soaps is that the producer has to be someone of great integrity as Gerry Glaister was all those years ago. Some of the writers on Holby were potentially very good but they got steered in the direction that the management pushed them. You could see their faces sag as they realised what had been done to their scripts. Poor Matt Tombs said, 'I long for the script that is not finalised until the seventh or eighth draft instead of the third or fourth,' thus leaving no room for flashes of brilliance or outrageous ideas by directors or writers. So, when a new character was introduced: Doctor Griffin played by that fine classical actor Hugh Quarshie, his character was established as having several failed marriages and he was strapped for cash paying enormous alimony. This meant that the writers were forced into making Doctor Griffin talk about his problems to all and sundry in every scene, in the operating theatre, in the street and in the locker room in front of very junior staff. Why on earth was he in the locker room anyway, as he had his own office? Hugh is a professional who managed to speak fast enough and to take attention away from the rubbishy dialogue to make the part interesting. In the scenes where he didn't have to talk about his wives he was very strong.

Many of the actors, Siobhan Redmond, Dominic Jephcott and others managed by sheer craftsmanship to make banality acceptable. They worked terribly hard and were a pleasure to direct.

The schedules were quite severe. We shot six minutes a day working from 8.00 a.m. until 7.00 p.m. This is quite possible if the cast and crew are totally committed to what they are doing and one can even make time for a rehearsal. I was used to producers being close colleagues of the actors and directors. On *Holby City* they seemed a race apart.

The surgeons who advised us on operating scenes were wonderful. Shyem Kolvokar and Rupert Kipping were inspiring. If one could get the public to watch the skilful business on the table they could blot out the poor dialogue.

To prepare for the series I went to the Middlesex Hospital to watch Shyem operate. It was amazing; he replaced an aortic valve and, unexpectedly, an atrio-ventricular valve. He worked with absolute confidence and precision. He and his staff were all Indian. In India a surgeon has first to qualify in general surgery before specialising in cardiac surgery. As the child of a very versatile general surgeon, it seems to me to be a very good idea. The operation lasted four hours. I was never further than eighteen inches from the patient's heart. Shyem kept calling for slush. I found that this meant crushed ice of which jugfulls were poured into the cavity to keep the heart fresh. Later Shyem instructed me how to reproduce a heart operation with a prosthetic figure. I said I wanted more blood so we wrote into the script that the surgeon had nicked the aorta and there was a great fountain of blood, which was speedily controlled.

My second episode was saved from banality by a strong storyline. A young girl with advanced cancer beautifully played by Hollie Chapman knew that she was about to die and wanted to be baptised. Her father hated the idea and thought it was all mumbo jumbo. The child was befriended by an outreach nurse, Keri McGrath, played by Anna Mountford, a regular in the series. Unsoapily, the child died and was given the last rites. Nick Warburton who wrote the scenes beautifully was persuaded to cut the actual death. I put it back in. I wanted to hear the words:

*Eternal requiem grant to her O Lord,*
*And let light perpetual shine on her.*

It was very moving.

In spite of everything I loved working with actors again and I think I made a lot of difference. The give-away dead-eyed look present in most soaps was mostly absent from my episodes.

On the last day a group of actors led by Siobhan Redmond grabbed hold of me and pushed me into Kathleen Hutchison's office. They said, 'This is the best director we have ever had and you've got to ask him back.' Kathleen's little eyes narrowed. I told my friend Peter Smith about it sometime later. 'I bet she never asked you back again,' he said.
'Right,' I said, 'Got it in one.'

There is a strange postscript to this story. Early in 2005 I was chairing a jury for the Directors' Guild awards. Among the contenders was a show called *Bodies* which had been shown only on BBC4. It was a hospital drama series, containing all the medical and social problems of a hospital, and it made *Holby City* look like what it was, a cynical piece of tired soap opera. It was written and produced by a doctor and brilliantly directed by John Strickland. It was everything that *Holby City* wasn't, but could have been. I am glad to say we gave it the award.

7. NOW IS THE TIME FOR ALL GOOD MEN...

I have always been of a liberal term of mind and for the last forty years have been a member of the Liberal Democratic party. I don't much like party workers of any stance. They seem, however worthy, to be nerdish anoraks, though the liberals were better than most. I used occasionally to do a bit of canvassing and sit outside the polling station smiling at the voters. The local Liberals used to use our garden for their annual fete until one of them found some dog poo and his little face creased up in horror and they stopped coming.

Many years later, during a period of enforced idleness, the headquarters of the party asked me to come and help give instruction to some of the MPs.

I found it interesting, I concentrated on looking at people's mannerisms both vocal and physical and I think I was able to be of some help. I always started off by saying 'You have a big advantage over the other two parties, you mostly believe what you are saying.'
I tried to give people advice quietly as I would an actor, but some of the party officials said, 'No we want all the criticism out in the open.'

I told Jenny Tonge, MP for Richmond, where I live, that when she was argued into a corner her voice went up an octive. She said, 'No it doesn't,' and immediately demonstrated the truth of what I had said and then laughed.

178

Generally speaking, the MPs and officials were extraordinarily pleasant and grateful. I was able to advise them of foolishly simple things, like which was their best side, a simple thing which any actor would know.

Simon Hughes, especially, realised at once that his left side was the best. It is quite difficult for MPs who are doing an interview in close up and who know which angle favours them most; often it is not a question about how pretty they are, but how honest they look. They often have to bully the interviewer into sitting at the side of the camera which will give them the best eye-line. and put up with the sneers which are every interviewer's stock in trade.

Another whom I liked very much was Lord Dholakia, who was extraordinarily humble and intelligent and only needed a little arrogance to make communicating easier. I think I was able to help him, though his inherent good nature, which was his warmest characteristic, would always shine through,.

I got the chance of directing a party politcal broadcast with Charles Kennedy, the Party leader. I put him at the window of the new building which houses MPs offices, Portcullis House, and was able to keep a bit of Westminster Hall in the background. Then I got him to turn and we cut inside. The cameraman and sound recordist were both giving their services for nothing, as I was, and we spent some time getting the lighting right and making it look rich and pleasant.

I sent out for a bunch of flowers, because the interior looked a little bit sterile and at the last moment took some petals off one of the flowers and spread them artistically on the table. Charles was absolutely charming and very amusing and easy to direct. I only had to say, 'I don't believe a word of it' and he would reply, 'Quite right neither do I,' and then we'd do it again. I think the party political broadcast looked good but, later on, a production company offered all their services free to the party and that included a director so I never did any more.


8. DRAGON'S BREATH


The little village of Pilton lies in the Vale of Avalon about six miles from Glastonbury. The church where Maggie and I were married, and forty years later Simon and Star, lies just above the Manor House. If you walk down the hill to the bridge where the little Whitelake river flows out into the flat lands of Somerset you come to a place known locally as the Harbour where, according to legend, Joseph of Arimathea landed and disembarked to found twelve churches including the Church of Our Lady of Glastonbury which was made of mud and wattles.

It is quite possible to believe that before the drainage of the levels, the water at high tide would come right up to the edge of the hills. When the land is covered with low lying mist the little hills stand out like an archipelago in a misty sea.

Joseph also supposedly stopped on Wearyall hill and stuck his staff, which had been made for him by Jesus, into the ground and it burst into a myriad white flowers. Since then, one of the Glastonbury thorn trees flowers every year at Christmas and a branch is taken and sent to the

Queen. The tree had a bit of difficulty in adjusting to the difference between the Julian and the Gregorian calendar but after three or four years it managed to do so.

The area is full of legends. King Arthur and his knights are supposed to be buried under Glastonbury Tor ready to rise and save Britain in her hour of need. The Holy Grail is supposedly buried somewhere under Chalice Hill.

Myth is myth and legend is legend and I only mention this to show how suffused with supposed magic this whole part of the country is. Worthy Farm is owned by Michael Eavis. When I first knew him it was a tiny dairy farm of 120 acres. Although the pasture land was good, it was a constant struggle to keep going. Michael was married to Ruth my sister-in-law. She was his first wife, the one that is never mentioned in the press reports. They both were involved in the first Glastonbury Festival which was then called the Pilton Pop Festival in 1970. It cost a pound to go in and you got free milk. When we went down there, there was a generator driver whom I knew and who said, 'Hello Jim, what's this film about then?'
I said, 'It isn't a film, Fred, it's some sort of festival,' and he said,'Where can I find a nice B & B?' The surrounding hippies all laughed and said, 'Man haven't you got your bed roll?' I think he slept under the Jenny.

There was a lot of serious New Age hippy talk about the first festival. People were convinced some great spiritual happening was going to occur. People even whispered about the Second Coming. The next day I said to some of the hippies, 'Well it didn't happen, did it?'
'Yes it did, man,' they all said. Well if it did happen, I didn't notice anything.

The festival grew and grew until in the end it was as if the land was occupied by a town the size of Bath. Although they were restricted to 100,000 tickets at least another 50,000 managed to break in.

I am not keen on pop music, nor do I love my fellow man in large quantities but I do see that Michael had to do something to save the farm. 120 acres is simply not viable. He now owns 800 acres.

Fifteen years ago we bought Worthy Cottage where Michael had previously lived. It was right on top of the festival site, but we couldn't complain, because we knew very well what went on every year in June for three days. The cottage was at least three hundred years old, had two and a half acres of land and was startlingly pretty. It needed quite a lot of work done on it. We got a marvellous builder called Chris Drew who did a lot of seriously difficult things like knocking down a structural wall and leaving the house for weeks on jacks while he looked for a beam. He needed paying in cash. We did have some cash, because Maggie had given a lot of money from the sale of Portugal to a friend of ours who was a millionaire and he said he would double it for us. I cannot believe we were so naïve. When we asked him how the money was doing he would say, 'It's rolling up nicely.'
Suddenly he wasn't a millionaire after all and we wanted our money back. He kept on saying: 'No problem, come and have lunch.'
Maggie said, 'I don't want lunch. I want my money back.'

By this time we had given up any hope of gaining any interest. Maggie followed him around to his place of work and to the metal market until she got the money though without any interest, and we used this to pay our builder. Quite suddenly we had a letter from the Inspector of Taxes who asked where the money had come from and told us we were under investigation. We went on being investigated for nearly three years.

My accountant who should have shouted at the Inspector, was absolutely craven and frightened and we had to keep going down to Hastings to be grilled by him. He would say:
'What is this sum of £1.43 from seven years ago?'
'I don't know,' I replied, 'Call it income and I'll pay tax on it.'
'That's not the point,' he said. 'What was it?'
I was nearly in tears. I got so worried that I couldn't sleep and would be taking the dogs out for walks at three o'clock in the morning. Eventually a young man took over the Inspector's job and said, 'I think we can sort your problems out in three days.'
He did, although I had to pay a massive amount of money.

Elsewhere in his book I have said how important it is if you are not working to find something creative to do. It is wonderful if you are a very skilled painter like Jim Goddard or Peter Smith, but I am not. We got a lot of creative satisfaction from doing up the cottage.

As the festivals continued year after year, we would have three days of quite serious trouble every June. We came back to the cottage one day and found an 18 year old looking very spaced out with his hand under the kitchen tap. I said, 'What are you doing in my house?'
He said, 'I cut my hand breaking in didn't I?'
I said, 'Well, get out of my house and go and find the first aid post.'

Another time a very bad tempered looking guy was leading a lot of people into our garden. Maggie called for me, I came out of the house with an armful of cans of beer. Maggie said, 'This is my house and you are not bringing all these people in.'
He said, 'Get out of my way, you fucking bitch. All property is theft.'
I didn't know whether to hit him with a beer can or try and get him tangled up in the barbed wire fence. Suddenly a police car came around the corner and I shouted 'Officer.'
They were there in a flash and one of them said, 'Now sir, we don't want to come into the nice gentleman's house, do we? So I think you'd better turn back or perhaps you'd like to come for a nice ride in our car?' He left muttering.

Every year our kids ask all their friends to the festival and we have lunch in the orchard, which was quite idyllic. It is very noisy but curiously comforting to sit in front of a log fire in the evening, listening to distant music and reading a book. Almost the only one of the stalls I liked at the festival was the Cider Tent run by Julian Temperley. They would bring several thousand gallons a day down to the site and we used to go backstage and drink a very great deal of dry cider. I once heard him on his mobile telephone asking for two more tankers full of cider. I worked out that this came to 18,400 pints.

Over seven years ago we made the house over to our children. Now when we go and stay there, it is with their permission and they could boot us out if they wanted to. When we first moved in, we could get eighty-five bales of hay off the land. Now no-one wants hay, they prefer silage, which stinks and is quite unpleasant. though very occasionally we can manage to make a few bales.

We decided that we wanted to build a barn. I was now getting much less work and we needed the familiar outlet for our creative energy. We were refused planning permission at first; the Parish Council said, 'What do you want with a stone barn anyway. Why don't you make one out of corrugated iron the same as everybody else?'

After we'd been turned down twice, we got the planning officer around and explained what we wanted to do. He was very reasonable and we decided to use a Chartered Surveyor, Chris Frewen instead of an architect. We found a marvellous builder called Tony Seller and dug up a lot of beautiful stone from down the road. It was wonderfully exciting to see it take shape and when it was finally finished we had a party in it just before Simon's wedding with all our American in-laws.

During this time, as the work began to dry up I was teaching and occasionally writing. I spent six months translating a Mystery (or Mistery) Play from the Middle English which was quite difficult, as I felt it necessary to keep the original rhyme scheme and this meant effectively re-writing it. I didn't have any luck selling it, though it was well enough thought of, and I conceived the idea eventually of shooting it as a film in another barn: the Pilton Tithe Barn. This dated from the twelfth century and in the late 1960s the thatched roof had been struck by lightning and all the thatch and timbers totally destroyed. Michael Eavis got some money from English Heritage and began to rebuild. The timbers, which looked amazing, were made by the same people that did the Globe Theatre in London, and because it was in the shape of a church with chancels going north and south, would be an ideal location for the play. It needed very little in the way of design. We would build a rood screen strengthened with tubular scaffolding but looking like carved wood on the down stage side. I gave the play to Michael to look at. He said, 'I don't read plays, I'll give it to Liz (his present wife) to look at.' That's the last I've heard of it. I still entertain hopes of mounting it there or somewhere else. It's really a very good script.

Michael Eavis asked me if he could show *A Bequest To The Nation* at the Festival, because it was the 200th anniverary of Trafalgar in 2005. You certainly can, I said. It was shown this year[20] and was surprisingly well-received.

We still go down to the cottage occasionally, with our children's permission. It looks wonderful in the spring when the apple blossom comes out. We planted an orchard but unfortunately lost the piece of paper telling us which variety was planted where, so we just called them cooking and eating apples. We also have a medlar tree; every monastery is supposed to have had one in the early days. We make jelly of the fruit; you have to wait until it's rotten and you add a little port wine as it cools.

This year we had over 300 cooking apples which the kids put aside in the top floor of the barn and they don't seem to be going rotten. They have also given away several tons of apples to anyone who wants some. We planted a mulberry tree. I long for it to bear fruit, but it's been about seven years and it doesn't look at the moment as if it's going to.

---

[20] 2005

We are asked often why we don't up sticks and move down to the West Country. Apart from the fact that we don't own the cottage, I really like the combination of town and country. We keep the London house going by taking in lodgers which some people call paying guests. This is an opportunity for acting which is quite creative and great fun.

## 9  CARRY ON UP THE BLACKPOOL TOWER

The worst film ever made was recently thought to be about gangsters fighting about chips. They can't have seen *Married To Malcolm*. It wasn't a very good script but I needed the money and more important, I needed to work with actors again.

Alex Swan had a production company called Uglybug, with an office in Greek Street; without having the money, we started casting and Alex started looking for backers. We had been at it for a while, when Alex came in carrying an enormous bunch of white carnations. I hadn't filmed in France for nothing. I knew what they meant; a death or its equivalent. We'd lost the money, and the film was postponed sine die.

After a few months Alex said he had got some money and we could go ahead. We started casting and getting together a crew. We were to be based in Liverpool and shoot a lot of the film in Blackpool.

We were walking in Kew Gardens and I asked Alex, 'Have I your word that we have got the money?'
'Yes, you have my word,' he said.
This was a Sunday.
Next day, twenty two cheques bounced and we lost sixteen valuable crew members.

Eventually some money came through and we did some casting; Mark Addy was to play the lead and Josie Lawrence and Tracey Wilkinson his two wives. The two girls were both very good and later ad-libbed some scenes with great skill. We cast Ronnie Fraser as the mad aristocratic Marxist taxi driver with a Rolls Royce. (It was that sort of film).

Not long after Ronnie, who was an old friend, died. I was very upset and went to the funeral; Alex came too. Jimmy Villiers was there and I pointed him out to Alex as a contender for the part, but Alex was terribly keen on Peter O'Toole, who was a pallbearer. After a decent interval we offered him the part. He didn't rule it out, but he naturally wanted a lot of money, which we didn't have.

Finally I persuaded Alex to offer the part to Jimmy. After a few days Jimmy rang me and bowed out, saying he had to go back to hospital for an operation. What he didn't say, was that he had been diagnosed with cancer of the oesophagus and he had only a few weeks to live. He was a very brave man, who wanted to spend his last weeks with his dear wife, and the fact that he was dying was nobody else's business. He was my good friend and I spoke at his memorial service and had some difficulty containing my emotion.

It seemed there was a jinx upon us (I was dead right) I went to the Garrick Club for lunch, and saw Freddie Jones and immediately cast him. He was and is as mad as a hatter which was just what I, and the film, needed. Later we both found a dear little bar at the base of the`Blackpool Tower where we could have what Freddie called a tincture.

All this time we laboured unaware of a dread cloud of disaster menacing us. I should have mentioned that Gary Glitter was to play an important part (Yes, it was that sort of film). Three days before we started shooting, Gary was arrested; I, rather pathetically said he was innocent until proven guilty, but when all our freebie locations started to disappear, I had to agree it was Bye Bye Gary. We had to do massive rewrites, and persuade the cast and crew that the film was going on.

We lurched on from crisis to crisis and when we lost another famous pop star, Noddy Holder (who he?) I had to make the speech to the whole crew which every director dreads, to the effect that they must stiffen up the sinew and summon up the blood and that we were going to finish the film no matter what. My heart was in my mouth and I don't know what I'd have done if we hadn't finished, but we limped on to the end.

Barry Peters and I spent some weeks in Munich editing it, and, of course, you always kid yourself that it isn't quite so bad. When it was shown at Cannes, we were proudly told by the distributors that we had a poster ten feet by seven. What they didn't say was that it was next to a poster that was seventy feet by ten.

I understand that it has covered its production costs and is in profit!

## 10. FAITH, HOPE AND CHARITY

P. D. James is a distinguished writer of detective stories. She is 82 years old, still working very hard and as sharp as anything. Sir Robin Chichester Clark was raising money for the Arvon Foundation, which helps young writers and had asked her to write a mistery play (no, not a mistery play[21]) which could be performed in front of an audience of very rich people to raise money for the charity.

I found Phyllis James an absolute delight and her script very funny and outrageous, if a little bit long. A distinguished film director had agreed to direct it but had bowed out and said his assistant director would do it. Not unnaturally Robin thought this was a lousy idea. He approached me. He and I and Phyllis had a convivial lunch together and I agreed to direct it.

The problem was that I had to get a fairly distinguished and well known cast. The audience would expect it and there was no money, not a cent. I had agreed to work for free and I had to persuade the actors to do so. Actors are extraordinary generous people and can always be prevailed upon to do something for charity though they are a little bit nervous of learning lines with a very short rehearsal. I managed to get Edward Fox and Joanna David to agree to be in it and Caroline Langrishe and Nicholas Palliser also agreed. After that it became much more difficult. I aimed always for the top, there's no point in doing otherwise. As soon as I managed to engage someone he would get a proper paying job and I would lose him. I must have gone

---

[21] A mistery play has a Biblical theme and was produced in the Thirteenth and Fourteenth centuries by groups of craftsmen (mistery = mastery)

through twenty actors like this, but I ended up with a good cast including the incomparable Freddie Jones.

I cast the last actor on the day before we were due to start rehearsal. We only had three days and, after the read through, I realised that the play was at least 20 minutes too long. It was to be performed in two acts, the first after the main course had been served (we were charging the customers £175 per ticket, that included dinner and wine) and in the second half after the pudding. The play was a mystery and there were prizes for guessing the murderer and the clues which had led to his or her arrest.

Having no money at all to spend made life quite difficult. I was desperately looking for a rehearsal room and had to tell people that I had no money to hire it. We eventually found a room over a pub in King's Cross and I had to promise that the actors would eat there. They didn't.

Only one person got paid anything at all and that was young Miles Palliser, Nicholas's nephew, who had been my stage manager on Pagan Saints and was incredibly hard working and inventive. He was paid below the national minimum wage. He found the props, which were very complicated, including a gramophone with a horn and some old telephones.

The action depended on the black out in the middle of the first act. I tried to get the exit signs turned off, but the Park Lane Hotel refused so I got a lot of pretty girls to walk across the stage space with black drapes on poles.

We needed a iced cake which was a fake; the top had to lift off revealing a space beneath containing a will. I got a distinguished lady who had a cake shop to put some icing on a plastic box. She said she didn't want to make money out of it as it was for charity but she didn't want to lose any either. She charged us £75.

We managed to get the show together but it was a close run thing. Christine Rawlins who had won the BAFTA award for *Fortunes Of War* came and did the costumes for nothing. Likewise Lizzie Moss with the makeup The action depended on the detective played by Nicholas Palliser apparently going and finding a member of the audience and putting him up on the stage. This of course was a fake and I played the man and very bad I was too.

We rehearsed assiduously and I had forgotten that when one did a charity performance all the members of the committee felt able to give free advice on how to direct it, but I smiled a lot and we got the thing together. When it came to the performance Phyllis, who was going to introduce it with a three page speech was nowhere to be found. We desperately asked the hotel staff if they knew where she was. They said she was lying down in her room and had given instructions not to be disturbed. We had to shake one of the managers like a rat to tell us where she was and we got her down just in time. She did the introduction with great style and aplomb. I over-acted quite a lot when I was brought up on stage but the others all did very well.

The performance was followed by an auction where people bid extravagant sums of money for bottles of champagne and signed copies of the programme and a lot of other expensive gifts. We earned £39,500 for the charity and a good time was had by all.

# Chapter Thirty-Nine

# Advice To The Young Director

How pompous that sounds! I intended, as I told you, at one stage to call this book *Screen Directing For Pleasure And Profit*, in the hope of sales to young aspirant directors. So what follows is a series of single words which they might find useful and you might find amusing.

1. LEARN

Keep your ears and eyes open every day of your life. People want to impart their knowledge to you. Let them know you really appreciate what they can tell you.

When I was young the first thing I had to learn was the lenses of a TV camera. They were measured in angles of acceptance. 9° 16° 24° and 35° a wonderfully easy way to envisage the shot each lens would take. Of course we quickly learnt that dividing the angles into 72 gave you the approximate focal length in inches.

By looking carefully at the pictures, you can see the characteristics of each lens. The longer the focal length the shorter the depth of field, and by choosing a lens carefully you can make an apparent change in a person's features. Thus, the best lens for a close up of Emma Thompson is a 37 mm (or 75 on 35 mm film) which will shorten her attractive but slightly long nose.

Lamps used to be, first, brutes which were in fact large arc lights; novelists and journos use the term to describe any bright light when they should really call them inkies. The other lamps were 10 kw, 5 kw, 2 kw, pups and inkiedinks.
Not long after I started, with the arrival of small or more portable lamps everything changed. When you see a lamp working look at what it does and remember.

As a Director you should be able to operate a camera, hold a boom, know the characteristics and field of a microphone, cleat a flat, paint a straight line, act small parts, know what good costume design and maintenance is, draw a scale plan of a set, write simple dialogue and do electronic editing.

You will not be able to do any of these quite as well as your crew. If you can, you shouldn't be employing them. Don't overstate your talents. A director I know likes to operate the camera himself on all the films he directs. He can do it reasonably well but not nearly as well as his operator and he is not nearly so inventive.

Learn from actors. If an actor says a line is unsayable he may be right but you must make him try to say it. Sometimes with experimenting it can be made to work and too many rewrites can turn into chaos. Listen to an actor who may have a very good grasp of his character. Don't let him subdue his instinct with his intellect. Above all don't let your intellect subdue his natural instinct. It's unforgivable.

KEEP ON LEARNING UNTIL YOU ARE DEAD.

## 2. TEACH

To be pompous for once (once?) you should give back something to the trade you love. (If you don't love it, you shouldn't be within a couple miles of it).

It's hard to avoid being didactic. It is useful to say: 'This is what I've found, your experience may be quite different.' Try and learn to make your students as excited about what they're doing as you do your actors - or at least you hope you do. Remember Reinhardt said, 'The director is the communicator of an enthusiasm.'

## 3. LOOK

An infantry soldier looks at country with a particular eye. If he is well trained and enthusiastic, he can scan a landscape for cover, obstacles, clear paths of advance and killing grounds.

You have to develop your own eyes so that on a recce you automatically store away shots in your mind and the problems you will have in shooting them. Carry a compass with you so that you always know where the light is coming from at any hour of the day.

A recce may happen long before the shoot; try and imagine what the land will look like in a few months' time.

## 4. LISTEN

Not just for problems like aeroplane noise but for the particularity of sound which complements the picture. Learn the quality of silence. The desert may seem awesomely silent but as night falls there is an almost unbearable fervid rustling as all the animals which have buried themselves beneath the sand to avoid the heat come to the surface. Listen together with your sound recordist and compare what you hear.

## 5. TALK

To other directors, it's a lonely job and it's difficult to find someone to share your hopes and fears. Producers are rarely suitable. Join the Directors' Guild and listen before you talk.

## 6. BEFRIEND

Technicians, actors and all other directors. They will want to talk about their problems. Let them talk. Sometimes they don't want advice they just want a sympathetic ear. Let them tell you about their problems before you burden them with yours.

## 7. BE MERCIFUL

Shouting or swearing at an incompetent actor or technician is not going to make his work better, quite the reverse. It's surprising how suddenly a performance can change and what seemed disastrous suddenly becomes better than you dared hope.

You may have to sack people. It is a cruel moment and you must do it as quickly and as cleanly as you can. Don't have the person's replacement waiting in the wings while you are doing the job.

I was doing a play in Scotland. One of the younger leading men was obviously not interested. During the rehearsals he would read a novel and never seem to be able to learn his words. It became obvious that I would have to sack him. I took him into the panelled boardroom at the theatre and explained that I was going to have to let him go.
'I'll kill myself,' he said.
'No you won't,' I said, 'I know you have got a good a part in the next play the theatre is doing and you'll make a great success of it.'
'I will, I'll kill myself,' he said.
I talked to him for some while and then said, 'Well I must go back to rehearsal.'

We had both seen Truffaut's film *La Nuit Americaine* recently. In it, the leading lady couldn't get her speech right and blew take after take. Finally she got it right and instead of going through the door made an exit into the broom cupboard and fell in a welter of brushes and buckets. The room was panelled like the room the actor and I were in. I made for the exit and walked straight into the broom cupboard falling most undignifiedly onto the floor surrounded by mops and buckets. The actor gave a sardonic smile and I left. I think it helped to soften the blow.

## 8. REST

The reason so many feature film directors (though not usually TV directors) carry on well into old age is that they learn to pace themselves. Take every opportunity to rest. I used to work with the actors in the morning, block a scene, rehearse it and when the set was being lit and the actors made up, lie down on the set and go to sleep. I learnt to have ten or even five minutes slumber and rise like a giant refreshed.

## 9. IMPROVISE

If it rains re-write the script and make it a sunlit scene. If an actor is missing try the scene without him. If you have to improvise, pretend to your actors that this is a wonderful chance to do something new and exciting. Sometimes you can make them think that they thought of it themselves.

## 10. NURTURE

When you find talent of any sort, nurture it, not for your own sake, but because a light hidden under a bushel is an offence to God and Man.

# Appendix One:
# Television Credits

---

*LORNA DOONE*
Produced by BBC West

Based on a book by RD Blackmore; From a treatment by AR Rawlinson;
Adapted by Constance Cox; Music by Dudley Simpson; Script Editor Joy Harington;
Produced by Douglas Allen; Film sequences directed by James Cellan Jones;
Directed by Brandon Acton-Bond.

---

*A Boy And A Girl* transmitted 16.06.63
Bill Travers (John Ridd), Jean Anderson (Mrs Ridd), Andrew Faulds (Carver Doone),
Norman Tyrrell (John Fry), Daphne Heard (Betty Muxworthy),
Terence De Marney (Counsellor Doone).
With Vincent Brimble, Michael Healey, Shusha Assar, Beth Harris, Edgar Harrison,
Thérese McMurray, Heather Bower, Ronald Russell, Joby Blanshard, David Morrell,
Carl Bernard, Fleur Shaw.

*A Brave Rescue* transmitted 23.06.63
Bill Travers (John Ridd), Jean Anderson (Mrs Ridd), Meg Wynn Owen (Annie Ridd),
Janet Pate (Lizzie Ridd), Daphne Heard (Betty Muxworthy), Norman Tyrrell (John Fry),
Andrew Faulds (Carver Doone), Mark Burns (Charleworth Doone),
Brian Hankins (Marwood De Whichehalse), John Bennett (Tom Faggus),
Terence De Marney (Counsellor Doone), Jane Merrow (Lorna Doone).
With Carl Bernard, Hedley Goodall, Robert Sansom, Julian D'Albie.

*A Summons To London* transmitted on 30.06.63
Bill Travers (John Ridd), Jean Anderson (Mrs Ridd), Janet Pate (Lizzie Ridd),
Meg Wynn Owen (Annie Ridd), Jane Merrow (Lorna Doone), Andrew Faulds (Carver Doone),
Norman Tyrrell (John Fry), Nigel Stock (Jeremy Stickles).
With Hedley Goodall, Phyllis Smale, Gerald Cowan, John Saunders,
Noel Coleman, Patrick Troughton.

*Harvest Festival* transmitted on 07.07.63
Bill Travers (John Ridd), Jean Anderson (Mrs Ridd), Jane Merrow (Lorna Doone),
Norman Tyrrell (John Fry), Meg Wynn Owen (Annie Ridd), Janet Pate (Lizzie Ridd),
Daphne Heard (Betty Muxworthy), John Bennett (Tom Faggus), Andrew Faulds (Carver Doone).
With Ronald Russell, Pat Pleasance, Hedley Goodall, Joby Blanshard, Ioan Jenkins, Carl Bernard.

*Sir Ensor* transmitted on 14.07.63
Bill Travers (John Ridd), Jean Anderson (Mrs Ridd), Andrew Faulds (Carver Doone),
Jane Merrow (Lorna Doone), Meg Wynn Owen (Annie Ridd), Nigel Stock (Jeremy Stickles),
Janet Pate (Lizzie Ridd), Norman Tyrrell (John Fry), Mark Burns (Charleworth Doone),
Patricia Brake (Gwenny Carfax), John Bennett (Tom Faggus), Terence De Marney (Counsellor Doone).
With Carl Bernard, Pat Pleasance, Norman Mitchell, David Morrell.

*The Great Frost* transmitted on 21.07.63
Bill Travers (John Ridd), Jean Anderson (Mrs Ridd), Norman Tyrrell (John Fry),
Janet Pate (Lizzie Ridd), Meg Wynn Owen (Annie Ridd), Daphne Heard (Betty Muxworthy),
 Terence De Marney (Counsellor Doone), Brian Hankins (Marwood De Whichehalse),
Mark Burns (Charleworth Doone), Andrew Faulds (Carver Doone),
Patricia Brake (Gwenny Carfax), Jane Merrow (Lorna Doone).
With David Morrell.

*The Glass Necklace* transmitted on 28.07.63
Bill Travers (John Ridd), Jean Anderson (Mrs Ridd), John Bennett (Tom Faggus),
Meg Wynn Owen (Annie Ridd), Terence De Marney (Counsellor Doone),
Andrew Faulds (Carver Doone), Janet Pate (Lizzie Ridd), Nigel Stock (Jeremy Stickles),
Daphne Heard (Betty Muxworthy), Jane Merrow (Lorna Doone), Patricia Brake (Gwenny Carfax),
Mark Burns (Charleworth Doone), Brian Hankins (Marwood De Whichehalse),
Norman Tyrrell (John Fry).
With David Morrell, Norman Mitchell.

*The Secret* transmitted on 04.08.63
Bill Travers (John Ridd), Jean Anderson (Mrs Ridd), Nigel Stock (Jeremy Stickles),
Janet Pate (Lizzie Ridd), Norman Tyrrell (John Fry), Terence De Marney (Counsellor Doone),
Daphne Heard (Betty Muxworthy), Jane Merrow (Lorna Doone), Meg Wynn Owen (Annie Ridd),
Patricia Brake (Gwenny Carfax), Mark Burns (Charleworth Doone),
Brian Hankins (Marwood De Whichehalse), Andrew Faulds (Carver Doone).
With Shusha Assar, Trevor Baxter, Patrick Kavanagh.

*Slaughter In The Marshes* transmitted on 11.08.63
Bill Travers (John Ridd), Jean Anderson (Mrs Ridd), John Bennett (Tom Faggus),
Norman Tyrrell (John Fry), Janet Pate (Lizzie Ridd), Meg Wynn Owen (Annie Ridd),
Nigel Stock (Jeremy Stickles), Andrew Faulds (Carver Doone), Mark Burns (Charleworth Doone),
Brian Hankins (Marwood De Whichehalse).
With Hedley Goodall, Pat Pleasance, Philip Morant, Norman Mitchell, Paul Nicholson,
Gordon Gostelow, Desmond Cullum-Jones.

*A Royal Favour* transmitted on 18.08.63
Bill Travers (John Ridd), Jean Anderson (Mrs Ridd), Jane Merrow (Lorna Doone),
Patricia Brake (Gwenny Carfax), Janet Pate (Lizzie Ridd), Meg Wynn Owen (Annie Ridd),
John Bennett (Tom Faggus), Nigel Stock (Jeremy Stickles)
With Edwin Brown, Alan Edwards, Maria Corvin, Paul Lorraine, John Laurie, Norman
Mitchell, Sid Dellar, Peter Thornton.

*A Long Account Settled* transmitted on 25.08.63
Bill Travers (John Ridd), Jean Anderson (Mrs Ridd), Andrew Faulds (Carver Doone),
Mark Burns (Charleworth Doone), Brian Hankins (Marwood De Whichehalse),
John Bennett (Tom Faggus), Nigel Stock (Jeremy Stickles),
Terence De Marney (Counsellor Doone), Daphne Heard (Betty Muxworthy),
Janet Pate (Lizzie Ridd), Jane Merrow (Lorna Doone), Meg Wynn Owen (Annie Ridd),
Patricia Brake (Gwenny Carfax), Norman Tyrrell (John Fry).
With David Morrell, Bridget Turner, Peter Layton, Hedley Goodall, Philip Morant,
Ronald Russell, Pat Pleasance, Joby Blanshard.

*Eleven twenty-five minute episodes, transmitted live with filmed inserts - no copies survive.*

---

## COMPACT
Produced for the BBC

Series created by Peter Ling and Hazel Adair.

---

*Happy New Year* transmitted on 31.12.63
Written by Bob Stuart; Produced by Morris Barry; Directed by James Cellan Jones.
Robert Flemyng (Bruce), Beryl Cooke (Mrs Chater), Ronald Allen (Ian),
David Langton (Marmot James), Basil Moss (Alan), Louise Dunn (Iris),
Pauline Munro (Jenny), Carmen Silvera (Camilla), Bill Kerr (Ben), Frances Bennett (Gussie),
Patricia Haines (Vivien Ames), Betty Cooper (Alison), Scot Finch (Tim),
Diana Beevers (Mitch), Vincent Ball (David), Shane Rimmer (Corrigan),
Douglas Blackwell (Gym Instructor), Gretchen Franklin (Ella Bedford).

*Weekend Guest* transmitted on 02.01.64
Written by Hazel Adair and Peter Ling; Directed by James Cellan Jones.

*One Of Us Must Go* transmitted on 28.01.64
Written by Martin Worth; Produced by Morris Barry; Directed by James Cellan Jones.
Shane Rimmer (Corrigan), Ronald Allen (Ian), Frances Bennett (Gussie),
Robin Hawdon (Barry), Lawrence James (Doug), Joanna Vogel (Sheila),
Robert Flemyng (Bruce), Robert Desmond (Adrian), Basil Moss (Alan), Pauline Munro (Jenny),
Hazel Penwarden (Rose), Vincent Ball (David), Diana Beevers (Mitch), George Roderick (Mr
Watson), Arnold Ridley (Harry), Patricia Haines (Vivien), Betty Cooper (Alison).

*Love You and Leave You* transmitted on 30.01.64
Written by Martin Worth; Produced by Morris Barry; Directed by James Cellan Jones.
Ronald Allen (Ian), Shane Rimmer (Corrigan), Lawrence James (Doug),
Frances Bennett (Gussie), Robin Hawdon (Barry), Joanna Vogel (Sheila),
Carmen Silvera (Camilla), Basil Moss (Alan), Robert Desmond (Adrian),
Diana Beevers (Mitch), Beryl Cooke (Mrs Chater), Robert Flemyng (Bruce),
Patricia Haines (Vivien), Vincent Ball (David).

*Walls Have Ears* transmitted on 18.02.64
Written by Peter Ling and Hazel Adair; Produced by Morris Barry; Directed by James Cellan Jones.
Basil Moss (Alan), Pauline Munro (Jenny), Johnny Wade (Stan), Beryl Cooke (Mrs Chater), Robert Flemyng (Bruce), Ronald Allen (Ian), Christine Pollon (Janet), Carmen Silvera (Camilla), Lawrence James (Doug), Frances Bennett (Gussie), Patricia Haines (Vivien), Louise Dunn (Iris), Betty Cooper (Alison), Bill Kerr (Ben), Vincent Ball (David), Alan Wheatley (Howard Norton), Colette Wilde (Barbara Clay), Aubrey Morris (Bobby Chandos), Joanna Vogel (Sheila).

*In The Air* transmitted on 20.02.64
Written by Hazel Adair and Peter Ling; Produced by Morris Barry; Directed by James Cellan Jones.
Aubrey Morris (Bobby Chandos), Betty Cooper (Alison), Vincent Ball (David), Colette Wilde (Barbara Clay), Alan Wheatley (Howard Norton), Charles Hodgson (Bill Blake), John Rolfe (Studio Manager), Carmen Silvera (Camilla), Bill Kerr (Ben), Louise Dunn (Iris), Joanna Vogel (Sheila), Robert Desmond (Adrian), Ronald Allen (Ian), Christine Pollon (Janet), Robert Flemyng (Bruce), Basil Moss (Alan), Johnny Wade (Stan), Patricia Haines (Vivien), Lawrence James (Doug), Frances Bennett (Gussie), Beryl Cooke (Mrs Chater).

*Plots And Plans* transmitted on 10.03.64
Written by Rosemary Anne Sisson; Directed by James Cellan Jones.

*Secrets And Lies* transmitted on 12.03.64
Written by Rosemary Anne Sisson; Directed by James Cellan Jones.

*Just Married - Good Luck!* transmitted on 31.03.64
Written by Bob Stuart; Produced by Morris Barry; Directed by James Cellan Jones.
Louise Dunn (Iris), Robert Desmond (Adrian), Audrey Noble (Mrs Alcott), Johnny Wade (Stan), Basil Moss (Alan), Norman Mitchell (Mr Alcott), David Craig (Milkman), Ronald Allen (Ian), Beryl Cooke (Mrs Chater), Sandra Payne (Wendy Millet), Lawrence James (Doug), Frances Bennett (Gussie), Robert Flemyng (Bruce), Eric Thompson (Mervyn Slater), Pauline Munro (Jenny), Joanna Vogel (Sheila), Bill Kerr (Ben), Vincent Ball (David), Carmen Silvera (Camilla), Freda Bamford (Mrs Millet), Ian Frost (Photographer), Howell Evans (Signalman), Jeremy Longhurst (Policeman).

*Honeymoon And Holidays* transmitted on 02.04.64
Written by Bob Stuart; Produced by Morris Barry; Directed by James Cellan Jones.
Louise Dunn (Iris), Johnny Wade (Stan), Harry Littlewood (Garage Man), Lawrence James (Doug), Pauline Munro (Jenny), Ronald Allen (Ian), Beryl Cooke (Mrs Chater), Robert Flemyng (Bruce), Vincent Ball (David), Chuck Julian (Paul Divine), Basil Moss (Alan), Ken Parry (Sydney Playfair), Frances Bennett (Gussie), Carmen Silvera (Camilla), Robert Desmond (Adrian), Bill Kerr (Ben).

*Ian In Danger* transmitted on 21.04.64
Written by Rosemary Anne Sisson; Directed by James Cellan Jones.

*Investigations* transmitted on 23.04.64
Written by Rosemary Anne Sisson; Directed by James Cellan Jones.

*Delicate Negotiations* transmitted on 19.05.64
Written by Rosemary Anne Sisson; Produced by Bernard Hepton; Directed by James Cellan Jones.
Joanna Vogel (Sheila), Margo Andrew (Dinah), Eric Barker (Mr Coombs), Brian Miller (Gary),
Frazer Hines (Ray), Johnny Wade (Stan), Sandra Payne (Wendy), Carmen Silvera (Camilla),
Robert Flemyng (Bruce), Beryl Cooke (Mrs Chater), Robert Desmond (Adrian),
Lawrence James (Doug), Bill Kerr (Ben), Ronald Allen (Ian), Vincent Ball (David),
Richard Coleman (Mike Fuller), Lew Luton (Norman Spring), Louise Dunn (Iris),
Bernard Kay (Farrow), Colin Douglas (Police Inspector).

*Parties And Quarrels* transmitted on 21.05.64
Written by Rosemary Anne Sisson; Directed by James Cellan Jones.

*To Catch A Thief* transmitted on 09.06.64
Written by Peter Ling and Hazel Adair; Script Editor Donald Tosh;
Produced by Bernard Hepton; Directed by James Cellan Jones.
Ronald Allen (Ian), Richard Beale (Inspector Birling), Christine Pollon (Janet), Bill Kerr (Ben),
Robert Desmond (Adrian), Lawrence James (Doug), Vincent Ball (David),
Sandra Payne (Wendy), David Nettheim (Arthur Plum), Eric Barker (Mr Coombs),
Frances Bennett (Gussie), Carmen Silvera (Camilla), Robert Flemyng (Bruce),
Beryl Cooke (Mrs Chater), Margo Andrew (Dinah), Judy Franklin (Paula),
Jack Hulbert (Smith), Malcolm Rogers (Mr Goodman).

*Play On Crime* transmitted on 11.06.64
Written by Hazel Adair and Peter Ling; Script Editor Donald Tosh;
Produced by Bernard Hepton; Directed by James Cellan Jones.
Robert Desmond (Adrian), Eric Barker (Mr Coombs), Malcolm Rogers (Mr Goodman),
David Nettheim (Arthur Plum), Margo Andrew (Dinah), Jack Hulbert (Smith),
Richard Beale (Inspector Birling), Frances Bennett (Gussie), Carmen Silvera (Camilla),
Basil Moss (Alan), Ronald Allen (Ian), Lawrence James (Doug), Sandra Payne (Wendy),
Polly Adams (Julia Preston), William Sherwood (Sir Duncan Wallace),
Robert Flemyng (Bruce), Christine Pollon (Janet), Hubert Rees (Waiter).

Twenty-five minute episodes - some transmitted live, some recorded on 405-line videotape.
Of the above, only *To Catch A Thief* and *Play On Crime* exist as a 16mm telerecording of an
omnibus transmission on BBC 2.

### *ESTHER WATERS*
Produced for BBC 2

Based on a book by George Moore; Adapted by Harry Green; Music by Dudley Simpson; Script Editor Michael Voysey; Produced by Douglas Allen; Directed by James Cellan Jones.

*The Lottery* transmitted on 14.11.64
Meg Wynn Owen (Esther Waters), Ruth Porcher, John Dearth, John Bennett, Daphne Heard, Elizabeth Bell, Gwendolyn Watts, Pauline Letts, Tracy Reed, Carl Bernard, Blake Butler, Linda Polan, Alan Kemp, Doris Hare.

*London Pride* transmitted on 21.11.64
Meg Wynn Owen (Esther Waters), Gwendolyn Watts, Elizabeth Bell, Daphne Heard, Tracy Reed, John Bennett, Pauline Letts, Ruth Porcher, John Dearth, Diana Hope, Faith Kent, Ann Lancaster, Dorothy Frere, Anne Ridler, Gordon Gostelow, Alex Allan, Howard Lockhart.

*Starter's Orders* transmitted on 28.11.64
Meg Wynn Owen (Esther Waters), Gwendolyn Watts, Elizabeth Bell, Daphne Heard, Tracy Reed, John Bennett, Pauline Letts, Ruth Porcher, John Dearth, Diana Hope, Faith Kent, Ann Lancaster, Dorothy Frere, Anne Ridler, Gordon Gostelow, Alex Allan, Howard Lockhart.

*The Favourite Wins* transmitted on 05.12.64
Meg Wynn Owen (Esther Waters), Gwendolyn Watts, Elizabeth Bell, Daphne Heard, Tracy Reed, John Bennett, Pauline Letts, Ruth Porcher, John Dearth, Diana Hope, Faith Kent, Ann Lancaster, Dorothy Frere, Anne Ridler, Gordon Gostelow, Alex Allan, Howard Lockhart.

Four forty-five minute episodes - recorded on 405-line videotape.  No copies survive.

### *THE AMBASSADORS*
Produced for BBC 2

Based on a book by Henry James; Adapted by Denis Constanduros;
Directed by James Cellan Jones.

*Arrival* transmitted on 31.01.65
David Bauer (Waymarsh), Alan Gifford (Lambert Stether), Lois Maxwell (Sarah Pocock), Harvey Spencer (Chadwick Newsome), Roy Stephens (Little Bilham), Bethel Leslie (Maria Gostrey).

*Encounter* transmitted on 07.02.65
David Bauer (Waymarsh), Alan Gifford (Lambert Stether), Lois Maxwell (Sarah Pocock), Harvey Spencer (Chadwick Newsome), Roy Stephens (Little Bilham), Bethel Leslie (Maria Gostrey).

*Departure* transmitted on 14.02.65
David Bauer (Waymarsh), Alan Gifford (Lambert Stether), Lois Maxwell (Sarah Pocock),
Harvey Spencer (Chadwick Newsome), Roy Stephens (Little Bilham),
Bethel Leslie (Maria Gostrey).

Three forty-five minute episodes - recorded at BBC Glasgow on 405-line videotape.
No copies survive.

---

### THE SCARLET AND THE BLACK
Produced for BBC 2

Based on a book by Stendahl; Translated by Margaret RB Shaw; Adapted by Michael Barry;
Music by Dudley Simpson; Story Editor Michael Voysey; Produced by Douglas Allen;
Directed by James Cellan Jones.

---

*Low Estate* transmitted on 09.05.65
John Stride, June Tobin, Anne Ridler, Elizabeth Bell, Ann Lancaster, Geoffrey Rose,
Derek Lamden, Carl Bernard, Thomas Gallagher, Noel Johnson, Henry Oscar, Emrys Jones,
George Roderick, Emrys James.

*A Town In The Country* transmitted on 16.05.65
John Stride, Noel Johnson, June Tobin, Anne Ridler, Emrys James, Emrys Jones,
Derek Lamden, Elizabeth Bell, George Roderick, Geoffrey Rose, Carl Bernard, Henry Oscar,
Ann Lancaster, Tom Conti, Hamilton Dyce.

*Entry Into Society* transmitted on 23.05.65
John Stride, Noel Johnson, Hamilton Dyce, Tom Conti, Michael Burrell, Geoffrey Hutchings,
Emrys James, William Sherwood, June Tobin, Anne Ridler, Gerald Cross, John Shedden,
Emrys Jones, Mark Burns, Karin Fernald, Maud Risdon, Michael O'Halloran, Brian Hankins,
Anthony Verner, Jerold Wells, Tony Lane, Donald Pickering.

*A Question Of S*tyle transmitted on 30.05.65
John Stride, Noel Johnson, Donald Pickering, Jerold Wells, Adrian Ropes, Karin Fernald,
Brian Hankins, John Shedden, Mark Burns, Maud Risdon, Hamilton Dyce, Gerald Cross,
Christopher Denham, Philip Madoc, George Roderick.

*A Man Of Intelligence* transmitted on 06.06.65

Five forty-five minute episodes. No copies survive.

---

**AN ENEMY OF THE STATE**
Produced for BBC 2

Written by Ken Hughes; Produced by Alan Bromly; Directed by James Cellan Jones.

---

*The Trouble With Harry* transmitted on 17.10.65
Charles Tingwell (Harry Sutton), Veronica Strong (Jennifer Sutton), James Maxwell (Colonel Rykov), Alfred Hoffman (Orlov), Dallia Penn (Karin), Jan Conrad (Boris), Peter Stephens (Simons), Robert Mill (Henderson), William Sherwood, Frederick Treves, David Langton, Alex Miller, Steve Plytas, Dorothy Frere, Christopher Denham, John Harwood, Blake Butler, Jane Evers.

*Point Of No Return* transmitted on 24.10.65
Charles Tingwell (Harry Sutton), Veronica Strong (Jennifer Sutton), James Maxwell (Colonel Rykov), Alfred Hoffman (Orlov), Dallia Penn (Karin), Jan Conrad (Boris), Peter Stephens (Simons), Adrian Ropes (Wilson-Nichols), Jane Evers, Nigel Bernard, Terry Wright, Ann Lancaster, John Pickles, George Herbert, Margareta Bourdin, Stephen Hubay, Roy Stephens, Alexis Chesnakov, John Luxton.

*Cause For Alarm* transmitted on 31.10.65
Charles Tingwell (Harry Sutton), Veronica Strong (Jennifer Sutton), James Maxwell (Colonel Rykov), Alfred Hoffman (Orlov), Dallia Penn (Karin), Jan Conrad (Boris), Peter Stephens (Simons), Adrian Ropes (Wilson-Nichols), Harold Lang, Peter Forest, Marguerite Young, Richard Kane, Richard Armour, David King, Bernard Monshin, Tom McCall.

*The Faceless Men* transmitted on 07.11.65
Charles Tingwell (Harry Sutton), Veronica Strong (Jennifer Sutton), James Maxwell (Colonel Rykov), Alfred Hoffman (Orlov), Dallia Penn (Karin), Jan Conrad (Boris), Peter Stephens (Simons), Adrian Ropes (Wilson-Nichols), Robert Mill (Henderson), David King, Jonathon Scott, Richard Armour, Harold Lang, Tony Poole, Richard Kane.

*The Blood Red Tape* transmitted on 14.11.65
Charles Tingwell (Harry Sutton), Veronica Strong (Jennifer Sutton), James Maxwell (Colonel Rykov), Alfred Hoffman (Orlov), Dallia Penn (Karin), Jan Conrad (Boris), Peter Stephens (Simons), Robert Mill (Henderson), Adrian Ropes (Wilson-Nichols), Monica Francis, Anna Marie, Anna Barrtea, David King, Alan Curtis, Michael Collins, George Pravda, Steven Berkoff, Michael Rix, Michael Seddon.

*The Reckoning* transmitted on 21.11.65
Charles Tingwell (Harry Sutton), Veronica Strong (Jennifer Sutton), James Maxwell (Colonel Rykov), Alfred Hoffman (Orlov), Dallia Penn (Karin), Jan Conrad (Boris), Peter Stephens (Simons), Robert Mill (Henderson), Adrian Ropes (Wilson-Nichols), Alan Curtis, George Pravda, Steven Berkoff, Michael Collins, Michael Rix, Michael Seddon, James Appleby, Bryan Kendrick, Michael Davis, Marc Malicz.

Six twenty-five minute episodes recorded on 405-line videotape. No copies survive.

**THE HUNCHBACK OF NOTRE DAME**
Produced for BBC 2

Based on a book by Victor Hugo; Adapted by Vincent Tilsley;
Produced by Douglas Allen; Directed by James Cellan Jones.

*Abduction* transmitted on 08.03.66
Peter Woodthorpe, Gary Raymond, James Maxwell, Emrys Jones, Gay Hamilton, Alex Davion, Suzanne Neve, Beatrix Lehmann, Jeffrey Isaac, Norman Mitchell, Jane Tann, Lucretia Burgess, Ann Windsor, Terry Wright.

*Torture* transmitted on 15.03.66
Peter Woodthorpe, Arnold Ridley, Norman Mitchell, Alex Davion, Gay Hamilton, Gary Raymond, Jeffrey Isaac, Wilfrid Lawson, Michael Beint, Derek Baker, James Maxwell, Suzanne Neve, Peggy Ann Wood, Susan Pitts, Marguerite Young, Winifred Hill, Neil Hunt.

*Seduction* transmitted on 22.03.66
Peter Woodthorpe, Gay Hamilton, Gary Raymond, Alex Davion, Peggy Ann Wood, Suzanne Neve, James Maxwell, Anthony Verner, John Devaut, Dorothy Reynolds.

*Interrogation* transmitted on 29.03.66
James Maxwell, Peter Woodthorpe, Gary Raymond, Gay Hamilton, Dorothy Reynolds, Roy Spencer, Beatrix Lehmann, Emrys Jones, Geoffrey Rose, Michael Burrell, Derek Baker.

*Accusation* transmitted on 05.04.66

*Repentance* transmitted on 12.04.66

*Retribution* transmitted on 19.04.66
Peter Woodthorpe, Wilfrid Lawson, Gary Raymond, Jeffrey Isaac, James Maxwell, Gay Hamilton, Michael Murray, Brian Cant, Beatrix Lehmann, Emrys Jones, Derek Baker, Bob Raymond, Campbell Godley, David Rayner.

Seven forty-five minute episodes, recorded on 405-line videotape.  No copies survive.

**THE FORSYTE SAGA**
Produced for BBC 2

Based on novels by John Galsworthy; Theme music by Eric Coates;
Story Editor Lennox Phillips; Produced by Donald Wilson.

*Encounter* transmitted on 01.04.67
Dramatised by Vincent Tilsley; Directed by James Cellan Jones.
Susan Hampshire (Fleur), June Barry (June), Martin Jarvis (Jon), Jonathan Burn (Val),
Suzanne Neve (Holly), Nicholas Pennell (Michael Mont), Kenneth More (Jo),
Eric Porter (Soames), Nyree Dawn Porter (Irene), Margaret Tyzack (Winifred),
John Barcroft (George), Maggie Jones (Smither), Christopher Benjamin, John Dunn-Hill.

*Conflict* transmitted on 08.04.67
Dramatised by Vincent Tilsley; Directed by James Cellan Jones.
Julia Whyte (Coaker), Susan Hampshire (Fleur), June Barry (June), Martin Jarvis (Jon),
Jonathan Burn (Val), Suzanne Neve (Holly), Nicholas Pennell (Michael Mont),
Kenneth More (Jo), Eric Porter (Soames), Nyree Dawn Porter (Irene),
Margaret Tyzack (Winifred), John Barcroft (George), Maggie Jones (Smither),
Christopher Benjamin, Richard Armour, Patricia Leventon, Stephen Hubay.

*To Let* transmitted on 15.04.67
Dramatised by Vincent Tilsley; Directed by James Cellan Jones.
Julia Whyte (Coaker), Susan Hampshire (Fleur), June Barry (June), Martin Jarvis (Jon),
Jonathan Burn (Val), Suzanne Neve (Holly), Nicholas Pennell (Michael Mont), Kenneth More
(Jo), Eric Porter (Soames), Nyree Dawn Porter (Irene), Margaret Tyzack (Winifred), John
Barcroft (George), Maggie Jones (Smither), Richard Armour, Christopher Benjamin, Patricia
Leventon, Rosemary Rogers

*A Family Wedding* transmitted on 22.04.67
Dramatised by Anthony Steven; Directed by James Cellan Jones.
Terry Scully (Bicket), Cyril Luckham (Sir Lawrence Mont), Derek Francis (Elderson),
Geraldine Sherman (Victorine Bicket), Donald Gee (Butterfield), Clifford Parrish (Gradman),
Robin Phillips (Wilfred Desert), Julia Whyte (Coaker), Susan Hampshire (Fleur),
June Barry (June), Martin Jarvis (Jon), Jonathan Burn (Val), Suzanne Neve (Holly),
Nicholas Pennell (Michael Mont), Eric Porter (Soames), Nyree Dawn Porter (Irene),
Margaret Tyzack (Winifred), John Barcroft (George), Maggie Jones (Smither),
Hugo Keith-Johnston, Brenda Cowling, Ian Fleming, Geoffrey Denton, Maurice Quick,
Hubert Hill, Colin Douglas, John Kidd.

*The White Monkey* transmitted on 29.04.67
Dramatised by Anthony Steven; Directed by James Cellan Jones.
Julia Whyte (Coaker), Terry Scully (Bicket), Cyril Luckham (Sir Lawrence Mont),
Derek Francis (Elderson), Geraldine Sherman (Victorine Bicket), Donald Gee (Butterfield),
Clifford Parrish (Gradman), Robin Phillips (Wilfred Desert), Susan Hampshire (Fleur),

June Barry (June), Martin Jarvis (Jon), Jonathan Burn (Val), Suzanne Neve (Holly),
Nicholas Pennell (Michael Mont), Eric Porter (Soames), Nyree Dawn Porter (Irene),
Margaret Tyzack (Winifred), Maggie Jones (Smither), Ian Fleming, Henry Longhurst,
Geoffrey Denton, Brenda Cowling, John Bailey, Hugo Keith-Johnston.

*The Afternoon Of A Dryad* transmitted on 06.05.67
Dramatised by Anthony Steven; Directed by James Cellan Jones.
Terry Scully (Bicket), Cyril Luckham (Sir Lawrence Mont), Derek Francis (Elderson),
Geraldine Sherman (Victorine Bicket), Donald Gee (Butterfield), Clifford Parrish (Gradman),
Robin Phillips (Wilfred Desert), Julia Whyte (Coaker), Susan Hampshire (Fleur),
June Barry (June), Martin Jarvis (Jon), Jonathan Burn (Val), Suzanne Neve (Holly),
Nicholas Pennell (Michael Mont), Eric Porter (Soames), Nyree Dawn Porter (Irene),
Margaret Tyzack (Winifred), Maggie Jones (Smither), John Bailey, Brenda Cowling,
Cicely Paget-Bowman, Steve Plytas.

No Retreat transmitted on 13.05.67
Dramatised by Anthony Steven; Directed by James Cellan Jones.
Terry Scully (Bicket), Cyril Luckham (Sir Lawrence Mont), Derek Francis (Elderson),
Geraldine Sherman (Victorine Bicket), Donald Gee (Butterfield), Clifford Parrish (Gradman),
Robin Phillips (Wilfred Desert), Julia Whyte (Coaker), Susan Hampshire (Fleur),
June Barry (June), Martin Jarvis (Jon), Jonathan Burn (Val), Suzanne Neve (Holly),
Nicholas Pennell (Michael Mont), Eric Porter (Soames), Nyree Dawn Porter (Irene),
Margaret Tyzack (Winifred), Maggie Jones (Smither), Brenda Cowling, Austin Trevor,
Ian Fleming, Jimmy Gardner, Maisie MacFarquhar, Phillip Ray, Henry Longhurst,
Maurice Quick, Mirabelle Thomas.

Fifty-minute episodes, originally recorded on 625-line monochrome videotape. All episodes
survive on a mixture of D3 and Digital Betacam videotape. Most recordings contain some
out-takes on the end of the reels.

---

## Z CARS
### Produced for BBC 1

---

*Calling The Tune: Episode 1* transmitted on 25.09.67
Written by Gerald Kelsey; Produced by Ronald Travers; Directed by James Cellan Jones.
John Barrie (Detective Inspector Hudson), James Ellis (Sergeant Bert Lynch),
Stephen Yardley (PC May), Ken Parry, Mollie Sugden, Brian Peck, Barry Jackson, Frank
Middlemass, Michael Earl, Bartlett Mullins, Bill Lyons, Michael Gordon, Sally Sanderson.

*Calling The Tune: Episode 2* transmitted on 26.09.67
Written by Gerald Kelsey; Produced by Ronald Travers; Directed by James Cellan Jones.
John Barrie (Detective Inspector Barrie), James Ellis (Sergeant Bert Lynch),
Stephen Yardley (PC May), Frank Middlemass, Barry Jackson, Brian Peck,
Mollie Sugden, Ken Parry, Peter Hempson, Michael Earl.

Twenty-five minute episodes, recorded on 405-line videotape. No copies survive.

---

**THE FIRST FREEDOM**
Produced for BBC 1

---

Transmitted on 19.11.67
Translated by Stuart Hood; Executive Producer Stephen Hearst;
Produced by Christopher Burstall; Directed by Christopher Burstall and James Cellan Jones;
Narrated by Stuart Hood.
Arthur Hill (Sinyavsky), Lee Montague (Daniel), Peter Vaughan (Public Prosecutor),
Godfrey Quigley (Judge), John Ringham (Clerk Of The Court), Anne Blake (Social Accuser),
David Blake Kelly (Social Accuser), Carl Bernard (Counsel For The Defence),
John Garvin (Usher), Kathleen Heath (People's Assessor), Leslie Pitt (People's Assessor),
James Mellor (Garbuzenko), Walter Gotell (Khmelnitsky), Jeffrey Segal (Petrov),
Daphne Slater (Elena Dokukina), Peter Clay (Golomshtok), John Cazabon (Duvakin),
George Roderick, Emrys James, Kenneth J. Warren, Peter Stephens, Aubrey Morris,
Mischa de la Motte, Michael Mellinger, Gerald Harper, David Bauer.

James Cellan Jones directed 'Scenes from Sinyavsky's Story'.

A one-hundred minute play recorded on 405-line video tape and preserved on Digital
Betacam.

---

**THE PORTRAIT OF A LADY**
Produced for BBC 2

Based on a novel by Henry James; Adapted by Jack Pulman;
Produced by David Conroy; Directed by James Cellan Jones.

---

*Proposals* transmitted on 06.01.68
Richard Chamberlain (Ralph Touchett), Suzanne Neve (Isabel), Edward Fox (Lord Warburton),
Sarah Brackett (Henrietta), Beatrix Lehmann (Mrs Touchett), Alan Gifford (Mr Touchett),
Susan Tebbs (Constance), Rachel Gurney (Madame Merle), Felicity Gibson, Margaret Corey,
Ed Bishop.

*Bequests* transmitted on 13.01.68
Richard Chamberlain (Ralph Touchett), Suzanne Neve (Isabel), Edward Fox (Lord Warburton),
Sarah Brackett (Henrietta), Beatrix Lehmann (Mrs Touchett), Alan Gifford (Mr Touchett),
Susan Tebbs (Constance), Rachel Gurney (Madame Merle), Angus Mackay, Richard Young,
Ed Bishop, Howard Charlton.

*Schemes* transmitted on 20.01.68
Richard Chamberlain (Ralph Touchett), Suzanne Neve (Isabel), Edward Fox (Lord Warburton),
Sarah Brackett (Henrietta), Beatrix Lehmann (Mrs Touchett), Alan Gifford (Mr Touchett),

Susan Tebbs (Constance), Rachel Gurney (Madame Merle), Sharon Gurney, James Maxwell, Rosalind Atkinson, Kitty Fitzgerald, John Devaut, Kathleen Byron, Angus Mackay.

*Decisions* transmitted on 27.01.68
Richard Chamberlain (Ralph Touchett), Suzanne Neve (Isabel), Edward Fox (Lord Warburton), Sarah Brackett (Henrietta), Beatrix Lehmann (Mrs Touchett), Alan Gifford (Mr Touchett), Susan Tebbs (Constance), Rachel Gurney (Madame Merle), Angus Mackay, James Maxwell, Michael Ruebens, Sharon Gurney, Ed Bishop, Kathleen Byron.

*Dissensions* transmitted on 03.02.68
Richard Chamberlain (Ralph Touchett), Suzanne Neve (Isabel), Edward Fox (Lord Warburton), Sarah Brackett (Henrietta), Beatrix Lehmann (Mrs Touchett), Alan Gifford (Mr Touchett), Susan Tebbs (Constance), Rachel Gurney (Madame Merle), James Maxwell, Sharon Gurney, Cavan Kendall, Kevork Malikyan.

*Revelations* transmitted on 10.02.68
Richard Chamberlain (Ralph Touchett), Suzanne Neve (Isabel), Edward Fox (Lord Warburton), Sarah Brackett (Henrietta), Beatrix Lehmann (Mrs Touchett), Alan Gifford (Mr Touchett), Susan Tebbs (Constance), Rachel Gurney (Madame Merle), Ed Bishop, Kathleen Byron, James Maxwell, Sharon Gurney, Marguerite Young.

Six forty-five minute episodes, recorded in colour on 2" videotape.  Copies of all episodes survive on D3 videotape.

---

### *THEATRE 625*
Produced for BBC 2

---

*Albinos In Black* transmitted on 22.01.68
Written by Alun Richards; Produced by Michael Bakewell; Directed by James Cellan Jones.
Gwen Ffrangcon-Davies (Acsa Beddgelert Williams), Gerald James (Joshua, Her Son), Meg Wynn Owen (Olwen, His Wife, Joan of Arc Reclaimed), Emrys Jones (Heulog Wynne-Jones, MA), Pauline Delany (Lena Ryan), Charles Williams (Ifor Williams), John Rees (Ben Boats), Ambrosian Singers (Hunting Miners), Roy Desmond (Secretary of the Miners), Sheila Irwin (Mona), Willie Jonah (Negro Student), Ilarrio Pedro (Negro Student).

Ninety-minute play recorded in colour on 2" videotape.  No copy survives.

---

**THIRTY MINUTE THEATRE**
Produced for BBC 2

---

*The Sinners* transmitted on 10.04.68
Written by David Hopkins; Produced by Innes Lloyd; Directed by James Cellan Jones.
William Mervyn (Father), Doris Hare (Mother), Geraldine Sherman (Girl),
Christopher Chittell (Son).

Thirty-minute play recorded in colour on 2" videotape. No copy survives.

---

**DETECTIVE**
Produced for BBC 1

Series 2: Script Editor Anthea Browne-Wilkinson; Produced by Verity Lambert.

---

*Eve Gill : The Golden Dart* transmitted on 04.08.68
Based on a book by Selwyn Jepson; Adapted by Donald Wilson;
Directed by James Cellan Jones.
Penelope Horner (Eve Gill), John Stride (James Belsin), John Laurie (Commodore Gill),
Andrew Faulds (Gonzalez), Angus Mackay (Jones), Michael Wynne (Hooker),
Anthony Corlan (Jonathan), Allan McClelland (George Wick), Frank Middlemass (Billy Bull),
Veronica Hurst (Sophie), Charles Hodgson (Boosie), Maurice Quick (John),
Iona Macrae (Phoebe), Patricia Mason (Jessie), Kitty Attwood (Mrs Garside).

Forty-seven minute play, recorded on 625-line monochrome videotape.
Survives as a 16mm telerecording.

*Auguste Dupin : The Murders In The Rue Morgue* transmitted on 01.09.68
Based on a book by Edgar Allan Poe; Adapted by James Mactaggart;
Directed by James Cellan Jones.
Edward Woodward (Auguste Dupin), Charles Kay (Edgar Allan Poe),
Christopher Benjamin (Rodier), Marguerite Young (Madame L'Espanaye),
Philip Anthony (Belair), Jimmy Gardner (Muset), Walter Horsbrugh (Duval),
John Devaut (Bird), Kevork Malikyan (Garcio), Guido Adorni (Montani),
Dennis Edwards (Dumas), James Hall (Clerk), Ray Callaghan (Le Bon),
Geoffrey Rose (Prefect), Beatrice Greeke (Madame Douterc), Charles Kinross (Gendarme),
Anthony Langdon (Sailor).

Fifty-four minute play, recorded on 625-line monochrome videotape. No copy survives.

---

*OUT OF THE UNKNOWN*
Produced for BBC 2

---

*Beach Head* transmitted on 28.01.69
Based on a story by Clifford Simak; Adapted by Robert Muller; Produced by Alan Bromly;
Directed by James Cellan Jones.
Ed Bishop (Decker), Helen Downing (Cassandra), Barry Warren (Ensign Warner-Carr),
James Copeland (Oliver McDonald), Vernon Dobtcheff (NB Waddron),
John Gabriel (Bertrand Le Maitre), Robert Lee (AG Tiosawa).

Fifty-two minute play, recorded on 2" colour videotape.  No copy survives.

---

*THE WAY WE LIVE NOW*
Produced for BBC 2

Based on a novel by Anthony Trollope; Adapted by Simon Raven;
Produced by David Conroy; Directed by James Cellan Jones.

---

*The Great Heiress* transmitted on 05.04.69
Colin Blakely (Augustus Melmotte), Rachel Gurney (Lady Carbury),
Cavan Kendall (Sir Felix Carbury), Adrian Ropes (Dolly Longestaffe),
Pieter Van Der Stolk (Vossner), Peter French (Miles Grendall), Jeremy Clyde (Lord Nidderdale),
Inigo Jackson (Roger Carbury), Richard Heffer (Paul Montague),
Sharon Gurney (Henrietta Carbury), Irène Prador (Madame Melmotte),
Angharad Rees (Marie Melmotte), Llewellyn Rees (Lord Alfred Grendall),
Phyllida Law (Georgiana Longestaffe), Charles Lloyd Pack (Adolphus Longestaffe),
Patricia Hastings (Lady Pomona Longestaffe), Freddie Earlle (Croll), Angus Mackay, Ed Bishop.

*Nothing Ventured* transmitted on 12.04.69
Colin Blakely (Augustus Melmotte), Rachel Gurney (Lady Carbury),
Cavan Kendall (Sir Felix Carbury), Adrian Ropes (Dolly Longestaffe),
Pieter Van Der Stolk (Vossner), Peter French (Miles Grendall), Jeremy Clyde (Lord Nidderdale),
Inigo Jackson (Roger Carbury), Richard Heffer (Paul Montague),
Sharon Gurney (Henrietta Carbury), Irène Prador (Madame Melmotte),
Angharad Rees (Marie Melmotte), Llewellyn Rees (Lord Alfred Grendall),
Phyllida Law (Georgiana Longestaffe), Charles Lloyd Pack (Adolphus Longestaffe),
Patricia Hastings (Lady Pomona Longestaffe), Freddie Earlle (Croll), John Wilding,
Otto Diamant, Sarah Brackett, Brigit Paul.

*Melmotte's Glory* transmitted on 19.04.69
Colin Blakely (Augustus Melmotte), Rachel Gurney (Lady Carbury),
Cavan Kendall (Sir Felix Carbury), Adrian Ropes (Dolly Longestaffe),
Pieter Van Der Stolk (Vossner), Peter French (Miles Grendall), Jeremy Clyde (Lord Nidderdale),
Inigo Jackson (Roger Carbury), Richard Heffer (Paul Montague),
Sharon Gurney (Henrietta Carbury), Irène Prador (Madame Melmotte),
Angharad Rees (Marie Melmotte), Llewellyn Rees (Lord Alfred Grendall),
Phyllida Law (Georgiana Longestaffe), Charles Lloyd Pack (Adolphus Longestaffe),
Patricia Hastings (Lady Pomona Longestaffe), Freddie Earlle (Croll), Peter Bartlett,
Brigit Paul, Sarah Brackett, Christopher Benjamin, Robert Mill, Anthony Langdon,
Eric Woodburn, Philip Anthony.

*Melmotte Contra Mundum* transmitted on 26.04.69
Colin Blakely (Augustus Melmotte), Rachel Gurney (Lady Carbury),
Cavan Kendall (Sir Felix Carbury), Adrian Ropes (Dolly Longestaffe),
Pieter Van Der Stolk (Vossner), Peter French (Miles Grendall), Jeremy Clyde (Lord Nidderdale),
Inigo Jackson (Roger Carbury), Richard Heffer (Paul Montague),
Sharon Gurney (Henrietta Carbury), Irène Prador (Madame Melmotte),
Angharad Rees (Marie Melmotte), Llewellyn Rees (Lord Alfred Grendall),
Phyllida Law (Georgiana Longestaffe), Charles Lloyd Pack (Adolphus Longestaffe),
Patricia Hastings (Lady Pomona Longestaffe), Freddie Earlle (Croll), Sarah Brackett,
Angus Mackay, Christopher Benjamin, Otto Diamant, John Kidd, Philip Anthony.

*Close Of Play* transmitted on 03.05.69
Colin Blakely (Augustus Melmotte), Rachel Gurney (Lady Carbury),
Cavan Kendall (Sir Felix Carbury), Adrian Ropes (Dolly Longestaffe),
Pieter Van Der Stolk (Vossner), Peter French (Miles Grendall), Jeremy Clyde (Lord Nidderdale),
Inigo Jackson (Roger Carbury), Richard Heffer (Paul Montague),
Sharon Gurney (Henrietta Carbury), Irène Prador (Madame Melmotte),
Angharad Rees (Marie Melmotte), Llewellyn Rees (Lord Alfred Grendall),
Phyllida Law (Georgiana Longestaffe), Charles Lloyd Pack (Adolphus Longestaffe),
Patricia Hastings (Lady Pomona Longestaffe), Freddie Earlle (Croll), John Devaut,
Christopher Benjamin, Philip Anthony, Sandy Stein, Peter Stephens, Geoffrey Rose,
Eric Woodburn, Angus Mackay, Ed Bishop.

Five forty-five minute episodes, recorded on 2" colour videotape. No copies survive.

## *W. SOMERSET MAUGHAM*
### Produced for BBC 2

Based on novels by W. Somerset Maugham; Produced by Verity Lambert.

*The Creative Impulse* transmitted on 17.06.69
Dramatised by Simon Raven; Directed by James Cellan Jones.
Brenda de Banzie (Mrs Albert Forrester), John Le Mesurier (Mr Albert Forrester),
Megs Jenkins (Mrs Bulfinch), Derek Hart (Narrator), Timothy Bateson (Simmons),
Arthur Hewlett (Publisher), Richard Matthews (Clifford Boyleston),
Liz Ashley (Rose Waterford), Peter French (Harry Oakland), Aubrey Morris (Oscar Charles),
Richard Davies (Labour Minister), Robert Henderson (American Ambassador),
Anna Fox (Carter), John Devaut (French Academician), Rosamund Greenwood (Miss Warren),
Robert Lee (Hu-Tzung), Alex Jawdokimov (Russian Prince), Marguerite Young (Duchess),
Aharon Ipale (Painter), Marian Forster (Adolescent Girl).

*Olive* transmitted on 28.05.70
Dramatised by David Turner; Directed by James Cellan Jones.
Eileen Atkins (Olive Hardy), Edward Fox (Tim Hardy), Martin Potter (Mark Featherstone),
John Bailey (District Officer), Kenneth Houng (His Clerk), Mary Yang (The Hardys' Amah),
Michael Beint (George Sergison), Liz Ashley (Ethel Sergison), Max Rahman (Barman),
Kim Kee Lim (Post Boy), Denis Cleary (Ship's Steward), Jimmy Fung (Mark's Servant),
Geoffrey Denton (Mr Richardson), Marguerite Young (Mrs Richardson), Clare Sutcliffe (Sally).

Fifty-minute plays, recorded on 2" colour videotape, both survive on D3 videotape.

## *SOLO*
### Produced for BBC 2

Produced by Cedric Messina; Directed by James Cellan Jones.

*A selection from EE Cummings* transmitted on 21.01.70
Read by Alec Guinness.

*Little Gidding by TS Eliot* transmitted 18.02.70
Read by Alec Guinness.

Twenty-minute programmes, recorded on 2" colour videotape and preserved on D3 videotape.

## THE ROADS TO FREEDOM
Produced for BBC 2

Based on a book by Jean-Paul Sartre; Adapted by David Turner;
Produced by David Conroy; Directed by James Cellan Jones.

---

*15 June 1938 - Evening* transmitted on 04.10.70
Michael Bryant (Mathieu), Daniel Massey (Daniel), Rosemary Leach (Marcelle),
Georgia Brown (Lola), Clifford Rose (Jacques), Anthony Corlan (Boris),
Heather Canning (Sarah), Donald Burton (Brunet), Alison Fiske (Ivich), Eamonn Boyce,
Robert Tayman, Rosamund Greenwood, Alfred Hoffman, David Gilmore, Keith Campbell,
Joy Hope.

*16 June 1938 - Afternoon* transmitted on 11.10.70
Michael Bryant (Mathieu), Daniel Massey (Daniel), Rosemary Leach (Marcelle),
Georgia Brown (Lola), Clifford Rose (Jacques), Anthony Corlan (Boris),
Heather Canning (Sarah), Donald Burton (Brunet), Alison Fiske (Ivich), Anna Fox (Odette),
Mischa de la Motte, Billie Hill, Bella Emberg, Charles Lloyd Pack, Anthony Pinhorn,
Roger Lloyd Pack.

*16 June 1938 - Evening* transmitted on 18.10.70
Michael Bryant (Mathieu), Daniel Massey (Daniel), Rosemary Leach (Marcelle),
Georgia Brown (Lola), Clifford Rose (Jacques), Anthony Corlan (Boris),
Heather Canning (Sarah), Donald Burton (Brunet), Alison Fiske (Ivich),
Anthony Corlan (Boris), Winifred Hill, John Devaut, Linda Priest, Cyril Cross,
Elizabeth Tyrrell, Winifred Braemar.

*17 June 1938 - Morning* transmitted on 25.10.70
Michael Bryant (Mathieu), Daniel Massey (Daniel), Rosemary Leach (Marcelle),
Georgia Brown (Lola), Clifford Rose (Jacques), Anthony Corlan (Boris),
Heather Canning (Sarah), Donald Burton (Brunet), Alison Fiske (Ivich),
Anthony Corlan (Boris), Frederick Beauman, Sally Corday, Mercia Mansfield.

*17 June 1938 - Afternoon* transmitted on 01.11.70
Michael Bryant (Mathieu), Daniel Massey (Daniel), Rosemary Leach (Marcelle),
Georgia Brown (Lola), Clifford Rose (Jacques), Anthony Corlan (Boris),
Heather Canning (Sarah), Donald Burton (Brunet), Alison Fiske (Ivich), Colin Baker (Claude),
Walter Swash, Vernon Dobtcheff, Alfred Hoffman, Betty Hare, Consuela Chapman, Ian Gray,
Myles Reitherman, Marguerite Young, Joyce Burton, Damon Sanders.

*17 June 1938 - Evening* transmitted on 08.11.70
Michael Bryant (Mathieu), Daniel Massey (Daniel), Rosemary Leach (Marcelle),
Georgia Brown (Lola), Clifford Rose (Jacques), Anthony Corlan (Boris),
Heather Canning (Sarah), Donald Burton (Brunet), Alison Fiske (Ivich), Frans Van Norde,
Marguerite Young.

*24 September 1938 - Morning* transmitted on 15.11.70
Michael Bryant (Mathieu), Daniel Massey (Daniel), Rosemary Leach (Marcelle),
Georgia Brown (Lola), Clifford Rose (Jacques), Anthony Corlan (Boris),
Heather Canning (Sarah), Donald Burton (Brunet), Alison Fiske (Ivich), Anna Fox (Odette),
Simon Cellan Jones (Pablo), Anthony Corlan (Boris), Alfred Maron, Michael Goodliffe,
Tenniel Evans, Paul Hansard, Andrew Faulds, Tom Marshall, Basil Henson, Susan Travers,
Frank Seton, John Bryans.

*26 September 1938 - Evening* transmitted on 22.11.70
Michael Bryant (Mathieu), Daniel Massey (Daniel), Rosemary Leach (Marcelle),
Georgia Brown (Lola), Clifford Rose (Jacques), Anthony Corlan (Boris),
Heather Canning (Sarah), Donald Burton (Brunet), Alison Fiske (Ivich),
Anthony Corlan (Boris), Anna Fox (Odette), Kathleen Heath, John Caesar, Frank Seton,
Michael Goodliffe, Giles Phibbs, Betty Hare, Simon Ward, Leon Vitali, Marty Cruickshank.

*28 September 1938 - Morning* transmitted on 29.11.70
Michael Bryant (Mathieu), Daniel Massey (Daniel), Rosemary Leach (Marcelle),
Georgia Brown (Lola), Clifford Rose (Jacques), Anthony Corlan (Boris),
Heather Canning (Sarah), Donald Burton (Brunet), Alison Fiske (Ivich),
Anthony Corlan (Boris), Anna Fox (Odette), Simon Cellan Jones (Pablo), Colin Baker (Claude),
Marty Cruickshank, Pat Gorman, Simon Ward, Christopher Benjamin, Frank Duncan,
Anthony Jacobs, Frederick Hall, Anthony Sagar, John Lawrence, Richard Beale, Roy Denton,
John Bryans, George Roderick, Michael David, Trevor Baxter, James Bree, Gerald Case,
Michael Goodliffe, Eric Longworth, Denis Cleary.

*15 June 1940 - Morning* transmitted on 06.12.70
Michael Bryant (Mathieu), Daniel Massey (Daniel), Rosemary Leach (Marcelle),
Georgia Brown (Lola), Clifford Rose (Jacques), Anthony Corlan (Boris),
Heather Canning (Sarah), Donald Burton (Brunet), Alison Fiske (Ivich), Andrew Faulds,
Warren Stanhope, Christian Rodska, John Cater, Norman Rossington, Christopher Heywood,
Freddie Earlle, Matthew Guinness, Andrew McCulloch, Peter French, Hugo Panczak,
Ray Chiarella, André Maranne, Robert Henderson.

*15 June 1940 - Afternoon* transmitted on 13.12.70
Michael Bryant (Mathieu), Daniel Massey (Daniel), Rosemary Leach (Marcelle),
Georgia Brown (Lola), Clifford Rose (Jacques), Anthony Corlan (Boris),
Heather Canning (Sarah), Donald Burton (Brunet), Alison Fiske (Ivich),
Anthony Corlan (Boris), Freddie Earlle, Peter Wyatt, Jane Woolnough, Paul Henry, John Cater,
Christian Rodska, Leon Lissek, Norman Rossington, Stephen Chase, Brian Grellis,
Clare Sutcliffe, Michael Mulcaster, Matthew Guinness, Brian Lawson, Patrick Durkin,
David Hargreaves, Robert Davis.

*16 June 1940 - Afternoon* transmitted on 20.12.70
Michael Bryant (Mathieu), Daniel Massey (Daniel), Rosemary Leach (Marcelle),
Georgia Brown (Lola), Clifford Rose (Jacques), Anthony Corlan (Boris),
Heather Canning (Sarah), Donald Burton (Brunet), Alison Fiske (Ivich), John Cater,

Paul Henry, Peter Wyatt, Robert Davis, David Hargreaves, Freddie Earlle, Simon Ward, Norman Rossington, Clare Sutcliffe, Christian Rodska, Arthur Brough, Blake Butler, Shirley Cooklin, Christopher Heywood, Michael Goldie, Michael Elphick, James Appleby, Donald Webster, Stephen Yardley.

*17 June 1940 - Night* transmitted on 27.12.70
Michael Bryant (Mathieu), Daniel Massey (Daniel), Rosemary Leach (Marcelle),
Georgia Brown (Lola), Clifford Rose (Jacques), Anthony Corlan (Boris),
Heather Canning (Sarah), Donald Burton (Brunet), Alison Fiske (Ivich), Michael Elphick,
Donald Webster, Norman Rossington, Stephen Yardley, James Appleby, David Hargreaves,
John Cater, Peter Wyatt, Paul Henry, Clare Sutcliffe, Jimmy Gardner, Kate Brown, Udo Schone,
Hugo Panczak, Donald Campbell.

Thirteen forty-five minute episodes, recorded on 2" colour videotape and preserved on D3 videotape.

---

### PLAY FOR TODAY
Produced for BBC 1

---

*The Piano* transmitted on 28.01.71
Written by Julia Jones; Produced by Graeme McDonald; Directed by James Cellan Jones.
Glyn Owen (Willie), Janet Munro (Mabel), Leo Franklyn (Edgar), Hilda Barry (Ada),
James Cossins (Jeremy), Brian Wilde (Ted), Harry Littlewood (Enoch),
Roy Barraclough (Claud)

Sixty-five minute play recorded on 2" colour videotape and, apart from the first minute, preserved on D3 videotape.

---

### SUNDAY NIGHT THEATRE
Produced for Granada Television

---

*Square* transmitted on 27.06.71
Written by Mark Priaux; Produced by Kenith Trodd; Directed by James Cellan Jones.
Hermione Baddeley (Amy Riordan), Elaine Taylor (Janet Turner),
Liam Redmond (Pat Riordan), Edward Fox (Michael Turner).

Fifty-minute play, recorded on 2" colour videotape and preserved on Digital Betacam videotape.

*EYELESS IN GAZA*
Produced for BBC 2

Dramatised by Robin Chapman; Based on a novel by Aldous Huxley;
Produced by Martin Lisemore; Directed by James Cellan Jones

*O Dark, Dark, Dark, Amid The Blaze Of Noon* transmitted on 12.09.71
Ian Richardson (Anthony Beavis), Lynn Farleigh (Helen Ledwidge),
Michael Gambon (Mark Staithes), Harry Brooks Jr (Ekki Giesebrecht),
John Laurie (James Miller), Adrienne Corri (Mary Amberley), Christopher Vale,
Jeremy Richardson, Gareth Forwood, Clifford Rose, Trader Faulkner, Marguerite Young,
Peter Stephens, Llewellyn Rees, Jonathan Scott.

*With Inward Eyes Illuminated* transmitted on 19.09.71
Ian Richardson (Anthony Beavis), Lynn Farleigh (Helen Ledwidge),
Michael Gambon (Mark Staithes), Harry Brooks Jr (Ekki Giesebrecht),
John Laurie (James Miller), Adrienne Corri (Mary Amberley), Gareth Forwood, Clifford Rose,
Brian Stirner, Mark Dignam, Philippa Markham, Peggy-Louise Vance, Saba Sarol,
Sharon Maughan, Paul Hardwick, John Glyn-Jones, Elspeth MacNaughton.

*Come, Come, No Time For Lamentation Now* transmitted on 26.09.71
Ian Richardson (Anthony Beavis), Lynn Farleigh (Helen Ledwidge),
Michael Gambon (Mark Staithes), Harry Brooks Jr (Ekki Giesebrecht),
John Laurie (James Miller), Adrienne Corri (Mary Amberley), Selma Vaz Dias, Juan Moreno.

*All Is Best, Though We Oft Doubt* transmitted on 03.10.71
Ian Richardson (Anthony Beavis), Lynn Farleigh (Helen Ledwidge),
Michael Gambon (Mark Staithes), Harry Brooks Jr (Ekki Giesebrecht),
John Laurie (James Miller), Adrienne Corri (Mary Amberley), Jouey Douben, Geoffrey Rose,
Jeremy Wilkin, Ingo Mogendorf, Hugh Cecil, Peter Stephens, Brian Anthony, Elspeth Charlton,
Michael Mulcaster, Walter Swash, Trader Faulkner, George Sweeney, John Caesar.

*And Calm Of Mind, All Passion Spent* transmitted on 10.10.71
Ian Richardson (Anthony Beavis), Lynn Farleigh (Helen Ledwidge),
Michael Gambon (Mark Staithes), Harry Brooks Jr (Ekki Giesebrecht),
John Laurie (James Miller), Adrienne Corri (Mary Amberley), Jeremy Wilkin, Stephen Greif,
Neil Phelps, Elspeth Charlton, Barbara Hickmott, David Firth, Gareth Forwood,
Philippa Markham, Christopher Vale, Nigel Read, Simon Thorne, Jeremy Richardson,
Bert Simms.

Five forty-five minute episodes, recorded on 2" colour videotape and preserved on
D3 videotape.

---

**PLAY OF THE MONTH**
Produced for BBC 1

---

*A Midsummer Night's Dream* transmitted on 26.09.71
Written by William Shakespeare; Produced by Cedric Messina; Directed by James Cellan Jones.
Eileen Atkins (Titania), Ronnie Barker (Bottom), Lynn Redgrave (Helena),
Robert Stephens (Oberon), Amanda Barrie (Hermia), Eleanor Bron (Hippolyta),
Jeremy Clyde (Demetrius), Edward Fox (Lysander), Michael Gambon (Theseus),
John Glyn-Jones (Egeus), Paul Henry (Flute), John Laurie (Quince), Bunny May (Puck),
Julian Orchard (Snug), Ken Parry (Snout), Clifford Rose (Starveling), Sarah Taunton (The Fairy).

A two-hour play, recorded on 2" colour videotape and preserved on D3 videotape.

---

**THE GOLDEN BOWL**
Produced for BBC 2

Dramatised by Jack Pulman; Based on a novel by Henry James;
Produced by Martin Lisemore; Directed by James Cellan Jones.

---

*The Prince* transmitted on 04.05.72
Cyril Cusack (Bob Assingham), Daniel Massey (Prince Amerigo),
Gayle Hunnicutt (Charlotte Stant), Barry Morse (Adam Verver),
Jill Townsend (Maggie Verner), Kathleen Byron (Fanny Assingham), Freddie Earlle,
Jonathan Scott, Carl Bernard.

*Mr Verver* transmitted on 11.05.72
Cyril Cusack (Bob Assingham), Daniel Massey (Prince Amerigo),
Gayle Hunnicutt (Charlotte Stant), Barry Morse (Adam Verver),
Jill Townsend (Maggie Verner), Kathleen Byron (Fanny Assingham), Kes Bohan-McGlashan,
Sarah Brackett, Billy Franks.

*Charlotte* transmitted on 18.05.72
Cyril Cusack (Bob Assingham), Daniel Massey (Prince Amerigo),
Gayle Hunnicutt (Charlotte Stant), Barry Morse (Adam Verver),
Jill Townsend (Maggie Verner), Kathleen Byron (Fanny Assingham), Henry Goodman,
Donald Gray.

*Fanny* transmitted on 25.05.72
Cyril Cusack (Bob Assingham), Daniel Massey (Prince Amerigo),
Gayle Hunnicutt (Charlotte Stant), Barry Morse (Adam Verver),
Jill Townsend (Maggie Verner), Kathleen Byron (Fanny Assingham), Anna Fox,
Terry Mitchell, Deborah Davies, Hilary Minster, Angus Mackay, Olivier Harari.

*Maggie* transmitted on 01.06.72
Cyril Cusack (Bob Assingham), Daniel Massey (Prince Amerigo),
Gayle Hunnicutt (Charlotte Stant), Barry Morse (Adam Verver),
Jill Townsend (Maggie Verner), Kathleen Byron (Fanny Assingham), Olivier Harari,
Angus Mackay, Anna Fox, Marguerite Young, Carl Bernard.

*End Game* transmitted on 08.06.72
Cyril Cusack (Bob Assingham), Daniel Massey (Prince Amerigo),
Gayle Hunnicutt (Charlotte Stant), Barry Morse (Adam Verver),
Jill Townsend (Maggie Verner), Kathleen Byron (Fanny Assingham), Mischa de la Motte,
Elizabeth Chambers, Hilary Minster, Andrea Addison.

Six forty-five minute episodes, recorded on 2" colour videotape and preserved on
D3 videotape.

---

**THE EDWARDIANS**
Produced for BBC 2

---

*E Nesbit* transmitted on 05.12.72
Written by Ken Taylor; Produced by Mark Shivas; Directed by James Cellan Jones.
Judy Parfitt (E Nesbit), James Villiers (Hubert Bland), Jane Lapotaire (Alice Hoatson),
Michael Menaugh (Paul Bland), Jenifer Armitage (Iris Bland), Simon Turner (Fabian Bland),
Rosalyn Landor (Rosamund Bland), Christopher Vale (John Bland), Brigid Erin Bates (Mary).

*Daisy* transmitted on 02.01.73
Written by David Turner; Produced by Mark Shivas; Directed by James Cellan Jones.
Virginia McKenna (Daisy), Thorley Walters (Edward, Prince of Wales),
John Bennett (Frank Harris), Bettine Le Beau (Maid), Mollie Maureen (Queen Victoria),
Vernon Dobtcheff (Disraeli), Julian Holloway (Lord Brooke), Myles Hoyle (Lord Beresford),
Karin McCarthy (Lady Beresford), Frank Middlemass (George Lewis),
Kenneth Benda (Archbishop of Canterbury), Llewellyn Rees (Salisbury),
Trevor Baxter (McDonnell), Marguerite Young (Nancy Galpin), Neville Barber (Robert Blatchford),
Philip Garston-Jones (Joseph Arch), Angus Mackay (Earl of Albemarle),
Frederick Treves (George Keppel), Patricia Nelligan (Alice Keppel), Colin Baker (Joseph Laycock),
Frank Gatliff (Viscount Esther), Philippa Markham (Marchioness of Downshire),
Elizabeth Reville (Shop Assistant), Simon Carter (Shop Manager),
Trader Faulkner (Arthur Du Cros), Charles Lloyd Pack (Stamfordham),
Philip Anthony (Charles Russell), Edward Harvey (Mr Justice Low), John McCarthy Singers.

Seventy-five minute plays, recorded on 2" colour videotape and preserved as 16mm
monochrome telerecordings.

---

### *AWAY FROM IT ALL*
Produced for BBC 1

---

*A Work Of Genius* transmitted on 13.05.73
Written by Evan Jones; Produced by Innes Lloyd; Directed by James Cellan Jones.
Michael Bryant (Chris), Ted Ray (Father), Suzanne Neve (Ann), Ernest Clark (Colonel),
Liz Ashley (Judith), Lorraine Peters (Barmaid).

Fifty-minute play, recorded on 2" colour videotape.  No copy survives.

---

### *BLACK AND BLUE*
Produced for BBC 2

---

*Secrets* transmitted on 14.08.73
Written by Michael Palin and Terry Jones; Script Editor Richard Broke;
Produced by Mark Shivas; Directed by James Cellan Jones.
Warren Mitchell (Rose), Clifford Rose (Villon), Julian Holloway (Robinson),
David Collings (Atkinson), George Innes (Saville), Hugh Walters (Jackson),
Brian Coburn (Foreman), Brian Wilde (Major Forster), Hilda Barry (Mrs Function),
Gretchen Franklin (Mrs Pitt), Betty Hare (Despatch Lady), George Tovey (Lorry Driver),
Godfrey Talbot (Handsome Man), Sarah Douglas (Beautiful Girl), Judy Robinson (Country Girl),
Pamela Coveney (Housewife), Kenneth Wolstenholme (Commentator).

Fifty-three minute play, recorded on 2" colour videotape.  Survives as a Digital Betacam copy
of a domestic video recording.

---

### *JENNIE, LADY RANDOLPH CHURCHILL*
Produced for Thames Television

Written by Julian Mitchell; Executive Producer Stella Richman;
Produced by Andrew Brown; Directed by James Cellan Jones.

---

*Jennie Jerome* transmitted on 22.10.74
Lee Remick (Jennie), Jeremy Brett (Count Kinsky), Rachel Kempson (Duchess of Marlborough),
Ronald Pickup (Randolph), Charles Lloyd Pack (Sir Henry Wolff), Adrian Ropes (Arthur Balfour),
David Steuart (Mr Gladstone), Barbara Parkins (Leonie), Thorley Walters (Prince of Wales),
Dan O'Herlihy, Helen Horton, Linda Liles, Joanna David, Peter Penry Jones, Hilary Minster,
Robin Sherringham, Thorey Mountain, John Westbrook, John Marquand, Cyril Luckham.

*Lady Randolph* transmitted on 29.10.74
Lee Remick (Jennie), Jeremy Brett (Count Kinsky), Rachel Kempson (Duchess of Marlborough),

Ronald Pickup (Randolph), Charles Lloyd Pack (Sir Henry Wolff), Adrian Ropes (Arthur Balfour), David Steuart (Mr Gladstone), Barbara Parkins (Leonie), Thorley Walters (Prince of Wales), Julia Sutton (Gentry), Barbara Laurenson, Virginia Denham, Cyril Luckham, John Westbrook, Michael Gough, Peter Cellier, Philippa Markham, Linda Liles, Paul Hardwick, Patrick Troughton, James Gregson, Susan Field, Joanna David, Helen Horton.

*Recovery* transmitted on 05.11.74
Lee Remick (Jennie), Jeremy Brett (Count Kinsky), Rachel Kempson (Duchess of Marlborough), Ronald Pickup (Randolph), Charles Lloyd Pack (Sir Henry Wolff), Adrian Ropes (Arthur Balfour), David Steuart (Mr Gladstone), Barbara Parkins (Leonie), Thorley Walters (Prince of Wales), Julia Sutton (Gentry), John Bailey, Patrick Troughton, Cyril Luckham, Marguerite Young, Anthony Langdon, John Dunbar, Juba Kennerley, Llewellyn Rees, Paul Ambrose, Alexander Scrivenor, Susan Field, John Port, Daniel Jones.

*Triumph And Tragedy* transmitted on 12.11.74
Lee Remick (Jennie), Jeremy Brett (Count Kinsky), Rachel Kempson (Duchess of Marlborough), Ronald Pickup (Randolph), Charles Lloyd Pack (Sir Henry Wolff), Adrian Ropes (Arthur Balfour), David Steuart (Mr Gladstone), Warren Clarke (Winston), Barbara Parkins (Leonie), Thorley Walters (Prince of Wales), Julia Sutton (Gentry), Marguerite Young, Dennis Edwards, Paul Ambrose, Michael Osborne, Charles West.

*A Perfect Darling* transmitted on 19.11.74
Lee Remick (Jennie), Jeremy Brett (Count Kinsky), Rachel Kempson (Duchess of Marlborough), Ronald Pickup (Randolph), Charles Lloyd Pack (Sir Henry Wolff), Adrian Ropes (Arthur Balfour), David Steuart (Mr Gladstone), Warren Clarke (Winston), Barbara Parkins (Leonie), Thorley Walters (Prince of Wales), Penelope Lee, Edgar Wreford, Patrick Macrae, Christopher Cazenove, Malcolm Stoddard, Zoë Wanamaker, Brenda Kaye, John Harvey, Patricia Garwood, John Barcroft, Roger Hammond.

*His Borrowed Plumes* transmitted on 26.11.74
Lee Remick (Jennie), Jeremy Brett (Count Kinsky), Rachel Kempson (Duchess of Marlborough), Ronald Pickup (Randolph), Charles Lloyd Pack (Sir Henry Wolff), Adrian Ropes (Arthur Balfour), David Steuart (Mr Gladstone), Warren Clarke (Winston), Barbara Parkins (Leonie), Thorley Walters (Prince of Wales), Christopher Cazenove, Malcolm Stoddard, Ciaran Madden, Anna Fox, Barbara Atkinson, Siân Phillips, Terence Alexander.

*A Past And A Future* transmitted on 03.12.74
Lee Remick (Jennie), Jeremy Brett (Count Kinsky), Rachel Kempson (Duchess of Marlborough), Ronald Pickup (Randolph), Charles Lloyd Pack (Sir Henry Wolff), Adrian Ropes (Arthur Balfour), David Steuart (Mr Gladstone), Warren Clarke (Winston), Barbara Parkins (Leonie), Thorley Walters (Prince of Wales), Julia Sutton (Gentry), Charles Kay, Ciaran Madden, Peter Dennis, Dennis Edwards, Anna Fox, David Dyke, Linda Liles, Malcolm Stoddard, Marty Cruickshank, John Boxer, Deddie Davies, Pat Conti, Michael Reeves, Willoughby Gray.

Seven fifty-minute episodes, recorded in colour on 2" videotape and preserved on D3 videotape.

---

### *DR WATSON AND THE DARKWATER HALL MYSTERY*
Produced for BBC 1

---

Transmitted on 27.12.74
Written by Kingsley Amis; Script Editor Richard Broke; Produced by Mark Shivas;
Directed by James Cellan Jones
Edward Fox (Doctor Watson), Christopher Cazenove (Sir Harry), Jeremy Clyde (Miles),
Terence Bayler (Carlos), Elaine Taylor (Emily), John Westbrook (Bradshaw),
Carmen Gomez (Dolores), Anthony Langdon (Black Paul),
Anne Cunningham (Black Paul's Woman), Marguerite Young (Mrs Hudson),
Derek Deadman (Maddocks).

Seventy-three minute play, recorded in colour on 2" videotape and preserved on D3 videotape.

---

### *PLAY OF THE MONTH*
Produced for BBC 1

---

*Strife* transmitted on 18.05.75
Written by John Galsworthy; Script Editor Alan Shallcross;
Produced by Cedric Messina; Directed by James Cellan Jones.
Colin Blakely (Roberts), Clifford Evans (John Anthony), Angela Down (Enid),
Nerys Hughes (Annie), Hugh Walters (Tench), Allan McClelland (Wanklin),
Clifford Rose (Wilder), Malcolm Stoddard (Underwood), George Waring (Scantlebury),
Jeremy Clyde (Edgar Anthony), Haydn Jones (Frost), John Bennett (Harness),
Aubrey Richards (Thomas), John Ogwen (George Rous), Betty Hare (Mrs Rous),
Victoria Plucknett (Madge Thomas), Fraser Cains (Jago), David Pugh (Lewis),
Mostyn Evans (Green), Mici Plwm (Henry Rous), Huw Ceredig (Bulgin),
John Pearce Jones (Blacksmith), Eilian Wyn (Youth), Gareth Lewis (Evans),
Olwen Rees (Parlourmaid)

Ninety-five minute play, recorded in colour on 2" videotape and preserved on D3 videotape.

---

### *THE ADAMS CHRONICLES*
Produced for the Public Broadcasting Service

---

*John Adams, Diplomat (1776-1783)*
Written by Sherman Yellan; Produced by Robert Costello; Directed by James Cellan Jones.
George Grizzard, Kathryn Walker, Robert Symonds

*John Adams, Minister to Great Britain (1784-1787)*
Written by Millard Lampell; Produced by Robert Costello; Directed by James Cellan Jones.
George Grizzard, Kathryn Walker, Robert Symonds.

*Charles Frances Adams, Minister To Great Britain (1861-1864)*
Written by Roger Hirson; Produced and directed by James Cellan Jones.
John Beal, Nancy Coleman.

---

### THE MADNESS
Produced for BBC 2

Written by John Elliot; produced by Rosemary Hill; directed by James Cellan Jones.

---

Transmitted on 21.07.76
Bill Fraser (Prieto), Patrick Stewart (Largo Caballero), Zena Walker (Dolores Ibarruri),
Clifford Rose (General Mola), Michael Goodliffe (General Queipo De Llano),
Tony Doyle (Andres Nin / Waiter in Café), Antony Sher (Militiaman / Young Man in Café),
Simon Prebble (Diaz), Timothy Davies (Radio Studio Manager / Young Man in Café),
Roberta Iger (First Telephone Operator / Prostitute), Vicki Woolf (Second Telephone Operator / Young Woman in Café), Adrian Ropes (General Asensio Torrado), Rosalind Bailey (Militia Girl),
Oliver Cotton (Jesus Hernandez), Alfred Hoffman (Vicente Uribe),
Lilita Barros (Federica Montseny), Juan Moreno (Garcia Oliver), Jan Conrad (Alvarez Del Vayo),
Garth Watkins (Negrin), Desmond Cullum-Jones (Giral), Colin Thomas (Galarza),
Charles Lloyd Pack (General Miaja), John Westbrook (General Rojo), Michael Byrne (Gorev),
Rachel Thomas (Rosario), Denis De Marne (Juan / First Largo's Aide),
Eric Francis (Old Man in Café), Marguerite (Carmela), Anthony Langdon (Anarchist),
Peter Miles (Orlov), Juan Martin (Guitarist).

Eighty-five minute play, recorded in colour on 2" videotape and preserved on D3 videotape.

---

### CENTRE PLAY SHOWCASE
Produced for BBC 2

---

*Sea Change* transmitted on 10.09.76
Written by Martin Thompson; Produced by Rosemary Hill; Directed by James Cellan Jones.
Michael Gough (Father), Edward Fox (Andrew), Marguerite Young (Mother),
Elizabeth Proud (Miss Yates), Ben Chapman (Cunningham), Simon Cellan Jones (Schoolboy),
Stephen Tacey (Schoolboy), Michael Stuckey (Organist), Barry Abbotts (Boy Singer).

Thirty-minute play, recorded in colour on 2" videotape and preserved on D3 videotape.

---

## THE FOUR OF US
### Produced for ABC Television

---

Transmitted November 1976
Written by Reginald Rose; Produced by Herb Brodkin & Robert Buzz Berger;
Directed by James Cellan Jones.

---

## CAESAR AND CLEOPATRA
### Produced for Southern Television
### in association with Talent Associates and Norton Simon Clarion

---

Transmitted on 04.01.77
Written by George Bernard Shaw; Music by Michael Lewis;
Associate Producer Margaret Matheson; Executive Producer Lewis Rudd;
Produced by David Susskind and Duane Bogie; Directed by James Cellan Jones.
Alec Guinness (Caesar), Genevieve Bujold (Cleopatra), Margaret Courtenay (Ftatateeta),
Jolyon Bates (Ptolemy Dionysus), Noel Willman (Pothinus), David Steuart (Theodotus),
Gareth Thomas (Achillas), Iain Cuthbertson (Rufio), Michael Bryant (Britannus),
Clive Francis (Apollodorus), Roy Stewart (Nubian Slave), Matthew Long (Wounded Soldier),
Michael Poole (Centurion), Neville Phillips (Major-Domo), Ludmila Nova (Charmian),
Kristin Hatfeild (Iras).

Seventy-five minute play, recorded in colour - and preserved - on 2" videotape.

---

## PLAY OF THE MONTH
### Produced for BBC 1

---

*The Ambassadors* transmitted on 13.03.77
Based on a book by Henry James; Adapted by Denis Constanduros; Music by Patrick Harvey;
Produced by Cedric Messina; Directed by James Cellan Jones.
Paul Scofield (Lewis Lambert Strether), Lee Remick (Maria Gostrey),
Delphine Seyrig (Marie De Vionnet), David Huffman (Chadwick Newsome),
Gayle Hunnicutt (Sarah Pocock), Don Fellows (Waymarsh), William Hootkins (Little Bilham),
Liz Ashley (Miss Barrace), Natalie Caron (Jeanne De Vionnet), Weston Gavin (Jim Pocock),
Toria Fuller (Mamie Pocock), Philippa Markham (Hotel Receptionist), Peter Banks (Clark),
Angus MacInnes (Williams), Richard Saire (McGregor), Penelope Beaumont (Louise, Sarah's
Maid), Mugette De Braie (Patronne of The Inn).

Ninety-five minute play, recorded in colour on 2" videotape and preserved on D3 videotape.

*You Can Never Tell* transmitted on 30.10.77
Written by Bernard Shaw; Music by Richard Holmes;
Produced by David Jones; Directed by James Cellan Jones.
Ernest Clark (Finch McComas), Warren Clarke (Bohun, QC), Cyril Cusack (Waiter),
Patrick Magee (Fergus Crampton), Kika Markham (Gloria Clandon),
Judy Parfitt (Mrs Clandon), Robert Powell (Valentine), Kate Nicholls (Dolly Clandon),
Richard Everett (Philip Clandon), Gina Rowe (Parlour Maid), Neville Phillips (Jo).

One hundred-and-thirty minute play, recorded in colour on 2" videotape and preserved on
D3 videotape.

*The Beaux' Stratagem* transmitted on 02.04.78
Written by George Farquhar; Script Editor Stuart Griffiths;
Produced by James Cellan Jones; Directed by David Jones.
Brenda Bruce (Lady Bountiful), Tom Conti (Francis Archer), Estelle Kohler (Mrs Sullen),
Ian Ogilvy (Thomas Aimwell), Zoë Wanamaker (Dorinda), David Waller (Boniface),
Julie Peasgood (Cherry), Jay Neill (Tapster/Sir Charles Freeman), Malcolm Terris (Squire Sullen),
Tony Haygarth (Scrub), Freddie Jones (Gibbet), Souad Faress (Gypsy),
Norman Rodway (Foigard), Carol Macready (Country Woman), Ray Callaghan (Hounslow),
Derek Fuke (Bagshot), Paul Froude (Fiddler).

One hundred-and-twenty-five minute play, recorded in colour on 2" videotape and preserved
on D3 videotape.

---

### PLAY OF THE WEEK
Produced for BBC 2

---

*Ice Age* transmitted on 17.05.78
Written by Tankred Dorst; Translated by Neville Plaice and Stephen Plaice;
Produced by James Cellan Jones; Directed by David Jones.
Anthony Quayle (The Old Man), Mike Gwilym (Oswald), Joyce Redman (Vera),
Michael Williams (Paul), Will Stampe (Gardener), Celia Imrie (Housemaid),
Phillada Sewell (Major's Widow), Aimee Delamain (Old Spinster), Ruby Head (Doctor's Widow),
Patrick Godfrey (Professor Jenssen), Hubert Rees (Pastor Holm),
Arnold Peters (Savings Bank Manager), David de Keyser (Axel Reich),
Boris Isarov (Latvian Cook), Clifford Mollison (Man With Compass), Ken Parry (Fat Man),
Judith Nelmes (Lady In Wheelchair), Janet Brandes (Sister Of Lady In Wheelchair),
John Herrington (Man With Monkey Mask), Anne Blake (Elegant Lady),
Charles Bentley (Blind Man), Llewellyn Rees (The Colonel), Robert Henderson (Berend),
George Cormack (Man With Camera), Gordon Gostelow (Kristian).

One hundred-and-twenty minute play, recorded in colour on 2" videotape and preserved on
D3 videotape.

*Langrishe, Go Down* transmitted on 20.09.78
Based on a book by Aidan Higgins; Adapted by Harold Pinter; Music by Carl Davis;
Produced by James Cellan Jones*; Directed by David Jones.
Judi Dench (Imogen Langrishe), Jeremy Irons (Otto Beck), Annette Crosbie (Helen Langrishe),
Harold Pinter (Barry Shannon), Margaret Whiting (Maureen Layde),
John Molloy (First Man On Bus), Niall O'Brien (Second Man On Bus),
Susan Williamson (Lily Langrishe), Arthur O'Sullivan (Joseph Feeney),
Liam O'Callaghan (Mr Langrishe), Joan O'Hara (Mrs Langrishe), Michael O'Briain (Priest).

A one-hundred-and-ten minute film, recorded and preserved on 16mm colour film.

*I produced, but did not take a credit as I could not attend the filming in Ireland.

*A Touch Of The Tiny Hacketts* transmitted on 31.10.78
Written by John Esmonde and Bob Larbey; Produced and directed by James Cellan Jones.
Ray Brooks (Raymond Collis), Tony Selby (Stan), Judy Cornwell (Sylvia Collis),
Brenda Bruce (Mrs Hackett), Rusty Goffe (Tiny Hackett), Nat Jackley (Norman Tuck),
Karl Howman (First Policeman), Hugh Walters (Second Policeman), Tim Meats (Ambulanceman),
Alec Linstead (CID Man), Doug Fisher (Terry), George Tovey (Old Spud),
George Innes (Graham), Anthony Langdon (Mike), Deborah Fairfax (Miss Benson),
Eamonn Boyce (Reporter), Patrick Newell (Mr Nesbitt), John Kidd (Mr Samson),
Esmond Webb (Court Attendant).

Sixty-five minute play, recorded in colour on 2" videotape and preserved on D3 videotape.

*Kean* transmitted on 26.11.78
Written by Jean-Paul Sartre; Translated by Frank Hauser; Music by Michael J. Lewis;
Produced by David Jones; Directed by James Cellan Jones.
Anthony Hopkins (Edmund Kean), Adrienne Corri (Amy, Countess Of Gosswill),
Barrie Ingham (Count De Koefeld), Sara Kestelman (Elena, Countess De Koefeld),
Cherie Lunghi (Anna Danby), Frank Middlemass (Solomon), Robert Stephens (Prince Of Wales),
Neville Phillips (Major-Domo), George Tovey (Peter Potts), Jennifer Granville (Sadie),

Roger Elliott (Constable), Julian Fellowes (Lord Neville), Helena Breck (Gidsa),
Hugh Walters (Darius), Mike Savage (Stage Manager).

One hundred-and-thirty-five minute programme, recorded and preserved on 16mm colour film.

---

### THE DAY CHRIST DIED
Produced for Twentieth Century Fox

---

Written by Edward Anhalt and James Lee Barrett; Based on a book by Jim Bishop;
Music by Laurence Rosenthal; Associate Producer Ted Butcher; Produced by Martin Manulis;
Directed by James Cellan Jones.
Chris Sarandon (Jesus Christ), Colin Blakely (Caiaphas), Keith Michell (Pontius Pilate),
Jonathan Pryce (King Herod), Barrie Houghton (Judas), Jay O Sanders (Peter),
Eleanor Bron (Mary), Tim Pigott-Smith (Tullius), Delia Boccardo (Mary Magdelene),
Oliver Cotton (John), Marne Maitland (Jacob), Ralph Arliss (Matthew).

---

### PLAYHOUSE
Produced for BBC 2

---

*School Play* transmitted on 07.11.79
Written by Frederic Raphael; Music by Iago Jones*; Produced by Richard Broke;
Directed by James Cellan Jones.
Denholm Elliott (Geoffrey Treasure), Jeremy Kemp (James Lombard),
Michael Kitchen (Rosie S.J.), Tim Pigott-Smith (Timothy Perkins),
Jenny Agutter (Miss P. Jackson), John Normington (Michael Bland),
Richard Warwick (R.D. Jackson), Jeremy Clyde (The Honourable C. St J. Denton),
Jeremy Sinden (J. D. Tupperman), Chuck Julian (Quinton C.C.), Richard Morant (Younger A.L.P.),
David Wilkinson (Forshawe J.R.), David Troughton (Hogg H.), Richard Clifford (A New Grunt).

Eighty-minute play, recorded in colour on 2" videotape and preserved on D3 videotape.

*Iago Jones is a pseudonym for James Cellan Jones.

---

***PLAY FOR TODAY***
Produced for BBC 1

---

*C2H5OH* transmitted on 28.10.80
Written by David Turner; Script Editor Brenda Reid; Produced by Innes Lloyd;
Directed by James Cellan Jones.
Dinsdale Landen (David Purser), Zena Walker (Mary Purser), Maureen O'Brien (Jill Secombe),
John Normington (Doctor Simpson), Keith Drinkel (Tony Secombe), Anne Ridler (Kate Wright),
Lavinia Cellan Jones (Lucy Purser), Deiniol Cellan Jones (Paul Purser),
Chris Sullivan (Doctor Jonson), Michael Halphie (Tommy), Brigid Mackay (Sister Wilson),
Caroline Holdaway (Jane), Roy Holder (Doug), John Eastham (Miguel), Patrick Duggan (Priest),
Shireen Haseen Shah (Doctor Garavandi), Deborah Grant (Louise Day),
Denyse Alexander (Patient), Alec Bregonzi (Patient), James Bryce (Patient),
Gordon Christie (Patient), Stacey Foster (Patient), Ray Gatenby (Patient),
David Hanson (Patient), Julian Hudson (Patient), Ceri Jackson (Patient),
Sydney Livingstone (Patient), John Pennington (Patient).

Seventy-minute play, recorded in colour on 2" videotape and preserved on D3 videotape.

---

***PLAYHOUSE***
Produced for BBC 2

---

*Unity* transmitted on 20.03.81
Based on a book by David Pryce-Jones; Adapted by John Mortimer;
Produced by Louis Marks; Directed by James Cellan Jones.
Lesley Anne Down (Unity Mitford), Nigel Havers (Philip Colindale),
Jeremy Kemp (Putzi Hanfstaengl), James Villiers (Hilary Martin), Ernst Jacobi (Hitler),
Ingrid Pitt (Fraulein Baum), Clare Higgins (Annie MacFarlane),
Emma Relph (Julia Owen Phillimore), Sarah Berger (Di Di Slingsby),
Clare Byam Shaw (Petra Plowright), Hilary Michel (Waitress), Kathleen Byron (Daphne
Martin), Terence Alexander (Sir Arnold Latimer), Ann Queensberry (Lady Latimer),
Hans Meyer (Janos Almasy), Brigitte Kahn (Maria Almasy), Eugene Lipinski (Max Leutgeb),
Richard Denning (Tony Albertini), Ingo Mogendorf (Lothar), Lex Van Delden (Bruckner),
Gertan Klauber (Streicher), Sheila Allen (Lady Redesdale),
Allan Cuthbertson (Lord Redesdale), Colin Rix (First Reporter),
Paul Henley (Second Reporter), Mischa de la Motte (Herr Deutlemoser).

One hundred-and-five minute play, recorded in colour on 2" videotape and preserved on
D3 videotape.

*A FINE ROMANCE*
Produced for LWT

*Series 1*

Written by Bob Larbey; Produced and directed by James Cellan Jones.
Judi Dench (Laura), Michael Williams (Mike), Susan Penhaligon (Helen),
Richard Warwick (Phil).

*The meeting* transmitted on 01.11.81
Angela Curran (Jean), Geoffrey Rose (Harry), Pola Churchill, Chris Holmes.

*The break-up* transmitted on 08.11.81

*Ethnic masks* transmitted on 15.11.81
Geoffrey Rose (Harry), Angela Curran (Jean), Neville Barber, Fernand Monast,
Charles Hodgson, Delia Lindsay.

*The dishy date is late* transmitted on 22.11.81
George Tovey (Charlie), Monica Grey, Glynis Barber, Michael Culver.

*Landscape business is threatened* transmitted on 29.11.81
George Tovey (Charlie).

*Laura pushes* transmitted on 06.12.81
Geoffrey Rose (Harry), Louisa Rix, Robert Swales.

*With Harry at the movies* transmitted on 13.12.81
Geoffrey Rose (Harry), George Tovey (Charlie).

Seven twenty-five minute episodes, recorded in colour on 2" videotape and preserved on
D2 videotape.

*Series 2*

Written by Bob Larbey; Produced and directed by James Cellan Jones.
Judi Dench (Laura), Michael Williams (Mike), Susan Penhaligon (Helen),
Richard Warwick (Phil).

*Again* transmitted on 17.01.82
John Baddeley, Sarah-Jane Varley, Jerold Wells.

*Gas* transmitted on 24.01.82
Paola Dionisotti, Corbet Woodall.

*Mike proposes* transmitted on 31.01.82
Leon Lissek, Hugh Walters.

*The new secretary* transmitted on 07.02.82
George Tovey (Charlie), Julian Curry, Suzie Cerys.

*Extra spice* transmitted on 14.02.82
Ken Wynne, Geoffrey Rose.

*Marriage?* transmitted on 21.02.82
Job Stewart, Derek Deadman, Harry Littlewood.

Six twenty-five minute episodes, recorded in colour on 2" videotape and preserved on D2 videotape.

---

### *HORACE*
Produced for Yorkshire Television

Written by Roy Minton; Executive producer David Cunliffe;
Produced by Keith Richardson; Directed by James Cellan Jones
Barry Jackson (Horace), Daphne Heard (Mrs Tiddy), Jean Heywood (Mother).

---

*Horace In The Swim* transmitted on 13.04.82
Anthony Wingate (Mr Frankel), Stephen Petcher, Johnny Maxfield, Julian Garlick,
Andrew Firth, Paul Tyreman, Howard Crossley, Alan Hulse.

*Horace Picks A Winner* transmitted on 15.04.82

*Horace Takes Charge* transmitted on 20.04.82
Anthony Wingate (Mr Frankel), Patrick Magee.

*Horace Finds A Friend* transmitted on 22.04.82

*Horace Steps Out* transmitted on 27.04.82
Alan Starkey, Margaret Burton, Mary Cunningham, Harold Goldblatt, Jonathan Thackwray,
Jeremy Armstrong, Stephen Thornley, Anthony Oughton.

*Horace And The Great Outdoors* transmitted on 29.04.82

Six twenty-five minute episodes, recorded in colour on 2" videotape and preserved on 1" videotape.

## *THE KINGFISHER*
Produced for Anglia Television

Transmitted on 23.12.82
Written by William Douglas Home; Executive Producer John Woolf;
Produced by John Rosenberg; Directed by James Cellan Jones.
Rex Harrison (Sir Cecil), Wendy Hiller (Evelyn), Cyril Cusack (Hawkins),
Gary Owen (Chauffeur).

A seventy-five minute play, recorded in colour on 2" videotape and preserved on
Digital Betacam.

## *LIVE FROM PEBBLE MILL*
Produced by BBC Birmingham for BBC 2

*Redundant! or The Wife's Revenge* transmitted on 20.02.83
Written by Fay Weldon; Produced by Robin Midgley; Directed by James Cellan Jones.
Leslie Phillips (Alan, A Husband), Judy Parfitt (Esther, A Wife),
Zia Mohyeddin (Mr Khan, A Cosmetic Surgeon), Connie Booth (Mrs Khan, A Brain Surgeon),
Nicola Pagett (Val, A Lover), Lucy Gutteridge (Hermes, A Daughter),
Dermot Crowley (Freddo, An Electrician), Marsha Fitzalan (Pony, A Nurse).

A live fifty-five minute production, preserved on Digital Betacam.

## *ALL FOR LOVE*
Produced for Granada Television

*Mrs Silly* transmitted on 18.09.83
Written by Bob Larbey; Based on a story by William Trevor; Produced by Roy Roberts;
Directed by James Cellan Jones.
Maggie Smith (Mrs Silly), Michael Culver (John), Deborah Grant (Gillian),
Salmaan Peer (Mr Ashraf).

A fifty-minute play, recorded on 2" videotape and preserved on D2 videotape.

---

### THE COMPLETE DRAMATIC WORKS OF WILLIAM SHAKESPEARE
Produced for BBC 2

---

*The Comedy Of Errors* transmitted on 24.12.83
Written by William Shakespeare; Music by Richard Holmes; Produced by Shaun Sutton;
Directed by James Cellan Jones.
Cyril Cusack (Aegeon), Charles Gray (Solinus, Duke of Ephesus),
Nicholas Chagrin (Master of the Mime), Michael Kitchen (The Antipholi),
Roger Daltrey (The Dromios), Suzanne Bertish (Adriana), Marsha Fitzalan (Luce),
David Kelly (Balthazar), Ingrid Pitt (Courtezan), Bunny Reed (Jailer),
Noel Johnson (First Merchant), Joanne Pearce (Luciana), Sam Dastor (Angelo),
Alfred Hoffman (Second Merchant), Frank Williams (Officer), Geoffrey Rose (Pinch),
Wendy Hiller (Aemelia), Peter MacKriel (Messenger), Ross Davidson, Nick Burnell,
Graham Christopher, Howard Lee, Daniel Rovai, Paul Springer, Jenny Weston (Mime Troupe).

A one-hundred-and-nine minute play, recorded in colour on 2" videotape and preserved on
D3 videotape.

---

### OXBRIDGE BLUES
Produced for BBC 2

---

Based on stories by Frederic Raphael; Music by Richard Holmes;
Produced by James Cellan Jones.

*Oxbridge Blues* transmitted on 14.11.84
Directed by James Cellan Jones.
Ian Charleson (Victor Geary), Malcolm Stoddard (Philip Geary), Amanda Redman (Maxine),
Rosalyn Landor (Wendy), Diane Keen (Carlotta), Michael Elphick (Curly (Bonaventura),
Clifford Rose (Sir Patrick (Hankey)), Norman Rodway (Narrator).

*That Was Tory* transmitted on 21.11.84
Directed by Rick Stroud.
John Bird (Clive), Joanna Lumley (Gigi), Malcolm Stoddard (Crispin), Christopher Good
(Duncan), Carol Royle (Tory).

*Similar Triangles* transmitted on 28.11.84
Directed by James Cellan Jones.
Malcolm Stoddard (Michael), Ciaran Madden (Rachel), Kate Fahy (Eileen), Julian Curry (Tom),
Niall Toibin (Minister), Timothy Carlton (Ned), Norman Rodway (Narrator), Tara Shah (Au Pair),
Jenny Wilson (Samantha), Sam Wilson (Sam)

*He'll See You Now* transmitted on 28.11.84
Directed by Frederic Raphael.
Susan Sarandon (Natalie Carlsen), Barry Dennen (Doctor Stein), Lou Hirsch (Sidney),
Philip O'Brien (Polska), Nancy Roberts (Mrs Stein), Andrea Browne (Marcia),
Jeff Harding (Rick's Voice).

*The Muse* transmitted on 05.12.84
Directed by Rick Stroud.
David Suchet (Colin), Frances Tomelty (Angela Lane), Carol Royle (Ellen), Holly Aird (Lucy),
Philip McGough (Albie Pocock), Robert Craig-Morgan (Michael), Natasha Richardson (Gabriella),
Dallas Adams (Watson), Milo Bell (Gareth), Jodene Bower (Justine),
Lizzie Spender (Girl At Party), Gavin Asher (Waiter), Paul Beech (Philosopher).

*Cheap Day* transmitted on 12.12.84
Directed by James Cellan Jones.
Ciaran Madden (Laura), Norman Rodway (Alec), Geoffrey Palmer (Fred), Kate Fahy (Lizzie),
Christopher Good (James), Ken Wynne (Ticket Seller), Steve Ismay (Ticket Collector),
Jabu Mbalo (Student).

*Sleeps Six* transmitted on 19.12.84
Directed by James Cellan Jones.
Ben Kingsley (Geoff Craven), Diane Keen (Sherry Craven), Jeremy Child (Philip, Lord Witham),
Alfred Marks (Bernie Pinto), Oona Kirsch (Alison Craven), Jackie Smith-Wood (Lady Jane),
Alisa Bosschaert (Chrissie), Nancy Roberts (Goldie Pinto), Stanley Davies (Pontecorvo),
Neil Nisbet (Rodney Craven), Francesca Hall (Polly), Roger Hammond (Father),
Robin Langford (Duke), Erika Hoffman (Girl At Picnic).

Seven plays, varying in length between thirty and eighty minutes in length. *Sleeps Six* was
recorded on 16mm colour film, the other episodes were recorded on 2" colour videotape. The
taped plays are preserved on D3 or Digital Betacam videotape, *Sleeps Six* on 16mm film.

---

## *MUSIQUE DE L'AMOUR: LA CHOUCHOU*
### Produced for Telfrance

---

Written by Eric-Emmanuel Schmitt; Directed by James Cellan Jones.
François Marthouret (Claude Debussy), Thérèse Liotard (Chouchou), Boris Sokolov (Bardac).

---

**SLIP-UP**
Produced for BBC 1

---

Transmitted on 30.12.86
Based on a book by Anthony Delano; Adapted by Keith Waterhouse; Script Editor Martyn Auty; Produced by Graham Benson; Directed by James Cellan Jones.
Jeremy Kemp (Slipper), Larry Lamb (Biggs), George Costigan (Jones),
Nicholas Le Prevost (Mackenzie), Tony Doyle (Vine), Fulton Mackay (McColl),
Barry Jackson (Hitchen), Desmond McNamara (Lovelace), Gwen Taylor (Charmian),
Philip Jackson (Purgavie), Michael Aitkens (Hinch), George Sweeney (Brennan),
Valerie Braddell (Anthea), Jack Watling (Champion), Julian Curry (Edwards),
Denys Hawthorne (Neill), Simon Cutter (Benckendorff), Ian Hastings (Steel),
John Flanagan (Monks), Daniel Webb (McCabe), Alastair Cumming (Australian),
Richard Ashley (Reporter), Richard Bonehill (Sub Editor), Desmond Cullum-Jones (Horace),
Dennis Edwards (Judge (Out of Vision)), Guy Standeven (Foreign Editor),
Silvina Pereira (Raimunda), Toze Martinho (Garcia), Armando Cortez (Flat Superintendent),
Suzanna Borges (Lucia), Adelaide Joao (Wife Favela), Antonio Evora (Husband Favela),
Eustasio De Abreu (Desk Sergeant), Angela Erreira (Phyllis), Rui Neves (TV Interviewer),
Lidia Franco (Receptionist), Rogerio Samora (Desk Clerk), Antonio Anjos (Taxi Driver),
Joao Sarababando (Anthea's Driver), Ricardo Luis Macedo (ITN Reporter),
Antonio Salgueiro (Old Prisoner), Silvina Pereira (Raimunda).

A ninety-five minute production, made and preserved on 16mm colour film.

---

**FORTUNES OF WAR**
Produced by Primetime for BBC 1

---

Based on a book by Olivia Manning; Adapted by Alan Plater; Music by Richard Holmes; Edited by Tariq Anwar; Produced by Betty Willingale; Directed by James Cellan Jones.

Emma Thompson (Harriet Pringle), Kenneth Branagh (Guy Pringle), Charles Kay (Dobson).

*September 1939* transmitted on 11.10.87
Ronald Pickup (Prince Yakimov), Vernon Dobtcheff (Hadjimoscos), Mischa de la Motte (Horvath),
James Villiers (Inchcape), Desmond McNamara (Galpin), Elena Secota (Sophie Oresanu),
Caroline Langrishe (Bella Niculesco), Magdalena Buznea (Despina), Nicholas Amer (Palu),
Mark Drewry (Dudedat), Harry Burton (Sasha Drucker), Barry Jackson, Richard Clifford,
Nicholas Chagrin, Vladimir Mirodan, Branko Miklavc, Branko Grubar, Snezana Savic, Relja Basic,
Andreja Saric, Vera Per, Polona Vetrih, Sreskco Ertavel, Iain Rattray, Andri Vasilescu.

*January 1940* transmitted on 18.10.87
Mark Drewry (Dudedat), Harry Burton (Sasha Drucker), Ronald Pickup (Prince Yakimov),
Elena Secota (Sophie Oresanu), James Villiers (Inchcape), Desmond McNamara (Galpin),
Caroline Langrishe (Bella Niculesco), Magdalena Buznea (Despina),

Vernon Dobtcheff (Hadjimoscos), Mischa de la Motte (Horvath), Nicholas Amer (Palu), Glyn Grain, Richard Clifford, Ronald Fraser, Vladimir Mirodan, Jo Kendall.

*June 1940* transmitted on 25.10.87
Alan Bennett (Lord Pinkrose), Ronald Pickup (Prince Yakimov), Christopher Strauli (Toby Lush), James Villiers (Inchcape), Mark Drewry (Dudedat), Elena Secota (Sophie Oresanu), Desmond McNamara (Galpin), Caroline Langrishe (Bella Niculesco), Harry Burton (Sasha Drucker), Magdalena Buznea (Despina), Vernon Dobtcheff (Hadjimoscos), Mischa de la Motte (Horvath), Nicholas Amer (Palu), Philip Madoc, Relja Basic, Glyn Grain, Gertan Klauber, Vladimir Bacic, Zdenka Hersar, Livius Omaran, Matija Rozman, Matko Ragus.

*October 1940* transmitted on 01.11.87
Alan Bennett (Lord Pinkrose), Ronald Pickup (Prince Yakimov), Christopher Strauli (Toby Lush), Mark Drewry (Dudedat), Harry Burton (Sasha Drucker), Clifford Rose, Peter Tilbury, Lollie May, Jeremy Brudenell, Beryl Cooke.

*April 1941* transmitted on 08.11.87
Rupert Graves (Simon Boulderstone), Alan Bennett (Lord Pinkrose), Robert Stephens (Castlebar), Ciaran Madden (Angela Hooper), Christopher Strauli (Toby Lush), Mark Drewry (Dudedat), Diana Hardcastle (Edwina Little), Greg Hicks (Aidan Pratt), Jack Watling, Clifford Rose, Jeff Rawle, Colin Foreman, Michael Cochrane, Esmond Knight, Anthony Calf, Leslie Southwick, Jeremy Sinden, Luke Bartley, Keith Edwards, Alix Refaie.

*September 1942* transmitted on 15.11.87
Rupert Graves (Simon Boulderstone), Alan Bennett (Lord Pinkrose), Robert Stephens (Castlebar), Ciaran Madden (Angela Hooper), Diana Hardcastle (Edwina Little), Greg Hicks (Aidan Pratt), Jeremy Sinden, Claire Oberman, Sam Dastor, Patricia Quinn, Anthony Calf, Erin Donovan, George Savides, Nicky Margolis, Abdallah Mahmoud, Salah Hamdi, Nigel Leach.

*January 1943* transmitted on 22.11.87
Rupert Graves (Simon Boulderstone), Ciaran Madden (Angela Hooper), Robert Stephens (Castlebar), Greg Hicks (Aidan Pratt), Diana Hardcastle (Edwina Little), Sam Dastor, Sam Miller, Jack Galloway, Patricia Quinn, Ahmed Mehrez, Esmond Knight, Claire Oberman, Erin Donovan, Hesham Salim, Paul Lacoux, Richard Linford, Mowaffa El Hakim.

Seven sixty-minute* episodes recorded on 16mm film and also preserved on Digital Betacam videotape.

*June 1940* runs for sixty-five minutes.

**THEATRE NIGHT**
Produced for BBC 2

*Arms And The Man* transmitted on 16.04.89
Written by Bernard Shaw; Produced by John Frankau; Directed by James Cellan Jones.
Helena Bonham Carter (Raina), Kika Markham (Catherine), Patsy Kensit (Louka),
Pip Torrens (Bluntschli), Nicolas Chagrin (Nikola), Dinsdale Landen (Major Petkoff),
Patrick Ryecart (Sergius), Mark Crowdy (Russian Officer).

A one-hundred-and-five minute play, recorded on 1" videotape and preserved on
Digital Betacam.

**THE BILL**
Produced for Thames Television

Series devised by Geoff McQueen.

*A Little Knowledge* transmitted on 24.08.89
Written by Christopher Russell; Executive Producer Michael Chapman;
Produced by Pat Sandys; Directed by James Cellan Jones.
Kevin Lloyd (DC Tosh Lines), Colin Fay (Andy), Richard Tate (Baz), Luke Hanson (Len),
Lynne Miller (WPC Cathy Marshall), Colin Blumenau (Police Constable 'Taffy' Edwards),
Nula Conwell (WPC Viv Martella), Mark Wingett (DC Jim Carver),
Ben Roberts (Chief Inspector Derek Conway), Andrew Mackintosh (DS Alastair Greig),
Huw Higginson (PC George Garfield), Susan Majolier (Marion, Brownlow's Secretary),
George Zenios (Levkas), Tony Sands (Damien), Eric Richard (Sergeant Bob Cryer),
Mark Powley (PC Ken Melvin), George Innes (China Seller), Clive Panto (Fruit Trader),
Gordon Winter (Balloon Man), Peter Ellis (Chief Superintendent Charles Brownlow),
Michael Ashforde (First Youth), Lee Chappell (Second Youth),
Gladis Robinson (First Wool Shop Lady), Kathleen Bidmead (Second Wool Shop Lady).

*Seen To Be Done* transmitted on 31.08.89
Written by Jonathan Rich; Executive Producer Michael Chapman;
Produced by Pat Sandys; Directed by James Cellan Jones.
Roger Leach (Sergeant Penny), Huw Higginson (PC George Garfield), Guy Williams (Lager Lout),
Birdy Sweeney (McPhee), Larry Dann (Sergeant Peters), Mark Powley (PC Ken Melvin),
Pauline Lewis-John (Cleaner), Jeremy Harrison (Desk Constable), Tony Scannell (DS Ted Roach),
Kevin Lloyd (DC Tosh Lines), Peter Ellis (Chief Superintendent Charles Brownlow),
Chris Humphreys (PC Turnham), Mark Haddigan (PC Able), James Cosmo (Detective Chief
Inspector Cameron), Michael Shaw (DS Chris Barry), Jeff Stewart (PC Reg Hollis),
Hilary Dawson (SOCO), Philip Bliss (Medic at Path Lab).

Twenty-five minute episodes, recorded on M2 videotape and preserved on D3 videotape.

***FREDERICK FORSYTH PRESENTS***
Produced by FFS Productions for LWT

*A Little Piece Of Sunshine* transmitted on 17.11.90
Introduced by Frederick Forsyth; Based on stories by Frederick Forsyth; Adapted by Murray Smith;
Executive Producers Murray Smith, Nick Elliott and Frederick Forsyth;
Produced by Frederick Muller; Directed by James Cellan Jones.
Alan Howard (Sam McCready), Lauren Bacall, Larry Lamb, Philip Michael Thomas,
Chris Cooper, Kitty Aldridge, Clarence Thomas, Robert Macbeth, Paul Bodie, Nelson Oramas,
Luis Alday, Ed Amatrudo, Jay Amor, John Archie, Phillip Astor, Alston L. Bair, June Barr,
Julian Bevans, Rex King, Chris MacCarty, Abraham Meeks, Ronald Shelley.

A one-hundred minute production recorded on 35mm colour film and also preserved on D2 videotape.

***A PERFECT HERO***
Produced by Havahall Pictures for LWT

Based on a book by Christopher Matthew; Adapted by Allan Prior;
Produced and directed by James Cellan Jones.
Nigel Havers (Hugh Fleming), James Fox (Angus Meikle).

*September, 1940* transmitted on 17.05.91
Bernard Hepton (Arthur Fleming), Barbara Leigh-Hunt (Iris Fleming),
Patrick Ryecart (Tim Holland), Nicholas Pritchard (Julian Masters), Fiona Gillies (Bunty Morrell),
Thomas Wheatley (Dickie Bird), Rosalind Knight, Rachel Fielding, Brian Mitchell,
Harry Burton, Nicholas Palliser, Joanna Lumley, Tacy Kneale, Beryl Cooke, Margaret John,
Tim Barker, Charles Pemberton.

Transmitted on 24.05.91
Fiona Mollison (Susan), Bernard Hepton (Arthur Fleming), Barbara Leigh-Hunt (Iris Fleming),
Nicholas Pritchard (Julian Masters), Fiona Gillies (Bunty Morrell), Amanda Elwes (Marjorie),
Thomas Wheatley (Dickie Bird), Brian Mitchell, Harry Burton, Rosalind Knight, Rachel Fielding,
Tacy Kneale, Nicholas Palliser, Jeff Rawle, Tony Collins.

Transmitted on 31.05.91
Amanda Elwes (Marjorie), Fiona Mollison (Susan), Georgia Allen (Nancy),
Bernard Hepton (Arthur Fleming), Barbara Leigh-Hunt (Iris Fleming),
Patrick Ryecart (Tim Holland), Nicholas Pritchard (Julian Masters), Jon Croft, Jane Wenham,
Leslie Southwick, Charles Collingwood, George Gilmore, Charles Gilmore.

# Forsyte and Hindsight

Transmitted on 07.06.91
Amanda Elwes (Marjorie), Georgia Allen (Nancy), Patrick Ryecart (Tim Holland),
Fiona Gillies (Bunty Morrell), Nicholas Pritchard (Julian Masters), Jeffrey Daunton, Jeff Rawle,
Andrée Evans, Joanna Lumley, Frederick Treves, Boris Isarov, Charles Daish, Ian Fitzgibbon,
Christopher Milburn.

Transmitted on 14.06.91
Amanda Elwes (Marjorie), Georgia Allen (Nancy), Bernard Hepton (Arthur Fleming),
Barbara Leigh-Hunt (Iris Fleming), Patrick Ryecart (Tim Holland),
Nicholas Pritchard (Julian Masters), Thomas Wheatley (Dickie Bird), John Bennett,
Jeffrey Daunton, Pearce Quigley, Sarah Hanna, Phil Horsley, David Trevena, Miriam Stockley.

Transmitted on 21.06.91
Amanda Elwes (Marjorie), Fiona Mollison (Susan), Bernard Hepton (Arthur Fleming),
Barbara Leigh-Hunt (Iris Fleming), Fiona Gillies (Bunty Morrell), Thomas Wheatley (Dickie Bird),
James Villiers, Jeff Rawle, Richard Butler, Martin Sadler.

Six fifty-minute episodes with stereo sound, recorded and preserved on 1" videotape.

---

## THE GRAVY TRAIN GOES EAST
### Produced by Portman Productions for Channel 4

Written by Malcolm Bradbury; Music by John Keane; Associate Producer Dickie Bamber;
Executive Producers Andrew Warren and Victor Glynn;
Produced by Ian Warren and Philip Hinchcliffe; Directed by James Cellan Jones.

---

*Episode 1* transmitted on 28.10.91
Ian Richardson (Spearpoint), Francesca Annis (Katya), Christoph Waltz (Dorfmann),
Jacques Sereys (Villeneuve), Anita Zagaria (Gianna), Jeremy Child (Steadiman),
Henry Goodman (Tankic), Cecile Paoli (Galina Vitali), John Dicks (Larson Parson),
Janek Lesniak (Lazlo), Judy Parfitt (Hilda), James Villiers (Penhurst), Sandor Szabo,
Frigyes Hollósi, András Bálint, Gyorgy Bardi, Roger Lloyd Pack, Antal Leisen, Ildiko Pecsi,
Zoltan Ratoti, Zsuzsma Manyai.

*Episode 2* transmitted on 04.11.91
Ian Richardson (Spearpoint), Francesca Annis (Katya), Christoph Waltz (Dorfmann),
Jacques Sereys (Villeneuve), Anita Zagaria (Gianna), Jeremy Child (Steadiman),
Henry Goodman (Tankic), Cecile Paoli (Galina Vitali), John Dicks (Larson Parson),
Janek Lesniak (Lazlo), Roger Lloyd Pack (Plitplov).

*Episode 3* transmitted on 11.11.91
Ian Richardson (Spearpoint), Francesca Annis (Katya), Christoph Waltz (Dorfmann),
Jacques Sereys (Villeneuve), Anita Zagaria (Gianna), Jeremy Child (Steadiman),

Henry Goodman (Tankic), Cecile Paoli (Galina Vitali), John Dicks (Larson Parson), Roger Lloyd Pack (Plitplov), Maggie Steed.

*Episode 4* transmitted on 18.11.91
Ian Richardson (Spearpoint), Francesca Annis (Katya), Christoph Waltz (Dorfmann), Jacques Sereys (Villeneuve), Anita Zagaria (Gianna), Jeremy Child (Steadiman), Henry Goodman (Tankic), Cecile Paoli (Galina Vitali), Janek Lesniak (Lazlo), Roger Lloyd Pack (Plitplov), Judy Parfitt (Hilda), James Villiers (Penhurst), Trevor Peacock, Mark Rogerson.

Four fifty-minute episodes with stereo sound, recorded and preserved on 16mm colour film.

---

## *MAIGRET*
### Produced for Granada Television

Based on novels by Georges Simenon; Music by Nigel Hess; Script Editor Craig Dickson; Executive Producers Sally Head, Arthur Weingarten and Rebecca Eaton; Produced by Jonathan Alwyn.

---

*The Patience Of Maigret* transmitted on 09.02.92
Adapted by Alan Plater; Directed by James Cellan Jones.
Michael Gambon (Chief Inspector Maigret), Geoffrey Hutchings (Sergeant Lucas), Jack Galloway (Inspector Janvier), James Larkin (Inspector Lapointe), Ciaran Madden (Madame Maigret), John Moffatt (Monsieur Comeliau), Christian Rodska (Moers), Cheryl Campbell, Trevor Peacock, Greg Hicks, Rachel Fielding, Ann Todd, Matyelok Gibbs, Robert McBain, Janos Gosztonyi, Ron Cook, Paul Bigley, Henry Goodman, Sandor Reisenbuchler, Agi Soproni, Robert Kovacs.

A seventy-eight minute episode, recorded on 16mm colour film and also preserved on Digital Betacam.

*Maigret Goes To School* transmitted on 23.02.92
Adapted by William Humble; Directed by James Cellan Jones.
Michael Gambon (Chief Inspector Maigret), Geoffrey Hutchings (Sergeant Lucas), Jack Galloway (Inspector Janvier), James Larkin (Inspector Lapointe), Ciaran Madden (Madame Maigret), Struan Rodger, Joanna David, Max Beazley, Jim Norton, Adrian Lukis, Godfrey James, Pip Donaghy, Eva Szabo, Guy Faulkner, Jamie Fletcher Lawson, Katie Marton, Istvan Hunyadkurthy, Laszlo Felhofi Kiss, Agi Csere.

A fifty-two minute episode, recorded on 16mm colour film and also preserved on Digital Betacam.

*Maigret On Home Ground* transmitted on 08.03.92
Adapted by Robin Chapman; Directed by James Cellan Jones.
Michael Gambon (Chief Inspector Maigret), Geoffrey Hutchings (Sergeant Lucas),
John Warnaby, James Clyde, Gareth Thomas, Paul Brightwell, Eva Orkenyi, Daniel Moynihan,
Jonathan Adams, Sue Withers, Sebastian Knapp, Charlotte Mitchell, Charlie Taylor-Coutts,
Sandor Szabo, Flora Kadar, Sandor Korospataki, Miklos Hajdu, Agi Margitay.

A seventy-eight minute episode with stereo sound, recorded on 16mm colour film and also preserved on Digital Betacam.

---

### RUMPOLE OF THE BAILEY
Produced for Thames Television

---

*Rumpole And The Children Of The Devil* transmitted on 29.10.92
Written by John Mortimer; Theme music by Joseph Horovitz; Associate Producer David Ball;
Executive Producer Lloyd Shirley and Brian Walcroft; Produced by Jacqueline Davis;
Directed by James Cellan Jones.
Leo McKern (Horace Rumpole), Julian Curry (Claude Erskine-Brown), Jonathan Coy (Henry),
Marion Mathie (Hilda Rumpole), Peter Blythe (Samuel Ballard, QC),
Camille Coduri ('Dot' Clapton), Denis Lill (Mr Bernard), Abigail McKern (Liz Probert),
Joanna Van Gyseghem (Lady Marigold Featherstone), Rowena Cooper (Marguerite Ballard),
Christopher Milburn (Dave Inchcape), Joanna David (Mirabelle Jones),
Chrissie Cotterill (Roz Timson), Paul Bigley (Cary Timson), Ron Pember (Dennis Timson),
John Bardon (Fred Timson), Amanda Dickinson (Peggy Molloy), Jennifer Piercey (Chairwoman),
Julian Gartside (Clerk Of The Court), John Warnaby (Charlie Wisbeach),
Philip Anthony (Master Of The Temple), Sandra Tallent (Isadora Fern),
Celestine Randall (Headmistress), Carly Maker (Tracy Timson), Luke Nugent (Dominic Molloy).

A fifty-one minute episode with stereo sound, recorded and preserved on 1" videotape.

---

### COMEDY PLAYHOUSE
A Humphrey Barclay production for Carlton

---

*Brighton Belles* Transmitted on 09.03.93
Written by Susan Harris; Executive Producer Al Mitchell;
Produced by Humphrey Barclay and Christopher Skala; Directed by James Cellan Jones.
Sheila Hancock (Frances), Wendy Craig (Annie), Sheila Gish (Bridget), Jean Boht (Josephine),
Harry Towb (Michael).

A twenty-five minute production with stereo sound, recorded and preserved on D2 videotape.

## THE BILL
Produced for Thames Television

Devised by Geoff McQueen.

*Divided We Fall* transmitted on 10.07.93
Written by Ron Rose; Executive Producer Michael Chapman; Produced by Mike Dormer;
Directed by James Cellan Jones.
Stephen Beckett (PC Mike Jarvis), Huw Higginson (PC George Garfield),
Richard Strange (Billy Staggers), Graham Cole (PC Tony Stamp), Eric Richard (Sergeant Bob Cryer),
Vivienne Burgess (Mrs Such), Daniel Illsley (Wayne Johnstone), Andrew Paul (PC David Quinnan),
Tom Butcher (PC Loxton), Tony O'Callaghan (Sergeant Matthew Boyden).

*A Malicious Prosecution* transmitted on 27.07.93
Written by Julian Jones; Executive Producer Michael Chapman; Produced by Mike Dormer;
Directed by James Cellan Jones.
Eric Richard (Sergeant Bob Cryer), Lynne Miller (WPC Cathy Marshall),
Huw Higginson (PC George Garfield), Timothy Walker (Counsel for the Plaintiff),
Adam Kotz (Counsel for the Defence), Christopher Ellison (DI Frank Burnside),
Trudie Goodwin (WPC June Ackland), Andrew Harrison (David Berne),
Graham Cole (PC Tony Stamp), Colin Tarrant (Inspector Andrew Monroe),
Tony O'Callaghan (Sergeant Matthew Boyden).

Twenty-five minute episodes, recorded and preserved on D3 videotape.

## BRIGHTON BELLES
A Humphrey Barclay production for Carlton

Written by Susan Harris; Executive Producer Al Mitchell;
Produced by Humphrey Barclay and Christopher Skala; Directed by James Cellan Jones.
Sheila Hancock (Frances), Wendy Craig (Annie), Sheila Gish (Bridget),
Jean Boht (Josephine), Harry Towb (Michael).

*Series 1*

*The Triangle* transmitted on 07.09.93
*Job Hunting* transmitted on 14.09.93
*The Tournament* transmitted on 21.09.93
*Guess Who's Coming To Dinner?* transmitted on 28.09.93
*Love In A Sea Mist* transmitted on 05.10.93
*The Transplant* transmitted on 12.10.93

Six twenty-five minute episodes with stereo sound, recorded and preserved on D2 videotape.

---

### HARNESSING PEACOCKS
Produced by Friday Productions for Meridian

---

Transmitted on 09.05.93
Based on a book by Mary Wesley; Adapted by Andrew Davies; Music by Richard Holmes;
Script Supervisor Sarah Garner; Executive Producer Colin Rogers;
Produced by Georgina Abrahams and Betty Willingale; Directed by James Cellan Jones.
Serena Scott Thomas (Hebe), Peter Davison (Jim), John Mills (Bernard), Tom Beasley (Silas),
Renée Asherson (Louisa), Brenda Bruce (Amy), Nicholas Le Prevost (Mungo),
Richard Huw (Rory), Abigail McKern (Hannah), David Harewood (Terry), Dilys Hamlett (Lucy),
Jeremy Child (Julian), Marsha Fitzalan (Alison), Delia Lindsay (Jennifer),
Richard Mathews (Grandfather), Elizabeth Ashley (Grandmother), Tom Beard (Robert),
Cara Konig (Ann), Nicholas Palliser (Delian), Helen Schlesinger (Cara), Buffy Davis (Patsy),
Jay Benedict (Eli), Jamie Groves (Giles), Jackson Kyle (Alistair), Ben Keyworth (Michael),
Jamie McClelland (Ian), Iago Jones* (Milkman).

*Iago Jones is a pseudonym for James Cellan Jones.

---

### CLASS ACT
Produced by Cinema Verity for Carlton

---

*"The bizarre death of an MP"* transmitted on 05.05.94
Written by Michael Aitkens; Produced by Verity Lambert; Directed by James Cellan Jones.
Joanna Lumley (Kate Swift), John Bowe (Jack Booker), Nadine Garner (Gloria O'Grady),
Richard Vernon (Sir Horace Mainwaring), John Bowe (Jack Booker),
Nadine Garner (Gloria O'Grady), Richard Vernon (Sir Horace Mainwaring),
James Gaddas (Detective Inspector Latham), Neil McCaul (Joe Addison), Ezra Bix,
Jeremy Clyde, Glyn Grain, Alastair Stewart, John Warnaby, Richard Dixon, Paul Clarkson,
Matthew Radford, Gillian Tompkins.

*"The chef's war"* transmitted on 12.05.94
Written by Michael Aitkens; Produced by Verity Lambert; Directed by James Cellan Jones.
Joanna Lumley (Kate Swift), John Bowe (Jack Booker), Nadine Garner (Gloria O'Grady),
Richard Vernon (Sir Horace Mainwaring), John Bowe (Jack Booker),
Nadine Garner (Gloria O'Grady), Richard Vernon (Sir Horace Mainwaring),
James Gaddas (Detective Inspector Latham), Neil McCaul (Joe Addison), Ian McNeice,
Peter Howitt, Jane How, Dorian Healy, Roger Griffiths, Andy Lucas, Richard Davies,
Wolf Christian.

Fifty-minute episodes, recorded on 16mm film, edited on video and preserved on
D2 videotape.

---

### *BRIGHTON BELLES*
A Humphrey Barclay production for Carlton

---

Written by Susan Harris; Executive Producer Al Mitchell; Produced by Humphrey Barclay and Christopher Skala; Directed by James Cellan Jones.
Sheila Hancock (Frances), Wendy Craig (Annie), Sheila Gish (Bridget),
Jean Boht (Josephine), Harry Towb (Michael).

*Series 2*

*That Was No Lady* transmitted on 07.12.94
*The Break In* transmitted on 14.12.94
*The Younger Man* transmitted on 21.12.94
*Gilbert's Return* transmitted on 28.12.94

Four twenty-five minute episodes with stereo sound, recorded and preserved on D2 videotape.

---

### *THE VACILLATIONS OF POPPY CAREW*
Produced by Bentley Films for Meridian

---

Transmitted on 05.03.95
Based on a book by Mary Wesley; Adapted by William Humble; Music by Richard Holmes;
Script Consultant Betty Willingale; Executive Producer Colin Rogers;
Produced by Brian True-May; Directed by James Cellan Jones.
Tara Fitzgerald (Poppy Carew), Joseph Fiennes (Willy), Owen Teale (Edmund),
Edward Atterton (Fergus), Samuel West (Victor), Charlotte Coleman (Mary),
Geraldine Alexander (Venetia), Helena Michell (Penelope), Siân Phillips (Calypso),
Daniel Massey (Dad), Thomas Wheatley (Anthony), Raouf Ben Amor (Mustafa),
Julian Rhind-Tutt (Sean), Sophie Linfield (Julia), Barbara Young (Mrs Frobisher).

A one-hundred minute production, recorded on 16mm colour film, edited on video and preserved on Digital Betacam.

**THE BILL**
Produced for Thames Television

Devised by Geoff McQueen.

*Russian Doll* transmitted on 24.08.95
Written by Sebastian Secker Walker; Executive Producer Michael Chapman;
Produced by Mike Dormer; Directed by James Cellan Jones.
Shaun Scott (DS Chris Deakin), Kerry Peers (WPC Croft), Susan Vidler (Anna McClellan),
Lynne Miller (WPC Cathy Marshall), Alan Westaway (PC Nick Slater), Peter Lindford (DI Egmont),
Neil Conrich (Matthew Goodman), Flip Webster (Sylvia), Sean Patterson (Mike),
Eric Richard (Sergeant Bob Cryer), Colin Tarrant (Inspector Andrew Monroe),
Raymond Johnson (Peter Hopkins), Christopher Saul (FME), Simon Rouse (DCI Jack Meadows),
Kevin Lloyd (DC Tosh Lines).

*Video Nasty* transmitted on 03.10.95
Written by David Hoskins; Executive Producer Michael Chapman; Produced by Mike Dormer;
Directed by James Cellan Jones.
Shaun Scott (DS Chris Deakin), Billy Murray (DS Don Beech),
Andrew Mackintosh (DS Alastair Greig), Mark Wingett (DC Jim Carver),
Robert Swann (James Hallet), Darren Tighe (Daniel Parks), Anhony Allen (Steve Cummins),
Abigail Rokinson (Karen), Marlene Sidaway (Mrs Smith), Michael Redfern (Landlord),
Ray Marioni (Ice Cream Shop Owner), Martin Oldfield (Fireman), David Blair (Simon),
Andrew Paul (PC David Quinnan), Huw Higginson (PC George Garfield),
Colin Tarrant (Inspector Andrew Monroe), Eric Richard (Sergeant Bob Cryer),
Lynne Miller (WPC Cathy Marshall), Robert Perkins (Sergeant Ray Steele),
Tom Cotcher (DC Alan Woods).

Twenty-five minute episodes, recorded and preserved on D3 videotape.

**THE RUTH RENDELL MYSTERIES**
Produced by Blue Heaven Productions for Meridian

*May And June*

Based on books by Ruth Rendell; Adapted by Ken Blakeson; Developed by John Davies;
Executive Producers Colin Rogers and Graham Benson; Produced by Neil Zeiger;
Directed by James Cellan Jones.
Phoebe Nicholls (May Thrace), Christine Kavanagh (June Symonds),
Julian Wadham (John Dyson), Albert Welling (Mr Thrace), Gabrielle Reidy (Mrs Thrace),
Elizabeth Ashley (Margery Lipton), Alistair Findlay (Doctor Kendrew),
Claire Szekeres (June, Aged 10), Jessica Fox (May, Aged 13), Charlotte Masson Apps (May, Aged 3),
William Scott-Masson (William Symonds), Dhurpal Patel (Asfa, Aged 8), Anisha Gangotra

(Amna, Aged 13), John Moreno (Taxi Driver), Lloyd McGuire (Man On Train), Lalita Ahmed (Asian Mother), Sally Sanders (Landlady), Stuart Fox (Vicar).

*Episode 1* transmitted on 07.02.97
*Episode 2* transmitted on 14.02.97

Fifty-one minute episodes, produced on 16mm in widescreen and stereo, edited on video and preserved on D2 videotape.

---

*MCLIBEL!*
Produced by Dennis Woolf Productions for Channel 4

Produced by Dennis Woolf; Directed by James Cellan Jones.

---

*Part 1* transmitted on 17.05.97
Clive Merrison (Mr Justice Bell), Angus MacInnes (Paul Preston),
Malcolm Sinclair (Richard Rampton QC), Peter-Hugo Daly (Dave Morris),
Julia Sawalha (Helen Steel), Joseph Marcell (Robert Beavers), Sheena McDonald (Host),
Jon Croft (Sid Nicholson), Crispin Letts, David Baxt, Richard Dixon, Natasha Pyne,
Martyn Stanbridge, Tim Preece, Vincent Marzello, Alec Linstead, Michael Begley.

*Part 2* transmitted on 18.05.97
Clive Merrison (Mr Justice Bell), Angus MacInnes (Paul Preston),
Malcolm Sinclair (Richard Rampton QC), Peter-Hugo Daly (Dave Morris),
Julia Sawalha (Helen Steel), Joseph Marcell (Robert Beavers), Sheena McDonald (Host),
Jon Croft (Sid Nicholson), Clyde Gatell, Malcolm Terris, Richard Howard, Vincent Pickering,
Cyril Appleton, Rolf Saxon, James Jordan, Terrence Hardiman, Nicholas Palliser, Bruce Byron,
Michael Sadler, Arthur Cox, Perry Fenwick, Tom Bowles, James Smith, Laurence Kennedy,
Rosie Cavaliero, Mary Woodvine, Wendy Lowder, Joseph O'Conor, Koroush Asad,
John Guerrasio, Jonathan Hackett, Andy Bowen.

One seventy-minute and one seventy-five minute episode with stereo sound, recorded and preserved on Digital Betacam videotape.

**_THE BILL_**
Produced for Thames Television

Devised by Geoff McQueen

*Straying* transmitted on 14.10.97
Written by Rod Beacham; Executive Producer Michael Chapman; Produced by Pat Sandys;
Directed by James Cellan Jones.
Trudie Goodwin (WPC June Ackland), Stephen Beckett (PC Mike Jarvis),
Colin Tarrant (Inspector Andrew Monroe), Lisa Geoghan (WPC Polly Page),
Tom Butcher (PC Loxton), Graham Cole (PC Tony Stamp), Billy Murray (DS Don Beech),
Mark Wingett (DC Jim Carver), Huw Higginson (PC George Garfield),
Gregory Donaldson (DC Tom Proctor), Jeff Stewart (PC Reg Hollis),
Andrew Conlan (Divisional Scene Examiner Colin Trevins),
Ben Roberts (Chief Inspector Derek Conway), Eric Richard (Sergeant Bob Cryer),
Tony O'Callaghan (Sergeant Matthew Boyden), Pauline Jefferson (Sally Jeavons),
Rowena Cooper (Margaret Miles), John Normington (Norman Miles), Peter Gunn (Barry Welsh),
Sanchia McCormack (Kelly Hammond), Daniel Forster-Smith (Ben Hammond).

*Crime Of A Lesser Passion* transmitted on 17.10.97
Written by Tunde Babalola; Executive Producer Michael Chapman; Produced by Pat Sandys;
Directed by James Cellan Jones.
Trudie Goodwin (WPC June Ackland), Stephen Beckett (PC Mike Jarvis),
Colin Tarrant (Inspector Andrew Monroe), Lisa Geoghan (WPC Polly Page),
Tom Butcher (PC Loxton), Graham Cole (PC Tony Stamp), Billy Murray (DS Don Beech),
Mark Wingett (DC Jim Carver), Huw Higginson (PC George Garfield),
Gregory Donaldson (DC Tom Proctor), Jeff Stewart (PC Reg Hollis),
Andrew Conlan (Divisional Scene Examiner Colin Trevins),
Ben Roberts (Chief Inspector Derek Conway), Eric Richard (Sergeant Bob Cryer),
Tony O'Callaghan (Sergeant Matthew Boyden), Alphonsia Emmanuel (Julia Herridge),
Charles Daish (Anton Haidge), Ray Fearon (Foley Marsh), Eileen Nicholas (Elspeth Merrick),
Sheila Whitfield (Brenda Marsh).

*Too Many Cooks* transmitted on 01.12.98
Written by Nigel Baldwin; Executive Producer Richard Handford; Produced by Pat Sandys;
Directed by James Cellan Jones.
Mark Wingett (Jim Carver), Trudie Goodwin (WPC June Ackland), Caroline Catz (WPC Fox),
Joy Brook (WDC Kerry Holmes), Aden Gillett (DS Lockyer), George Rossi (DC Duncan Lennox),
Anthony Valentine, Isla Blair, Flora Montgomery, Teowa Vuong, Choy Ling Man, Shaun Stone,
Daryl Kwan, Adrian Pang, Anne Ridler, Nigel Anthony, Richard Huw

*Look Away Now* transmitted on 22.04.99
Written by Michael Jenner; Executive Producer Richard Handford; Produced by Pat Sandys; Directed by James Cellan Jones.
Mark Wingett (Jim Carver), Trudie Goodwin (Woman Police Constable June Ackland), Caroline Catz (Woman Police Constable Fox), Joy Brook (Woman Detective Constable Kerry Holmes), Aden Gillett (Detective Sergeant Lockyer), George Rossi (Detective Constable Duncan Lennox), Rae Baker (Detective Constable Juliet Becker), Nicola Alexis (Police Constable Ruby Buxton), Jason Watkins, John O'Toole, Daniel Wilson, Andrew Mckay, Matthew Thomas, Anita Pashley

Twenty-five minute episodes with stereo sound, recorded and preserved on Digital Betacam videotape. *Look Away Now* was the last episode of *The Bill* before production changed to wide-screen format.

---

## *HOLBY CITY*
Produced for BBC 1

---

Created by Mal Young; Executive Producers Mal Young and Kathleen Hutchinson; Produced by Matt Tombs; Series Producer Richard Stokes.

*Mother Knows Best* transmitted on 20.11.01
Written by Dan Sefton; Directed by James Cellan Jones.
Thusitha Jayasundera (Tash Bandara), Jan Pearson (Kath Fox),
Jeremy Edwards (Danny Shaughnessy), Laura Sadler (Sandy Harper),
Jeremy Sheffield (Alex Adams), Dawn McDaniel (Kirstie Collins),
Peter De Jersey (Steve Waring), Colette Brown (Samantha Kennedy),
Dominic Jephcott (Alistair Taylor), Tina Hobley (Chrissie Williams),
Hugh Quarshie (Mr Ric Griffin), Mark Moraghan (Owen Davis), Miles Anderson (Terry Fox),
Siobhan Redmond (Janice Taylor), George Irving (Anton Meyer),
Deborah Poplett (Anna Chandler), Ian Burfield, Ruby Snape

*Forgiveness Of Sins* transmitted on 27.11.01
Written by Nick Warburton; Directed by James Cellan Jones.
Jan Pearson (Kath Fox), Thusitha Jayasundera (Tash Bandara),
Jeremy Edwards (Danny Shaughnessy), Laura Sadler (Sandy Harper),
Dawn McDaniel (Kirstie Collins), Jeremy Sheffield (Alex Adams),
Peter De Jersey (Steve Waring), Dominic Jephcott (Alistair Taylor),
Colette Brown (Samantha Kennedy), Tina Hobley (Chrissie Williams),
Hugh Quarshie (Mr Ric Griffin), Martin Ledwith (Father Michael),
Mark Moraghan (Owen Davis), Miles Anderson (Terry Fox), Ian Aspinall (Mubbs Hussein),
Siobhan Redmond (Janice Taylor), Anna Mountford, Sandy McDade.

Sixty-minute episodes in widescreen and with stereo sound, recorded and preserved on Digital Betacam.

# Cinema Credits

---

***A BEQUEST TO THE NATION***
Released in 1973

---

Written by Terence Rattigan; Music by Michel Legrand; Produced by Hal B Wallis; Directed by James Cellan Jones.

Peter Finch (Admiral Lord Horatio Nelson), Glenda Jackson (Lady Hamilton), Michael Jayston (Captain Hardy), Anthony Quayle (Lord Minto), Margaret Leighton (Lady Frances Nelson), Dominic Guard (Master George Matcham), Nigel Stock (George Matcham), Barbara Leigh-Hunt (Catherine Matcham), Roland Culver (Lord Barham), Richard Mathews (Reverend William Nelson), Liz Ashley (Sarah Nelson), John Nolan (Captain Blackwood), André Maranne (Admiral Villeneuve), Pat Heywood (Emily).

---

***MARRIED 2 MALCOLM***
Released in 1998

---

Music by John Scott; Script Supervisor Carol Saunderson; Associate Producer Beth Pinkerton; Executive Producers Rainer Bienger, Marie Hoy and Paul Luke; Produced by Alex Swan; Co-produced by Jürgen Biefang; Directed by James Cellan Jones.

Mark Addy (Malcolm), Josie Lawrence (Natalie), Tracey Wilkinson (Norma), Freddie Jones (Jasper), Steven Speirs (Sam Tex), Hywel Bennett (Reg), Liz Ashley, Tom Barlow, Helen Benoist, Moya Brady, Chris Brailsford, Elianne Byrne, Ina Clough, Daryl Fishwick, Anita Germaine, Emma Goodfield, Stewart Harvey-White, Jane Hogarth, Ennis Jackson, Vicki Lee, Peter Lorenzelli, Tina Malone, Lisa Millett, Stephen Omer, Beth Pinkerton, Adrian Plant, Robin Polley, Bob Ramsay, Drew Rhys-Williams, Bill Rogers, Philip Ross, Georgina Smith, Deborah Tinsley, James Wilde.

# Index